an introductio: METAPHYSICS

MARTIN O. VASKE, S.J.
CREIGHTON UNIVERSITY

IMPRIMI POTEST:

John J. Foley, S J.
Provincial, Wisconsin Province

IMPRIMATUR:

✠ Gerald T. Bergan
Archbishop of Omaha
May 18, 1962

PREFACE

A philosopher, according to the etymology of the term, is a lover of wisdom. The study of philosophy springs from man's natural love for knowledge.[1] It is an intellectual endeavor through the natural light of unaided reason[2] to attain an ever-deeper understanding of reality.

One does not learn philosophy once and for all as one learns the multiplication table. Rather, philosophy is the kind of knowledge in which one's progress is marked by a more and more profound grasp of the real. One does not encompass the intelligible splendors of being in a single gaze. There are always greater riches to be discovered by the sincere seeker after wisdom in the realities that confront him on all sides. And, we may add, these riches are the riches of the mind, apart from any practical use to which this knowledge may be ordered.

Throughout our study of philosophy, it is important to remember that the philosophical enterprise differs from other approaches to reality. Philosophy is not a science in the narrow, modern sense of the term; it is not a mathematicized expression of the sensible, measurable aspects of material being. Nor, on the other hand, is it poetry or art. Rather, it is a distinct kind of knowledge and as such has its distinctive method. Moreover, it is learned in a distinctive way. One cannot memorize philosophy. It can only be understood; and understanding, or insight, ordinarily comes only after prolonged pondering, extensive reading, and lively discussion.

Although philosophy is usually divided into various "courses" for pedagogical reasons, nevertheless it is a whole, a unified knowledge, and its various parts are interdependent. In this particular course, we shall be concerned with philosophy in the basic sense of the term, that is, with the philosophy of being, or *metaphysics*, as it is more commonly called. Of the edifice of philosophical

---

[1] "All men by nature desire to know" (Aristotle, *Metaphysics*, I, 1, 980ª).

[2] Sacred doctrine, or "theology," makes use of the supernatural light of Revelation as well as the natural light of reason.

knowledge which we are about to erect, metaphysics is the foundation on which everything else rests. This foundation, moreover, is not laid once and for all. Rather, it must be strengthened and deepened as the edifice grows taller.

Progress in philosophy, however, is organic rather than structural. If growth in philosophical knowledge is compared to the growth of a tree, then metaphysics is the root system and trunk. As the various branches grow, the trunk must become stronger and the root system deeper. One simply cannot make progress in philosophical wisdom without an ever-deeper understanding of metaphysics.

Many things are learned simply by doing. Little boys, for example, are sometimes taught to swim by throwing them into the water and letting them thrash about a bit. We shall do something similar to the student beginning the study of metaphysics. We shall omit the usual introductory chapter describing what kind of knowledge metaphysics is (accepted for the most part on the authority of the teacher) and hurl the student at once into the metaphysical swim.

Martin O. Vaske, S.J.

CONTENTS

I

Existents

At the outset of our philosophical study of reality, it is important that we begin at the beginning. We shall start with the most fundamental fact—the fact that things exist.[1] And more precisely, we shall begin with the very things which exist and confront us in our experience.

[1] The statement that *things exist* expresses the starting point of philosophy as a whole. See Jacques Maritain, *The Degrees of Knowledge*, translated from fourth French edition under supervision of Gerald B. Phelan, Charles Scribner's Sons, New York, 1959, p. 76; see also p. 57 of the same work.

1

A. THINGS EXIST

Point of Departure

Things confront us. They act upon us: they stop us, push us, pull us, strike us, and may even kill us. That things *are*, that they exist, is quite evident and need not be proved.[2] Indeed, this primordial fact may be even painfully evident, as it is to the mailman confronted by an angry, canine existent which is nipping his leg. A denial of reality, of being, is impossible to make and impossible to maintain in the face of the stirring, pulsing, beating existents that confront us on all sides.

We Exist

That we ourselves exist is also quite evident and need not be proved, nor can it be proved.[3] However, we do not know our (conscious) selves directly and immediately, or even primarily. Moreover, our knowledge is not primarily, directly, and immediately of knowledge.[4] Rather, we know primarily, directly, and immediately the sensible, bodily beings which confront us—"shoes, ships, sealing-wax, cabbages, kings." We know the self in the act of knowing such beings. We catch ourselves in the act of knowing something else; we know ourselves (and our knowledge) in the act of knowing objects; and these objects are primarily not God

[2] Only the nonevident needs proof. The evident neither needs proof nor can it be proved. It is its own "proof."

[3] Proof, in the sense of demonstration, moves from the nonevident to the evident in the light of the evident. That we exist is implicitly known in our knowledge of being and is made evident by a reflection on this knowledge.

[4] "No one perceives that he understands except from this that he understands something: because understanding something is prior to understanding that one understands; and so the soul comes to understand actually that it exists, from the fact that it understands . . ." (St. Thomas Aquinas, *De Veritate*, X, 8c).

Compare the following statement by Maritain: "The first thing thought about is being independent of the mind. The *cogitatum* of the first *cogito* is not *cogitatum*, but *ens*. We do not eat what has been eaten; we eat bread" (*op. cit.*, p. 108; reprinted by permission).

and the angels, or our intellect, or knowledge, or the self, but
sensible, corporeal existents.[5]

B. MAN'S INITIAL KNOWLEDGE OF BEING

Man's Twofold Knowledge

Man's knowledge of the sensible, bodily existents which confront him is twofold: sensory and intellectual. Through his senses,
man apprehends these beings according to their sensible characteristics: he grasps their sensible qualities—their color, sound,
taste, odor, and tactile qualities; he knows also their size, shape,
number, distance, movement, or rest. Such knowledge man has
in common with the brutes. Indeed, many of the brutes excel
man in sense knowledge; dogs, for example, excel man in the
sense of smell; eagles excel him in sight.

Man, however, is not limited to a knowledge of the *sensible*
attributes of bodily beings; he is not restricted to knowing what
color, shape, size, etc., they have. Man knows *what* they are and
that they *are:* he knows their essence, or nature;[6] and more profoundly he knows that they exist, that they exercise existence. In

---

[5] The human intellect precisely as *human* has for its first and direct object
material, sensible being; nevertheless, as *intellect* it has for its object all being.
Cf. Maritain, *op. cit.*, p. 248; also pp. 67 and 94.

[6] We do not claim that man has a direct intuition of essences, or natures;
they are known through the activities of a being. Nor do we claim that man
knows the essences of those things below man in their specificity. Cf. Maritain,
op. cit., pp. 30, 38, 205, 207. Nevertheless, it is obvious that we do know the
essences of things in some way, though for the most part in a very general
and descriptive manner. Another name for essence is *quiddity*, the *whatness*
of a thing. Every positive answer to the question "What is that?" reveals the
essence in some way. The answer may vary in definiteness from a most general and indeterminate expression of the essence to a definition which expresses the essence in its specific nature. When we say that the intellect grasps
essence, the term must be understood in its widest sense; the determinate,
specific essence is attained only by long and careful observation and comparison. Actually, we know the specific essences of very few things.

brief: man knows bodily beings intellectually as well as sensibly; human experience is sensory-*intellectual*.[7]

Man's Basic Intellectual Knowledge

The most fundamental intellectual knowledge which man has of any sensible existent is the knowledge "that something is." [8] As a consequence of, and simultaneous with, sense knowledge of an existent, the intellect grasps *what* the thing is (at least in a general or descriptive way) and at the same time affirms that it *is*. Thus, the sensible, corporeal existent is attained by the intellect in a twofold way: (1) according to its mode, or manner, of existing (its essence, or nature) in the act of apprehension and (2) according to its very act of existing in the judgment.[9]

Expressed in Existential Propositions

Such a judgment, the *existential* judgment, must be distinguished carefully from what is called an *attributive* judgment,[10] the type of judgment studied in classical Logic. Examples of attributive judgments are the judgments expressed in propositions such as these: "A snake is a limbless, scaly reptile," "A lion is a

[7] "In the concrete network of our cognitive operations, sense and intellect work together; our *direct knowledge* has its start in a sensible perception that is shot through with an intelligibility that is still not explicitly aware of itself" (*ibid.*, p. 92; reprinted by permission); see also p. 96.

[8] ". . . knowledge that a thing exists always precedes knowledge of its determinate nature, for it would be absurd to look for a thing's quiddity before having observed its existence" (L. M. Régis, *Epistemology*, translated by I. C. Byrne, The Macmillan Company, New York, 1959, p. 350).

[9] "The operation of the intellect is twofold: one . . . by which it knows concerning each thing what it is; the other, in which it composes and divides by forming affirmative or negative enunciations. And indeed these two operations correspond to two elements which are in things. The first operation is concerned with the nature of the thing, according to which the thing understood has a certain level among beings. . . . The second operation is concerned with the very existence . . ." (Aquinas, *In Librum Boethii De Trinitate*, V, art. 3).

[10] We cannot begin to study metaphysics unless we recognize and attend to this important distinction. Its meaning will become more evident as we progress.

dangerous animal." Such judgments are made, and formulated in propositions, in answer to the question "*What* is it?" They express the manner of be-ing (existing), the "way," or mode, of existing,[11] whether or not anything exists that "way," in that "manner," or according to that mode.

Examples of existential judgments are the judgments formulated in the following propositions: "There is a snake," "There is a lion."[12] Such judgments are made, and formulated in propositions,[13] in answer to the question "Is it?" "Is there?" or "Does it exist?" In such judgments, the intellect recognizes its *confrontation by an existent:* a slithering, serpentine existent in the first case above; a roaring, leonine existent in the second case. Such judgments are concerned with the *real* and differ profoundly from attributive judgments, which might be made and expressed more or less calmly in answer to a biology teacher's questions: "What is a snake?" "What is a lion?"

The "Is" of Attributive Judgments

Attributive judgments are concerned with *what* a thing is and do not express whether such a thing *is* (exists). Attributive judgments express a mode, manner, or way of existing, either a primary mode (substantial essence, or nature) such as human or canine, or a secondary mode (accidents) such as white, brave, wise. But the attributive judgment does not affirm the very *existing* according to such a mode. Thus, to judge that "a dinosaur *is* an animal" is not the same as to judge that "a dinosaur *is* (exists)." The "is" of attributive judgment is a link, or *copula,* between

[11] Either the *primary* mode of existing (the substantial essence), for example, "Dinosaurs are animals," or a *secondary* mode of existing (an accident), for example, "Dinosaurs are ferocious."

[12] Other examples: "Whooping cranes exist. Dodoes do not exist. I exist. God exists." In the case of living beings, since life (in the most profound sense) is their existence, the proposition may use some form of the verb "to live"; for example, "Fido still lives (exists)."

[13] Sometimes a simple "Yes" expresses the complex knowledge of an existential judgment; for example, "Do whooping cranes still exist?" "Yes." Such a judgment may also be negative; for example, "Do passenger pigeons still exist?" "No."

subject and predicate, and expresses the mind's act of composing. It does not signify the act of existing, of be-ing (*esse*).

Existential Judgments Affirm Existence

Existential judgments, on the other hand, are concerned with whether or not something *is* (exists). The two types of judgments reflect the difference between merely *thinking* about something (irrespective of whether it exists or not) and being sensibly and intellectually *confronted* by a real something—an existent.[14]

In brief: attributive judgments are expressions of our knowledge of *what* a thing is (the way, manner, or mode of existing); existential judgments express our knowledge that it *is* (exists).

Indeterminacy of First Intellectual Knowledge

In our first intellectual knowledge of a sensible, material existent, we may not know precisely and determinately *what* it is, but we do know that it *is*, that some individual (or individuals) exists. I may not know, for example, who is at the door, but I do know that someone *is* at the door from hearing him knock. I know that I am confronted by an existent of some sort, either a human existent or, perhaps, a well-trained, canine existent who has been taught to tap at the door with his paws.

This first intellectual knowledge of being is so basic and fundamental that we are apt to overlook it.[15] And yet when we reflect, we must admit that we possess such knowledge, even though we do not always make it explicit or express it in complex fashion.

Let us consider another example to bring out the content of this knowledge. A householder, when awakened in the dead of night by something stirring in a room below, knows that

[14] We shall see in the philosophy of God that even the judgment "God exists" rests on the judgment that sensible beings *exist* as effects requiring an *existing* cause to explain their very existing.

[15] Indeed, it has been overlooked even by philosophers of note or has been dismissed as not being of great philosophical moment.

something is (exists), that there is something or someone below; he is confronted by an existent (or existents).[16] As yet he does not know determinately and specifically what it is, whether a burglar or his pet cat—whether he is confronted by a human or by a feline existent. The mode, manner, or way of existing is not known as yet in any determinate way. So far he knows only that some sounding, sensible, corporeal object is. To discover determinately and specifically what that something is, he must leave his warm and comfortable bed and make further investigation.

Intellectual Reflection on Our First Knowledge

We see, then, by reflecting on our intellectual knowledge, that "being" (something exists) is what our intellect first knows.[17] What the thing is specifically and determinately (its essence, or nature) and many of the characteristics (accidents) of the existent are known only after closer observation and scrutiny. For example, the householder mentioned above, after making further investigation, finds himself confronted by a prowling, feline existent, not a burglarizing, human existent, as he had feared.

In this initial knowledge of the real, the intellect affirms that

[16] This knowledge does not *exclude* essense, but the essence is not known determinately. Moreover, in this first intellectual knowledge, the *number* of existents, whether one or many, is sometimes not known determinately; for example, a "single dim star" when viewed through a large telescope may turn out to be a cluster of thousands of stars or even an entire galaxy of stars

[17] The common content of this basic conceptual and judgmental knowledge of sensible existents is expressed in a notion, or concept. This notion is not a direct and immediate knowledge of the sensible existent. Rather, it is a conceptualization of the mind expressing that in its first knowledge of any existent, the mind knows that *something is*. (This notion, since it delivers only sensible being, is not the metaphysical knowledge of being.)

Without such notions, or concepts, a science of metaphysics cannot be formulated, much less written down in textbooks. Metaphysics is not a series of existential judgments recognizing the existence of singular, sensible beings. It is truly a science (necessary and universal knowledge), although unlike any other science. As such it is expressed in attributive judgments and propositions, which logically are reducible to subject, copula, predicate form.

something is; it knows "being." It recognizes a confrontation by an existent; it judges something *to be,* TO EXIST.

Attainable by All Who Intellectually Know Being

Thus far we have been concerned with our basic, experiential[18] knowledge of "being," of existents. Such a knowledge, which delivers sensible, material existents, is attained by all who intellectually know the real. Moreover, the reflection needed to see some (analogously[19]) common content of this first knowledge is not very difficult to make and, perhaps, is made by many adults who never formally study metaphysics.

Not the Metaphysical Knowledge of Being as Being

The scientific, metaphysical knowledge of being *as being,* however, is more difficult to reach. To know being on the metaphysical plane, we must know it as separated from those determinations and limitations that do not belong to being as such. To attain a metaphysical knowledge of the real, we must separate from the sensible, material "being" delivered in our initial knowledge, all those aspects of being that do not belong to being precisely as being, especially the restriction and limitation that come from matter.[20]

We will accomplish this by using a twofold method: (1) by reflectively considering the sensible, material existents presented in our experience and (2) by a brief critique of the answers given (explicitly or implicitly) by the principal philosophical systems to the question: What does it mean *to be?* At this point, we must ask ourselves: Since "being" (*ens*) is that which *is,* what does "is" mean?

[18] The term is used here to signify man's sensory-intellectual knowledge of sensible being—a sense knowledge permeated with intellectuality. See footnote 7 of this chapter.

[19] This term will be explained more fully in a later section of this chapter.

[20] Cf. Maritain, *op. cit.,* p. 36. It should be noted that Maritain uses the term "abstraction" where perhaps the term "separation" would more aptly convey the meaning. Cf. Régis, *op. cit.,* p. 305.

C. MEANING OF "TO BE" (*esse*)

What does it mean "to be"? What meaning[21] do we attach to existing, to being real? This is the most fundamental and radical question we can ask, and the answer we shall give will have far-reaching consequences throughout our philosophical view of reality. Philosophers throughout the history of thought have (implicitly or explicitly) given various answers to this crucial question: What is it to-be? [22]

Idealism

A pure idealism, or subjectivism, would identify reality with thought. For a radical idealism, such as that of the English philosopher Berkeley (1685–1753) to-be is *to-be-perceived* (*esse est percipi*); the entire reality of sensible objects consists in their being perceived; and if they are not perceived, they are not real.[23] In a pure idealism, the intellect produces its objects: beings are *what* they are because we think they are what they are; moreover, they *are* precisely because we think they are.[24]

[21] A "meaning" is ordinarily a restrictive, or definitive, meaning, which sets limits to (defines) a mode of existing, and hence is aptly expressed in a "definition." It should become clear in this section that "to be" of itself is not a restrictive meaning, or intelligibility

[22] We do not claim that any philosophers actually hold the philosophical positions as they are presented here. One will probably never, for example, encounter a pure idealist. Let us regard these "pure" philosophical positions as trends in philosophical thinking or as the fundamental insight that characterizes a philosopher's view of reality. One might also regard them as brief and oversimplified presentations of positions used as a pedagogical device for throwing light on a difficult philosophical problem. Cf. Reginald F. O'Neill, S.J., *Theories of Knowledge*, Prentice-Hall, Inc., Englewood Cliffs, N. J., 1960, pp. 123–124.

[23] Berkeley's God, however, in the absence of human perceivers ". . . constantly perceives the sensible world and gives it thereby its exterior reality" (*Three Dialogues between Hylas and Philonous*, Dialogue 1).

[24] The student who is tempted to be overcritical of the idealist's claim that the mind constructs its objects is reminded that the Ptolemaic explanation of planetary and stellar movements was indeed a gigantic *mental construction* (now fortunately abandoned). The world of learned men, however, accepted it for more than fifteen centuries. Today light phenomena are *inter-*

The realist, on the other hand, contends that the human intellect *discovers* its object, that it does not create its object. True, things are what we *know* they are, and are *when* we know they are (at least for the most part), but our knowing neither makes them be *what* they are, nor does it make them *be* (exist). Rather, the human intellect is confronted by existents; it does not produce them; it discovers them. True, it is only in and through *knowledge* that we attain being,[25] but in our knowledge of being we know that things exist (and a fortiori can exist) independently of our knowledge of them. What we assert, or affirm, is not our *knowledge* of the things which are, but that *they are*.

Moreover, not all objects of thought are real, for example, a dinosaur. Hence, when we know that something *is*, "is" means something more fundamental than our knowledge. In other words: things do not exist because we know them; our knowledge is not the reality principle.

Materialism

Another answer to the question "What is it to-be?" is the answer of materialism: to-be is to-be-material; to-be is to-be-quantitative, extended, dimensional, measurable; and any "thing" not extended, not dimensional, not quantitative, not measurable, simply is not. In this view of reality, a thing is real inasmuch as it is material. The position is not that all the beings a materialist experiences are material *de facto* and that, perhaps, some beings he does not know about can be immaterial. Rather, the position is that to be *at all* is to-be-material, that matter is the reality principle. (This statement, of course, is an alleged induction based on a materialist's knowledge of only some beings. They make their induction concerning the "nature" of reality from only some beings; and so shall we.)

---

preted either as waves or as particles or as a combination of the two—"wavicles," as Eddington would have it.

[25] The student who is inclined to regard the idealist position as completely unfounded is asked to consider these questions: Are there any realities apart from our knowledge? Are there any realities which we do not *know*? If so, how do we *know* this?

Materialism is of various kinds, but it will be sufficient for our purposes here to consider two principal types: mechanistic materialism and dialectical materialism.

Mechanistic Materialism. In a mechanistic materialism, reality is considered as identically "matter," and matter is regarded ultimately as solid, homogeneous, and inert particles which are united in various configurations, thus accounting for the many differences we find among things.[26] In one of its crudest forms, man is considered to be literally what he eats (*man ist wass er isst*).[27] Today mechanistic materialism is largely an obsolete philosophical position, especially because of its failure to explain adequately thought and other psychic activities by attempting to reduce them to material processes of the central nervous system.

Dialectical Materialism. The dialectical materialism of Karl Marx (1818–1883), however, is a much more influential and, we might add, a much more sophisticated brand of materialism. Many Marxists today, although still according the primacy to matter, admit thought as a reality apart from matter, but claim that thought has "emerged" from matter as a result of the evolutionary process along with life itself. Hence, even for these more recent materialists, matter remains the reality principle.

In making a brief critique of this metaphysical position, we must keep in mind that the beings of our direct sensory-intellectual experience are indeed material; they have matter as a

[26] This form of materialism dominated the thinking of philosophizing physicists during the eighteenth and early nineteenth centuries, who saw in it the philosophical generalizations of Newtonian physics. The more recent mechanists, mistaking a physicist's constructural explanations of phenomena for a philosophical account, tend to conceive matter, not as small, homogeneous particles, but as energy, mass, force, radiation or as an underlying mass-energy matrix.

[27] This remark credited to the German philosopher Feuerbach is not, however, representative of the general tenor of his position, which recognizes that thought is not itself material or merely an activity of the brain. See Sidney Hook, *From Hegel to Marx*, The Humanities Press, Inc., New York, 1958, p. 238.

constituent element. Nevertheless, these material beings are existents (are beings) not because they are material, but simply because they *are*, because they *exist;* matter is not the principle of their reality. True, these beings are quantitative, dimensional, spatiotemporal, measurable—in a word, *material,* but that is not what we mean when we say they *exist.*

Matter explains only why these beings exist with the limitations of space and time, why these beings are extended, dimensional, massive, inertial, measurable, quantitative. Such beings are corporeal (bodily); they are material; they are not matter itself. Matter, the common principle of material beings, does not explain what they are specifically, or formally: for example, why one material being is canine, another feline, another aquatic, etc.[28] Now, the principle which accounts for the specific nature of the material being—form—is a more fundamental reality factor than is matter. Thus, matter cannot be the ultimate reality principle itself. It merely makes material beings be material; it does not make them formal (specific); much less does it make them be (exist).

Even if all limited beings were material, it would not follow that to-be is to-be-material; nor would it follow that the reality principle is matter. Indeed, it will be proved in the philosophy of man and in natural theology that some beings are immaterial; it will be shown that man's intellectual knowledge is strictly immaterial and that God is a strictly immaterial being; but we do not need to prove this at this point. True, if we know that immaterial

[28] Matter, even in the materialistic view, is something of itself quite indeterminate. When we name a corporeal being, we do not call it *matter.* Rather, we name it according to its species, or formal type, for names are imposed to signify the kind, type, species, or *form* of corporeal being. Thus, we speak of canine, feline, and human corporeal beings—dogs, cats, men. In all these instances, we are stating the species, or form, of the corporeal (material) existent. To call all three (dog, cat, man) *matter* would deny the differences among them.

It is clear, then, that the source of specification (form) is a more important factor in material beings than matter. And yet even form is a factor on the side of determination, or restriction, of being.

We see, then, that both form and matter are limiting factors of a corporeal existent; they are not the existential factor, the reality principle; they are not the act of existing.

beings exist, we must conclude that to-be is not necessarily to-be-material,[29] but that is not the precise point at issue here. At this juncture, by reflecting on being as given in sensory-intellectual experience, we see that even though these beings are material, the reality principle is not that principle which restricts them to being material. Thus, we understand that a thing *can be* without being material,[30] that matter is not the reality principle.

An example may help us here. To-be-human is not necessarily to-be-shod, although all humans here are indeed shod. Shoes don't make the man; that is to say, shoes do not make one human. This intellectual insight is easy to make. More difficult is the insight that matter does not make a thing (even a material thing) BE. Although all beings of our direct experience are indeed material, nevertheless, by reflection we are able to see that the principle which restricts them to one place at one time (cutting them off from all other things) is not the selfsame principle which ranges them in the all-encompassing order of being. Thus, we come to understand that the principle of their *materiality* is not the principle of their *reality*.

Dynamism—Philosophies of Flux

Another major position on the "nature" of reality is one originally formulated by the Greek philosopher Heraclitus (540–465 B.C.), whose doctrine is summarized in a famous remark: "all things flow and nothing remains" (*panta rei kai ouden menei*).[31] For Heraclitus, reality is like a river, in which one cannot bathe

[29] However, even an immaterial being is a being, not because it is immaterial, but because it *exists*. The mode of existing does not explain the fact of existing.

[30] "It is extremely remarkable that being, the first object attained by our mind in things—which cannot deceive us since being the first, it cannot involve any construction effected by the mind nor, therefore, the possibility of faulty composition—bears within itself the sign that beings of another order than the sensible are thinkable and possible" (Maritain, *op. cit.*, p. 214, reprinted by permission).

[31] This, indeed, is a valuable philosophical insight. All the things of our experience are truly in flux; their very existence is a *flux* existence. "To be" (*esse*) is, indeed, a dynamic act and yields in no way to the dynamism of Heraclitus and Bergson.

twice since the waters flow ever onward. He also compares reality to fire, which cannot stop burning without stopping to exist and maintains itself by feeding on new material. Although Heraclitus does not expressly say so, it would seem that he rejects "being" in favor of "becoming" (change), that for him not only is to-be to-be-changed, but change is the only reality and reality is identically change.

A more recent philosophy of flux is that of the French philosopher Henri Bergson (1859–1941). In his view, what we call things, or beings, are intellectual stoppages of the mobile real— so many "still pictures" of the fluid real, which the concept-forming intellect constructs to manipulate and control the real. Reality, however, is duration, flux, or change itself.

In evaluating this position, we must note that the beings of which we have immediate knowledge are indeed changing; they are in flux. Nevertheless, it is not because they change that they exist. Rather, it is because they exist that they can change. (If nothing existed, there would be no change; or, to speak more concretely, only *existing* things change.) Nor do we mean that things are changing when we say that they exist. Although the beings of our experience do change, we understand that to-be is not the same as to-change, and that something can be without changing.

Activism

Closely allied to the philosophies of flux is the view that reality is identified with activity: that to-be is to-act; that existence is identically activity. According to this position, what we call a "being" is merely a complex, or collection, of activities to which we give a name; there is no "being," no substance, which acts.

In criticizing this view, we must grant that all beings act, and that it is only through activity that we know *what* things are and that they *are* (exist). The mode of existing is known through the (highest) mode of operation: barking, for example, manifests a canine existent; speech manifests a human existent. We depend on the mode of activity to know *what* something is and on the fact that it acts to know that it *is* (exists).

However, a being does not exist because it acts. It is the other way about: a being acts, or at least can act, insofar as it exists. What does not exist neither acts nor can act. Moreover, what exists does not always act, at least not to the full extent of its power to act. Thus, a student sometimes sits in class and thinks; at other times he merely sits. While merely sitting, he still exists as a human existent though he does not then act precisely as human. We see, then, that activity is not existence itself (at least not in the case of limited existents); activity is not the reality principle.

Essentialism

The position which attributes the reality of a being to its whatness, essence, or nature is called essentialism. This doctrine has taken various forms, the most important being that of Plato (429–347 B.C.),[32] but all forms of essentialism hold this in common: to-be is to-be-an-essence (or at least to-have-an-essence); *what* a thing is, is the very reality principle of a being; things are real by being *what* they are.

According to Plato, an individual dog, Fido, for example, since he is not dog (as such), but only *a* dog (a participant in canine essence, or nature), is not fully real. To be fully real, Fido would need to be the universal essence, "Dog in himself," existing in a separate world of universal Essences (subsisting forms, or Ideas). But since Fido is merely *a* dog, he is not fully real; his reality is merely a participation in the reality of the universal essence. Hence, he is merely a shadow (albeit a real shadow) of the "really" Real, the separated Form, or Idea, existing in the World of Ideas.

In the essentialism of Duns Scotus (1266–1308), to be real in the highest degree is to be this or that *individual*. In the Scotistic view, a thing is constituted an individual by a special principle,

[32] According to Plato, only the universal essences (for example, dog as such) existing in a separate World of Ideas are fully real. The sensible, individual existent merely participates in the universal nature and hence is not fully real, being merely a shadow reality though a real shadow. See his *Republic*, Book VII, for the famous allegory of the men in the cave, to whom the shadows are more real than the realities in the world of sunlight.

"thisness" (*haecceitas*), added to a universal essence, thus determining it to be this singular essence.[33] Thus, singularity, or "thisness," makes something to be fully real.

In criticizing the general essentialist position, we shall content ourselves with two considerations:

1. An essentialist philosophy cannot explain the various *kinds,* or modes, of existing of the various existents which confront us. If, for example, to-be were to-be-canine, only dogs would exist. If to-be were to-be-human, only humans could exist. The fact is, however, that we are confronted by existents of many different kinds. Hence, to-be (to exist) cannot be identified with any determinate kind, or mode, of existing; that is to say, (specific) essence is not the reality principle. Nor can the act of be-ing (*esse*) be identified with any individual of our experience which participates in a (specific) essence, or nature. To-be is not to-be-human; nor is to-be to-be-John Doe.

2. Moreover, an essentialism cannot distinguish between (1) what actually and presently exists, on the one hand, and (2) what did, will, or could exist, on the other. We can know, for example, *what* a thing is (a mode, manner, or way of existing) and still be in the dark as to whether any being (*ens*) exercises (or will exercise, or has exercised) existence according to that mode. I may know, for example, what a whooping crane is and still not know whether one is (exists), since the few survivors observed along the Missouri Valley flyways in the last flight northward may have perished in a blizzard and may no longer exist.

Moreover, I can know who an individual is (for example, a single, tagged whooping crane) and still not know whether he, she, or it still is (exists, lives). We sometimes ask whether so-and-so is still living (still exists). This means that we know who he is but do not know whether he still is (exists).

However, if being is essence (the essentialist position), then to know essence is to know being; knowing what-a-thing-is is to know that it is; for example, knowing what a hundred dollars are is to know that they are. But obviously such is not the case.

[33] See François J. Thonnard, *A Short History of Philosophy,* translated by Edward A. Maziarz, Desclée et Cie., New York, 1955, p. 443.

All this implies that essence (whether universal or individual) is not identical with the very existing of a being and the other way about. Essence is not the core reality factor of the existent; essence is merely the "kind," or mode, factor. We see, then, that to-be is not to-be-an-essence, whether specific essence, such as human, canine, whooping crane, or individual essence, such as the essence of John Doe, Fido, or this individual, tagged whooping crane.[34]

Thomistic Existentialism[35]

The position of many modern interpreters of the philosophy of St. Thomas Aquinas (1225–1274) is this: The question "What does it mean to-be?" is a double-meaning question, and in one sense it is an irrelevant question, that is, a question that should not even be asked. For "to be" is not a whatness,[36] which can be defined in a concept. When we are confronted by an existent, we grasp what it is in a *concept* and affirm (judge) that it is. The "is," or act of existing, is simply not an essence, nature, whatness, or quiddity; it is not the mode, way, or manner of existing;

[34] The positions we have criticized (with the exception of activism) were presented to help us make an "ascending" series of judgments of separation, in which we disengaged "being" from the restrictions of matter, change, and (limiting) essence. Of less importance to the metaphysician is the "descending" series of judgments of separation: for example, to-be is not necessarily to-be-Divine (once the existence of God is proved); to-be is not necessarily to-be-intellectual, sensitive, or even organic.

[35] Thomistic existentialism should not be confused with some other "existentialist" philosophies, that is, philosophies which tend to emphasize the primacy of the act of existing over essence, such as the philosophy of Kierkegaard, Heidegger, Jaspers, and others. Especially, it should not be confused with the thought of Jean-Paul Sartre, an atheistic and pessimistic philosophy, in which existence is regarded as absurd, the source of anxiety and even of nausea. In such a view, to-be is "too bad," a far cry from the position of St. Thomas Aquinas: "To be is . . . the perfection of all perfections" (*De Potentia*, VII, 2, ad 9[m]). Maritain considers Thomism the only "authentic" existentialism. See his *Existence and the Existent*, Doubleday & Company, Inc., Garden City, N.Y., 1956, pp. 11–13.

[36] This point can be more clearly expressed in cryptic Latin: "*Quid est* EST? *Non est* QUID." (What is *is?* Not a *what*)

it is not the determining and limiting whatness of the existent; it is the very act of existing, of be-*ing*, itself and cannot be grasped in a proper concept.[37]

True, we do form an abstract and nonproper[38] concept of the "existing" of beings (*entia*), and we express it by using the abstract term "existence." In this concept, we intellectually present to ourselves the act of existing as if it were a whatness, or essence. However, we must guard against confusing this abstract conception with the judgmental operation in which we affirm the concrete act of existing.

There will always be a certain mystery to the human mind as regards the act of existing, even in the beings which confront us; it is not attainable by our intellects in the concepts with which our intellects feel most at home. But this does not mean that the act of existing is not attainable at all, that it is not meaningful to our intellects. The "is" of existential judgments is meaningful, but its meaning is not a conceptual meaning. "Is" is not unintelligible; rather, it is *super*intelligible to the conceptualizing intellect; it can be reached only in another operation of the mind, the judgment.

Although as regards the beings of our experience, we always recognize and affirm an act of existing which is restricted, or limited, according to the mode (essence, nature) of the existent, nevertheless we understand that "to be" of itself is not restricted, since it is not the mode of existing. Rather, we see that "to be" is the core reality principle of the existent, its basic perfecting principle[39]—not its limiting whatness, essence, or nature. And we understand that a thing qualifies as a being in virtue of this principle.

[37] The question "What is to-be?" cannot be answered through an abstract, "static" concept, since to-be is a *dynamic* act and can be intellectually grasped (be meaningful) only in a similarly dynamic, mental act (the existential judgment) whose object is not form, or whatness, but existential act.

[38] We have proper concepts only of the essences of material beings.

[39] St. Thomas calls it the perfection of all perfections. See footnote 35 of this chapter.

Summary of Judgments of Separation

Thus, after considering the sensible, material existents presented in our experience, and after making a brief critique of the principal philosophical positions on the "nature" of the real, we may state by way of summary:

1. To-be is not to-be-perceived: a thing is not real because it is perceived; being as being need not be an object of human thought.
2. To-be is not to-be-material: a thing is not real because it is material; being precisely as being need not be material.
3. To-be is not to-be-changed: a thing is not real because it undergoes change; any existent precisely as existing need not be changing.
4. To-be is not to-act: a thing is not real because it acts; a being as being need not be acting (at least not in all its possible ways).
5. To-be is not to-be-an-essence, or nature: a thing is not real because it is of this or that specific or individual essence; any existent precisely as an existent need not be of this or that specific essence (nature) or of this or that individual essence.

In brief: things do not exist *because* they are perceived by us, are material, are undergoing change, are acting, or because of what they are. Rather, it is because of a more profound intrinsic factor that a thing is real; and that factor is the act of *existing*.

Thus, by a series of judgments of "separation," we have disengaged, or separated, a "meaning" (or intelligibility) from all limitations and restrictions. We have thereby discovered a meaning which *transcends* the determinations, limitations, and restrictions of the particular categories of being and applies (analogously) to all things that are regardless of how, or what, they are.[40] Hence, this notion is rightly called a *transcendental* notion.

[40] We have used an "ascending" series of judgments of separation, an upgrading of our knowledge of being, disengaging its content from restrictions, especially those that come from matter and motion (change).

Being as Being

Judging negatively, we find that "being as being" need not be confined to being perceived, to being material, to being changed; nor need it be confined within the determining limits of any specific or individual essence. "The ultimate meaning of 'being' is not to be in this or that way; it is *to be*."[41] Thus, by a series of judgments of separation, we purify our initial knowledge of "being" (material-sensible-thing-which-is) and are able to rise to the strictly metaphysical knowledge of being *as being*.

These negative judgments, however, presuppose *positive* knowledge: namely, the affirmative judgments that things exist and the positive, metaphysical insight (intuition, or vizualization) that *"to be" of itself transcends its determinations*. This insight may aptly be called a *transcendentalizing* judgment.

Thus, we come to understand that it is in proportion to the act of existing that anything makes the grade as a being. It is not the essence, the determining mode, manner, or way, of existing that primarily and radically makes a being qualify as an existent. Nor does matter, or motion, or its being known by us make a being *be*. True, the beings of our experience are material, are changing, are of a specific and individual essence, are known by us. Moreover, being as such does not *exclude* any of these determinations, but these determinations do not explain the reality of a being. It is insofar as they *exercise the act of existing* that things qualify as being.

Hence, we may aptly describe "being" (*ens*) as *that which is*.

D. "BEING" (*ens*) AS ATTRIBUTIVE NOUN

In the preceding section, we were concerned with the meaning of "being" as a verb. The term "being," however, is sometimes also used as a *noun* and attributed as a predicate[42] to various

---

[41] Étienne Gilson, *Elements of Christian Philosophy*, Doubleday & Company, Inc., Garden City, N.Y., 1960, p. 133.

[42] An opposing view holds that such a predication is tautological: ". . . in *I am being* or *God is being*, the predicate is but a blind window which is put there for mere verbal symmetry. There is no predicate . . . in the thus-

subjects: for example, I am a being, God is a being, a dinosaur is a being, a doughnut hole is a being, space is a being.

Strict and Proper Sense

In the strict and proper sense, "being" as an attributive noun signifies that which is actually and presently. Thus, the teacher and the students of this class are "beings" in the strict sense. The members of the past generation[43] and your future great-grandchildren, since they do not exist actually and presently, cannot be called "beings" in the strict and proper sense.[44]

Moreover, it is the unitary, "total" existent (the supposit) which is "being" in this proper sense, not the "parts" or coexisting principles which constitute it.[45] For example, it is not a man's

---

developed proposition . . ." (Étienne Gilson, *Being and Some Philosophers,* Pontifical Institute of Mediaeval Studies, Toronto, 1949, p. 193).

Another view attaches only *constructural* value to this concept but admits that it has some direct use as a predicate in some contexts, especially in criticism of those philosophers who hold that the First Principle of reality is nonbeing though real, for example, Plotinus. "To say in the context of an analysis, or criticism of such a position, 'God is a being,' means 'God can be truly understood by us as something which is' " (George P. Klubertanz, S.J., *Introduction to the Philosophy of Being,* Appleton-Century-Crofts, Inc., New York, 1953, pp. 285–286).

[43] Only their separated souls exist. The separated human soul is not a human person. This point will be discussed at length in the philosophy of man.

[44] "In the strictest sense of the phrase 'that which is' indicates 'that which is realized at this moment' . . ." (Louis De Raeymaeker, *The Philosophy of Being,* translated by Edmund H. Ziegelmeyer, S.J., B. Herder Book Co., St. Louis, 1954, p. 88; reprinted by permission).

[45] "To be properly belongs to subsistents, whether they are simple, as in the case of separated substances, or whether they be composite, as in the case of material substances. For to be properly belongs to that which has to be, namely, the subsistent exercising existence. But forms and accidents and the like are not called beings (*entia*) as if they themselves were, but because by them something is; as whiteness is called being (*ens*) because by it a subject is white. Wherefore, according to the Philosopher, an accident is more properly called of a being (*entis*) rather than being (*ens*). Therefore, . . . accidents and forms and the like, which do not subsist are coexistents rather than existents . . ." (Aquinas, *Summa Theologiae,* I, 45, 4c).

"Only that which subsists, *is:* the parts and the principles are not in

arms, feet, or other parts which are "being" in the proper sense; rather, that which exists is the individual who *has* arms and feet, who maintains these parts, and even originally evolved them by his own vital activity.[46]

It is "being" in the proper sense which is the point of departure of metaphysics and is its primary object of study. (Such beings are said to be "in act"; all others are said to be "in potency.") It is from these real beings, the existents exercising the act of be-*ing* actually and presently, that the human metaphysician derives his knowledge of "being as being" and formulates the principles and laws which are valid for every being.

Wider Sense

In a wider sense, "being" is sometimes used to designate even things which existed in the past or will exist in the future —which have been or will be. The last rose of (last) summer, which once actually did exist, may be called "being" in this sense. In the strict sense, however, it no longer exists; only the memory of it exists. Also, the roses which will bloom next summer—which actually will exist—may be called "being" in this wider sense. For the present, however, "beings" of this sort exist only in thought; the thought of them exists in someone's mind; or, to be precise, someone exists and thinks about them now and then.[47]

---

themselves, but they exist in the subsistent reality with which they communicate, with which they are united, and to which they belong as constitutive elements . . ." (De Raeymaeker, *op. cit.*, p. 245; reprinted by permission).

"Too often the manner in which it [the doctrine of composition in being] is presented seems to compromise the fundamental unity of subsistent being . . . :" (*ibid.*, p. 334; reprinted by permission).

[46] An organism is not the mere sum total of its parts, as if the parts were assembled as we assemble a machine. An organism is one being, a substantial unity. In the case of accidental units, on the other hand (for example, a house, automobile, typewriter), it is not the accidental unit which is "being" in the proper sense, but whatever are the ultimate, unitary beings which are the parts that compose the accidental unit. The difference between substantial units and accidental units will be discussed in a later chapter.

[47] It is true, however, and eternally true, that they did or will exist and

Moreover, it is only in a wider and derivative sense that the parts, or principles, which constitute a being in the strict sense (the unitary existent, or supposit) can be called "being." As we have seen, it is the being which *has* the parts, which exists and hence is a "being" in the proper sense.

Widest Sense

"Being" is also sometimes predicated even of things which are not, have not been, nor will be, but *could* be. Moreover, "being" is even predicated of that which can only be *considered* or signified as being, though it cannot be (exist).

As to the things which merely could be, the *possibles*, the predication of "being" signifies that such a *mode* of existing is conceivable and not contradictory; it also implies that a being exists which can produce them.[48] Thus, a "square circle" cannot be called "being," not even in the widest sense of the term. On the other hand, a "twin brother" (provided you do not have one), may be called "being" in the sense that he at least could have been under different circumstances. Certainly, a twin brother can be thought of; he is an intelligible object. But a square circle, a four-sided figure which is not four-sided, namely a circle, is

---

that the principles of metaphysics either did or will apply to them, as the case may be.

[48] Such beings are said to be "in potency" according to St. Thomas's division of being: "In an absolute sense (*simpliciter*), those things exist which are in act. Those things which are not in act are in potency either of God Himself or of the creature: whether in an active potency or in a passive potency; whether in the power (*potentia*) of thinking, or of imagining, or of signifying in any way whatsoever. . . . But of those things which are not in act a distinction must be noted. For some things, although they are not presently in act, nevertheless, either have been or will be. . . . But there are other things, which are in the potency [power] of God or of the creature, which, nevertheless, are not, nor will be, nor have been" (*Summa Theologiae*, I, 14, 9c).

Our division of "being" into a strict sense, wider sense, and widest sense is based on this text.

It should be noted that "to be in potency" means that some *existent* has either active potency or passive potency.

not even a conceivable object; it cannot even be thought; it is not possible.[49]

Even "things" which can only be discoursed about when considered as "being" can be called "being" in this widest sense, although they can never be (exist) in the primary sense of the term. Thus, we speak of doughnut holes, which are really nothing surrounded by something. We speak of outer space, which is "a tremendous amount of nothing" between the planets, the stars, and galaxies. We speak of the many evils (deficiencies in being) "existing" in the world. All such mental constructs (*entia rationis*) can be called "being" only in the widest sense of the term.[50]

From this division, it should be obvious that the term "being" is capable of the widest signification. Primarily and directly metaphysics is interested in "being" in the strict, or proper, sense of the term and takes its point of departure from the things which are (exist) actually and presently. Secondarily, however, and indirectly, metaphysics directs its interest to "being" in the wider and even in the widest sense.[51]

[49] Concerning the "possibles" and "being in potency," Hawkins, a contemporary British Thomist, has this to say: "A passing mention is all that is deserved by the attempt to attribute some sort of reality to the possible by saying that it exists in those minds which can conceive it and in the power of those agents which could bring it into existence. To say that a thing exists in thought is only a misleading way of saying that the thought of it exists; it confers no reality on the contents of the thought. In the same way, to say that a thing exists in the power which could bring it about is only a misleading way of saying that some existent thing could bring it about; the thing itself remains as non-existent as before" (from *Being and Becoming* by D. J. B. Hawkins, Copyright 1954, Sheed & Ward, Inc, New York, p. 109).

The following classic remark is from the same author: ". . . there is no need to postulate a mysterious class of possibilities halfway between being and not-being" (*ibid.*, p. 108).

[50] Cf. Maritain, *Degrees of Knowledge*, pp. 94–95.

[51] This at present is a controverted point among Thomists. For a similar position see "What Is Really Real?" by Wayne Norris Clarke, S.J., in *Progress in Philosophy*, edited by James R. McWilliams, S J , The Bruce Publishing Company, Milwaukee, 1955, p. 89.

E. THE SCIENCE OF BEING AS BEING

Metaphysics is the speculative science which studies being as being and formulates the principles and laws which are true of being as such.

Science in General

By *science* (*scientia*) we understand a certain, evident, and organized body of knowledge proceeding from principles, the meaning which Aristotle (384–322 B.C.) gave to the term. In such a knowledge, we understand that something is true, why it is true, and that it cannot be otherwise.[52] Much of our certain and evident knowledge is merely factual; for example: yesterday it rained; this chair is sturdy; that chalk is white. Science, however, in our sense of the term,[53] is unified (or organized) knowledge, and the basic organizing elements are the principles with which the science begins.[54] Much of our knowledge, too, is merely opinion; for example, it is my opinion that it will rain this afternoon. Science, on the other hand, is certain and evident knowledge: either with the evidence and certainty of first principles or made evident by reasoning to necessary conclusions from such principles, so that the conclusions are seen in the light of the principles.

Speculative vs. Practical Science

Many sciences seek truth primarily as a means to an end to which the truth is subordinated and directed; for example, the science of engineering may entail the study of stresses and strains

[52] An example of such a knowledge, which most college students will readily recognize, is that of a demonstration in Euclidean geometry.

[53] The contemporary sciences, the "experimental" sciences, have largely appropriated the term. Nevertheless, they are only approximations to the ideal type. They are best called "empiriological" sciences. See Maritain *Degrees of Knowledge*, pp. 22–23.

[54] The principles of one science may be borrowed from, and proved in, another science; for example, the science of shipbuilding presupposes the principles of the science of engineering, which in turn presupposes the principles of physics.

so that bridges, buildings, and other structures may be properly constructed and not collapse. Such a science is primarily *practical*.[55] Other sciences seek truth primarily as the end in itself, simply to understand the real, that is, to satisfy the intellect's desire for truth.[56] Such sciences are primarily *speculative*. Sought for their own sake and not subordinated as means to something else, such knowledges are themselves superior to the practical sciences.[57]

Material Object of a Science

Every science has a material object and a formal object. By *material object* we mean the subject matter of the science—what the science is concerned with, what the scientist studies, the scope of the science. Biology, for example, has for its material object all living bodies, the organisms. Inorganic chemistry has for its material object nonliving bodies.

The *material object* of metaphysics embraces all being—whether material or immaterial, finite or infinite, potential or actual, real or intentional, substantial or accidental. Metaphysics is not restricted in its scope as are the other sciences. True, as we have seen, metaphysics is primarily interested in being in the proper sense, that which actually and presently exists.

[55] However, even such an eminently practical science has a speculative element about it, and students of engineering may, for example, pursue a knowledge of stresses and strains for its own sake, simply to understand, or, as we often say, out of pure intellectual curiosity.

[56] Such speculative knowledges, however, may have a practical result as well. For example, what we hold philosophically concerning the nature of man can greatly influence one's actions toward others. If one regards his neighbor as little better than a canine existent, he will more readily treat him as such.

[57] Spectators watching spectator sports are acquiring a speculative knowledge, though (ordinarily) not a highly organized knowledge. In a sports-loving nation, not many question the value, or worth, of such a knowledge. It is an end in itself and does not depend on something else (to which it might be subordinated as a means) for its intrinsic worth. The same holds for the speculative sciences, and especially for the speculative science par excellence, metaphysics.

Formal Object of a Science

The formal object of a science is the aspect, or viewpoint, from which the science (or scientist) studies the material object, the subject matter; or, in more realistic terms, it is the intelligible aspect in the subject matter which presents itself to (or confronts) the scientist regarding it from that particular point of view.

Various sciences may study the same subject matter; that is to say, they may have the same material object and still be distinct sciences. Various sciences study man, for example, but owing to differences in methods, they study man from different and restricted points of view: e.g., anatomy (structural aspect), anthropology (origins), psychiatry (mental health), psychology (behavior), sociology (group activity), etc.[58] It is the formal object which differentiates sciences whose material object is the same. Hence, to define such sciences adequately, we must state both the material object and the determining, or specifying, formal object.

Metaphysics, we have seen, has for its material object, or scope, all being. Its *formal object,* however, is being precisely *as being.*[59] It studies the things which are insofar as they *are.* Although this formal object is, in a certain sense, a restricted aspect, or viewpoint, nevertheless it is an aspect that is presented in *every* being; it is the most common and most universal aspect; and for that reason the truths which metaphysics discovers will hold for all being. On the other hand, a particular science, let us say the science of chemistry, studies (among many other things) water (aquatic being) precisely as water and formulates the principles and laws (e.g., freezing point, boiling point) which are true of all aquatic being but are not true of other kinds of being.

[58] The restriction in formal object is due to the restricted type of analysis, or methodology, employed in the science. For example: spectroscopic analysis is helpful in physics and in chemistry; structural analysis is helpful to the biologist. Neither type of analysis is of use to the psychiatrist (who may rely instead on psychoanalysis) or to the philosopher.

[59] The student will gradually come to a realization of the meaning of this phrase as he makes progress through this course of study.

Absolute Universality and Necessity of Metaphysical Principles

Since metaphysics studies all being and studies being under its most universal aspect, the primary principles and laws formulated in this science must be true (analogously[60]) of all being. There can be no exceptions to these principles: only nonbeing, which does not exist, does not fall under these most general principles and laws. Such principles are unqualified, unconditioned, necessary, universal—in a word, *absolute*.[61]

On the other hand, the principles we discover concerning one type of existent, for example, water, are not absolute. Water precisely as water tends to freeze at 32 degrees Fahrenheit under standard conditions. What is true of water (aquatic being) precisely as water is true (within limits) of all water, wherever and whenever we find it, but is true only of water, of aquatic being, alone. However, what is true of being precisely *as being* must be true of every being regardless of its mode, manner, or way of existing,[62] whether material or immaterial, whether according to a finite mode or according to no limiting mode. For metaphysics is not concerned directly with the mode, or manner, of existing (though it does not exclude these modes, or essences), but precisely with being as being. It considers existents as existing, regardless of their individual, specific, and generic differentiating modes. Hence, the primary principles and laws which metaphysics discovers in being are absolute.

F.   FIRST PRINCIPLES CONCERNING BEING

The beings which confront us are the initial source, or principle, of our knowledge. Without being, without the *things which are,* no sensory experience of being would arise. Without sensory

---

[60] True but with a difference.

[61] Other principles may be absolute within a mode of being (for example, *human* beings are mortal). The primary, metaphysical principles, however, are absolute even in the order of be-ing (existing) itself. Hence, they are truly transcendental; that is to say, they cut across the modes of be-ing.

[62] Though always analogously, that is, in a way proportionate to its mode.

awareness, we would have no intellectual knowledge of being, much less a metaphysics. Implicit in our initial knowledge of "being" (that something is) are the principles, or laws, which are true of all being precisely as being. The content of this knowledge is made explicit, however, only by a reflection on our knowledge of being.[63]

Principle of Noncontradiction

A thing cannot both *be* and *not be* at the same time; either a thing is or it isn't; an existent cannot exercise the act of existing and not exercise it at the same time; being is, nonbeing is not. All these statements are various formulations of the law of non-contradiction regarding "being" itself. An existent, a being, is in opposition to not-existing, to nonbeing; it is opposed to nothingness; it *is*.

Nor can the same existent be *what* it is and be something else at the same time. A canine existent cannot be feline at the same time. A being existing according to one essential (substantial) mode cannot exist according to another mode at the same time. This is the principle of noncontradiction as regards the essential (substantial) order.

Nor can the same existent be accidentally modified in one respect and not so modified at the same time. A white dog can-not at the same time be a brown dog. A learned man cannot at the same time be an ignorant man concerning the same object of knowledge. This is the principle of noncontradiction with reference to the accidental order (which is concerned with sec-ondary, not primary, modes of existing).[64]

[63] Such principles are not mere laws of thinking, as the German philoso-pher Kant (1724–1804) held; they are laws of be-ing, of existing, as well. We must think of reality according to these principles ultimately because reality *is* (exists) that way and affects our minds that way.

[64] In the logical order, the principle of contradiction means that affirma-tion and negation (whether attributive or existential) are incompatible si-multaneously. It is impossible to affirm and deny the same thing about the same subject at the same time. The logical order, however, is based on the real order.

Principle of Intelligibility of Being

(1) Being is knowable, intelligible; it can move our intellects to knowledge.[65] (2) The intellect in turn can know being; it is the power of knowing being even precisely as being. (3) The concepts and judgments by which intellect knows correspond to the real which it knows. These three statements are various formulations of the principle of intelligibility of being in terms of (1) being itself, (2) intellect, (3) knowledge.

As regards our ability to know being, the principle of intelligibility implies two distinct elements: (1) that the thing *is*, is attainable in the judgment; (2) the essence of the being, its mode of existing, is attainable in the concept.[66]

Moreover, the intellect can conceive modes of existing though no existent may be exercising existence according to such a mode. I can, for example, conceive *what* a 30-foot-tall man would be; such a mode of existing is conceivable, though no individual human exercises existence according to that (accidental) mode. Such conceivable modes of existing are called the "possibles."

No Inconceivable Modes of Existing. On the other hand, a square circle is said to be *impossible;* such a mode of existing is not conceivable in any concept. No matter how hard we try to combine the concepts square and circle, we cannot put them together into one conceivable mode of existing. A square circle says a square which is not a square or a circle which is not a circle. Hence, a square circle is said to be impossible. Impossibles will never exist; or, to say the same thing more precisely, such modes of existing are inconceivable, and no existent will ever exercise existence according to such a mode. Nonbeings, nonexistents, cannot be judged to *be* in an existential judgment; contradictory "modes" of be-ing, of existing, such as square circle, cannot even be conceived in a concept.

[65] Being can, as it were, speak to intellect and evoke a response; *res ipsa loquitur.*

[66] At least in a general or descriptive way. We do not, however, have a direct intuitive knowledge of essences. We know them only through their activities. Cf. footnote 6 of this chapter.

Intellect's Ability to Know Being. That the intellect can know being cannot be demonstrated nor need it be demonstrated; it is obvious. One who universally doubts and rejects the intellect as the power of knowing reality must henceforth stop all discourse about reality and retire from any serious philosophical argumentation.

True enough, the intellect can make mistakes in judgments under certain conditions, but we cannot be universally and absolutely mistaken. A mistake cannot be made unless we MIS-TAKE something for something else already known with certainty. Thus, I cannot mistake a bird for an airplane unless I do know with certainty *what* an airplane is and that something *is*.

Descartes's Universal Doubt. It is impossible to start philosophizing by universally doubting the ability of our intellects to know being,[67] as Descartes (1596–1650) attempted to do. By intellect we mean precisely the ability to know being. One should not then make a complete about-face and ask whether this power (of knowing being) has the capacity to know being.[68] Another question, however, is perfectly in place: Under what conditions can the intellect (which obviously does attain reality) mistake one thing for something else? The answer to this question constitutes part of a special philosophical discipline—epistemology, or the critique of knowledge.

Principle of Explanation, or Accountability, of Being

Another first principle concerning being we shall call, for lack of a better term, the principle of "explanation," or "accountability," of being.[69] *Whatever exists,* rather than not, *must have an explanation for its very existing.* Otherwise, being would be in-

---

[67] Cf. Maritain, *Degrees of Knowledge,* p. 78.

[68] Of one who universally doubts whether he can know reality it is a fair question to ask, "What reality?" "The reality *certainly* out there?"

[69] This principle is sometimes referred to as the principle of "sufficient reason," an unfortunate term, since it suggests there might be an "insufficient reason" as explanation. Moreover, the principle is not to be understood in the sense in which Leibniz (1646–1716) understood it, for that would seem to involve a confusion of the essential and existential orders.

different to being (existing); in other words, an existent could simultaneously be and not be. This, of course, would imply a violation of the principle of noncontradiction.

The principle of accountability, or explanation, applies also to the events, or changes, that occur in being. Whenever a change occurs, rather than no change, there must be an accounting, or explanation, of the change.[70] For example, whenever smoke rises, rather than not, there must be an accounting, or explanation, for the smoke's rising. From past experience, we know that fire is the accounting, or explanation, of this particular type of event, or change. But we also know that *every* event, every change, requires an accounting, or explanation; we know that every effect requires a cause to explain the effect.

We must note carefully that the principle of explanation applies not merely to the events, or changes, which occur in (limited) beings; it applies even to the very be-ing (existing) of an existent. That which exists, rather than not, has a reason, an accounting, or explanation, why it is at all.[71]

Various Accounts of Being and of Change. Explanations of events, or changes, differ. The experimental, empirical, or "empiriological"[72] sciences endeavor to give *proximate* explanations of events that occur in beings (whose existence they take as given) with a view to predicting and controlling events. For example, the death of a man may be explained biologically as due to a temperature of 108 degrees Fahrenheit, although, to be sure, it was not the temperature reading but the microbes which did the man in. Such explanations are very useful, for once the inseparable connection between antecedent and consequent phenomenon is seen, we can predict the consequent from the known antecedent or avoid the consequent (sometimes) by avoiding the antecedent. Such expla-

---

[70] In this sense, the principle is the same as the principle of efficient causality regarding change and applies only to limited beings. The principle of efficient causality will be discussed in a later chapter.

[71] This point too will be considered at length in the chapter on efficient causes.

[72] The term is Maritain's. See his *Philosophy of Nature*, Philosophical Library, Inc., New York, 1951, *passim*.

EXISTENTS   33

nations, however, are not ultimate explanations, nor do they pretend to be ultimate explanations.

Philosophy, on the other hand, must give an *ultimate* explanation of changes, or events, and not through antecedent-consequent sequences, but through strict causal explanations.[73] Moreover, philosophy must give an account for the very *existence* of the beings which change, a problem which does not come up in the empiriological sciences, since they take the existence of their objects of study as given.

The empiriological sciences do not claim to study beings as they are in themselves; that is the work of philosophy.[74] Rather, these disciplines study (corporeal) beings according to their *sensible phenomena* and insofar as these phenomena are measurable and can be correlated; that is to say, these sciences try to discover inseparable antecedent-consequent relations among the sensible phenomena of material beings but do not attempt to reach the (substantial) essences of things, much less try to account for the very existing of things.

Nor are the findings of these sciences always expressed in terms of the beings themselves which are studied. Some findings are expressed in a set of *numbers;* that is to say, these findings are expressed in units of certain sensible standards existing in a national or international bureau of standards—so many feet, so many meters, pounds, grams, etc. For example, a man may be scientifically described by a set of numbers: 6 feet tall, 180 pounds in weight, 98.6 degrees Fahrenheit in temperature. To be meaningful, these numbers must be related to an existing sensible standard of measurement. Thus, they express a knowledge of one thing in terms of some other sensible thing used as a standard of measurement. Other findings are expressed in *mathematical constructs,* such as ergs, dynes, amperes, volts, calories, BTUs, ang-

[73] The "causes" of the empiriological sciences are usually antecedent phenomena which have inseparable consequents in time. Such antecedents can be called "causes" only in a highly analogous sense. The "causes" of Thomistic philosophy are contemporaneous to their effects.

[74] For the distinction between the "perinoetic" knowledge of the empiriological sciences and the "dianoetic" knowledge of philosophy, see Maritain, *Degrees of Knowledge,* p. 207.

strom units, horsepower units, etc. We may say, for example, that we are eating 3,000 calories a day, when as a matter of fact we eat food (meat, potatoes, etc.). The 3,000 figure is a mathematicized and very indirect expression of our knowledge of the energy output of the food.[75]

Thus, the empiriological sciences are explanations of the (corporeal) beings of the universe and their changes in terms of something *sensible;* they are verifiable either directly or indirectly through the sensible elements of our sensory-intellectual experience. Philosophy, on the other hand, must try to give an explanation of the entire universe of beings (known by the natural light of reason), not in terms of the sensible but in terms of the *intelligible*—being. The two knowledges are on different levels; they are not opposed to each other; neither can substitute for the other.

G. ANALOGY OF BEING[76]

Individual Differences of Being

Each and every existent is an individual. As an individual, it is different from every other being; it exists in a specifically, or at least individually, different way, or manner, from every other existent. Some beings are only individually different while specifically the same: for example, Tom, Dick, Harry or Rover, Fido, Fifi. Others are even specifically different: for example, men, brutes, plants, minerals. No two beings in the universe are abso-

---

[75] Ultimately, in these sciences, we are describing things and their changes in terms of our measuring devices. The descriptive, or "operational," definitions based on measurements are most useful to the scientist, since they enable him to predict and control events. This does not necessarily imply that these sciences are merely a knowledge of "pointer readings" as Professor Eddington would have it.

[76] This section is a brief presentation of the fundamentals of analogy and is presented early in the course lest the student get off to a false start by thinking that the principles of metaphysics apply to being in a univocal way. A fuller treatment will be given in the last chapter of this book.

lutely and entirely the same; otherwise, they would be identical
—not two, but one. Not even two "identical" twins are absolutely
the same.

Similarity and Difference

On the other hand, no two beings in the universe are absolutely different; for they both exist. All beings are similar in that
they exist. And yet all beings are simply different; that is to say,
they exist in a different manner, some only individually different,
some even specifically different.

There is a certain paradox as regards a universe of many (different) beings. Only similars (beings) can differ; only different
beings can be similar. Obviously, nothing can be similar to itself;
it is identical with itself. A being can be similar only to something
else (from which it differs). To express this in another way: only
things which exist (hence, similar) can differ from each other. On
the other hand, nonbeing is neither different nor similar; it simply
is not.

In a universe of many beings, a *pluralistic* universe, amid the
vast diversity of existents, there is a unity, a community. Amid the
manifold differences, there remains a similarity. We must be careful not to overstress or misinterpret the similarity and unity among
beings. To do so is to pave the way to a monistic conception of
the universe, which would reduce the many to one. We must beware of overextending the significance of statements such as this:
"The universe truly exists." In the strict and proper sense, only
individuals exist, each of them different from every other, although
there is a similarity, or commonness, among them in that they all
exist.

Predication of "Being" as Attributive Noun

To express this similarity amid differences, we may use the
noun "being" as a predicate and affirm it of various things. We
may say, for example: I am a being, Fido is a being, this rose is a
being. Such a predication is not univocal, nor equivocal, but *analogous.* These terms must be explained.

Univocal, Equivocal, and Analogous Predication

A term is predicated *univocally* of various subjects when it is said of these subjects according to exactly the same meaning; e.g., Tom is a man, Dick is a man, Harry is a man. In each of these predications, the meaning of man is exactly the same—rational animal. The individual differences (black-haired, blond-haired, no-haired, etc.) have been "dropped out" by *abstraction* in forming the common, or universal, concept. Hence, this concept, "meaning," or intelligibility, can be predicated of all the individuals that participate, or share, in that nature. The knowledge expressed by such a univocal term is a *common* knowledge, common to all the individuals of which the term is predicated.

A term is predicated *equivocally* when it is said of various subjects according to a meaning which is entirely different in every predication; for example, the covering of a tree is bark, the sound a dog makes is a bark, a small boat is a bark. Here we have three distinct concepts, meanings, or intelligibilities, expressed by one and the same spoken or written term.

A term is predicated *analogously* of various subjects when it is said of these subjects according to a meaning, or intelligibility, which is simply different but somewhat the same; for example: this is my foot, that is the foot (of the table), that is the foot (of the mountain), that is the foot (of the class). In these instances, the term "foot" signifies the lowermost part, whether of the body or in position, rank, etc. Hence, the meaning of the term is somewhat the same. And yet a human foot is living while the foot of a table, mountain, etc., is not. Hence, the meaning (intelligibility) is simply different.

Analogous Predication of "Being"

When "being" as an attributive noun is predicated of various subjects, it is not predicated *univocally* (according to the same meaning as an abstract universal), since no two beings exist in absolutely the same way, manner, or mode.

Nor is the predication of "being" *equivocal* (according to entirely different meanings), since totally and absolutely different from "being" is only nonbeing, which can properly be predicated of nothing. Now, no two beings are that different—not even humans and electrons—since they both exist.

Consequently, the predication of "being" must be *analogous* (according to a meaning, or intelligibility, simply different in every instance though somewhat the same). For, as we have seen, all beings are simply different though somewhat the same, and our predication to be true must reflect this difference amid similarity.

Analogy of Proper Proportionality

When "being" is predicated as an attributive noun of various subjects, it expresses the similarity between beings, which, nevertheless, are simply different. This similarity, however, is not a univocal similarity. The commonness, or community, in "being" is not that expressed by a universal concept, such as "man" when predicated (univocally) of Tom, Dick, and Harry.

In what does this community, or commonness, consist? How is "being" common to all things, which truly differ? And how is this commonness reflected in our knowledge of being? This is the heart of the problem of the analogy of being.

In every instance of (limited) being, an act of existing is proportioned to some individual essence; the exercise of existence is "on a level with" the capacity of the essence. In each and every existent, we discover an "is" factor and a "what" factor proportioned to each other. These factors are never twice the same, but they are always present. Without the "is" principle, nothing *is;* without the "what" principle, no*thing* is, no *kind* of existent results. In the analogous predication of "being," we express our knowledge of this proportional similarity between beings.

For the purpose of clarifying the analogy of proportionality, which is proper to "being," it may help to examine other proportions, or relationships, of paired terms. Let us consider, for example, the case of doubling. We may say, "These windows are double, those doors are double, those beds are double." Now, windows, doors, and beds are simply different. And yet, since there is a doubling of them, these simply different things are similar; there is a commonness, or community, among them owing to a *proportion,* and this commonness amid differences is expressed in the "analogous" predication.

Another example may be borrowed from *mathematical proportions:* for example, 1 : 2 as 3 : 6 as 7 : 14. Here again there are two elements involved, and the two elements are always different numbers. Nevertheless, there is a common proportion of one to the other; the first number is half of the second, and the second number is double the first. Thus, there appears to be some sort of proportional similarity (at first glance, but on closer examination we find that this is an identity, not a similarity, of proportions; the commonness turns out to be univocal).

Perhaps the most helpful in throwing light upon the analogy of proportionality between (limited) beings are the *metaphorical proportionalities.* We may say, for example: "Baudouin is king (of the Belgians), the lion is king (of the animals), John Doe is king (of the promenaders)." In every case, there is a similarity of relation, or proportion: there is a relation of ruler to ruled; Baudouin, the lion, John Doe all rule subjects. Nevertheless, there is a difference in these relations, or proportions: Baudouin rules by political power, the lion by physical power, while John Doe rules for one night by make-believe power. Thus, there is a relational similarity which is truly different in every case.

Although these various examples of paired terms, whether mathematical or metaphorical, may help us to come to an understanding of the analogy of being, we must remember that the proportional similarity between beings differs from that in any examples we may propose. This analogy between (limited) beings is aptly called the analogy of proper proportionality.

Analogous Affirmation of Existence

More fundamental than the analogous predication of the attributive noun "being," and underlying this predication, is the analogous *affirmation* of the act of existing itself. The existential act (to be) affirmed in the existential judgment is never twice the same. Although we affirm that men exist, dogs exist, roses exist (and use the same word), we never affirm the act of existing in absolutely the same way, since it is always proportioned to the capacity of the essence of the existent. A man, for example, could not exist with the existence of a dog. Nevertheless, in all these affirmations we do affirm something *to exist, to be;* we do affirm an act of existing proportioned to an essence. There is a commonness amid difference in our affirmation of existence. In brief: we affirm existence analogously.

Analogy of Existents

Ultimately, the analogous predication of the attributive noun "being" and the analogous affirmation of existence is grounded in the existents themselves. Every existent differs from every other existent; that is, it exercises the act of existing in an essentially (either specifically or at least individually) different way; the mode of existing, the manner of be-ing, of any two "be-ers" [77] is never absolutely identical. Nevertheless, every existent is similar to every other existent by a similarity of proportions. In every existent (of our experience), no matter how diverse, whether a human existent or an electronic existent, we discover a proportion between the act of existing and the essence. Every existent *is,* and is in its own unique, individual way, or mode.

Analogous Application of Metaphysical Principles

In conclusion to this chapter, we must call attention to a matter of the highest importance which follows from our consideration of the analogy of being. It is this: All the principles and laws which the science of metaphysics formulates regarding being as being must be *understood,* not univocally, but in an analogous

[77] An existential metaphysics is badly in need of terms which the English language does not provide, but new coinages are apt to encounter strong opposition from our colleagues in the English departments and, perhaps, rightly so from their point of view. Hence, it is with a certain hesitancy that we venture the term "be-er." A "be-er" is one who exercises the act of be-ing (existing), as a runner is one who exercises the act of running. Every bee is busy be-ing a bee, but whether we be bees or not, we be-ers are all busy be-*ing* It should be obvious now that the English word "being" is hopelessly ambiguous for our purposes in metaphysics; nevertheless, we can scarcely avoid using it.

way and *applied* analogously, since no two beings are exactly the same.

SUMMARY

A. Things Exist: Things confront us. We encounter them. We too exist, but we know ourselves only in the act of knowing being. The being first known by us is sensible, corporeal being, things other than ourselves.

B. Man's Initial Knowledge of Being: Man's knowledge is twofold; human experience is sensory-intellectual. Man's first intellectual knowledge is "that something is"—"being." This knowledge is expressed in an existential, not in an attributive, proposition. Reflection on this primary knowledge discovers a common intelligible content—"being" (something is)—but a content as yet not separated from matter. Such a knowledge is attainable by all who intellectually know being, but it is not the metaphysician's notion of "being."

C. Meaning of "to Be":   The most fundamental question about reality, the metaphysical question, is "What is it to-be?" For idealism to-be is to-be-thought; beings are because we think they are. For materialism to-be is to-be-material; whatever is not quantitative, extended, dimensional, measurable simply is not. For dynamism to-be is to-be-changed; reality is identically change, or flux. For activism to-be is to-act; beings are because they act. For essentialism to-be is to-be-an-essence; beings are insofar as they participate in a universal essence (Plato) or by being an individual essence (Scotus). For Thomistic existentialism to-be is to-exist; to-be is the perfection of all perfections (not an absurdity as in some contemporary forms of existentialism); to-be is not an essence and cannot be grasped in a concept. By a series of judgments of separation we purify the "being" of our initial sensory-intellectual experience and come to understand that a thing qualifies as a being, not by reason of its being known, nor by reason of its matter, nor by reason of any essential determination (whether specific or individual), but solely because of the act of existing. We may, then, aptly describe "being" as *that which is*.

D. "Being" as Attributive Noun: In the strict and proper sense, "being" signifies that which actually and presently is. In a wider sense, it signifies also that which was or will be. In the widest sense, it signifies even that which could be (although it never was or will be), or at least can be considered and signified as "being."

E. The Science of Being as Being: A science is certain, evident, and organized knowledge through principles. The material object of a science is that which the science studies. The formal object is the aspect under which it studies the material object, or the aspect presented by the material object. The material object of metaphysics is all being; the formal object is being as being. Since the formal object (as being) is most universal, the primary principles and laws of metaphysics must be absolute and necessary, not only as regards one mode of being, but even as regards any act of being.

F. First Principles Concerning Being: The principle of *non-contradiction:* the same thing cannot both *be* and *not be* at the same time. The principle of *intelligibility:* being is intelligible; the intellect can know being; the concepts and judgments by which intellect knows correspond to being. The principle of *explanation,* or accountability: whatever exists (rather than not) has an explanation; whatever events, or changes, occur (rather than not) have an explanation.

G. Analogy of Being: Only individuals exist. All beings differ from each other. All beings are similar to each other. The predication of "being" as attributive noun expresses this similarity amid differences. Such a predication is not univocal or equivocal, but analogous; that is to say, "being" is predicated according to a meaning somewhat the same but simply different. This analogy is the analogy of *proper proportionality*. It consists in a proportional similarity between limited beings; in every instance, an act of existing (never the same) is proportioned to an essence (never the same). The existential act affirmed in an existential judgment is never the same twice, but is always proportioned to some essence. It follows that the principles of metaphysics must be understood and applied in an analogous sense, since no two beings are exactly the same.

SUGGESTED READINGS

Anderson, James F.: *Metaphysics of St. Thomas Aquinas*, Henry Regnery Company, Chicago, 1953, pp. 3–18; on *what* is metaphysics. The author has gathered into one small volume many choice quotations of a metaphysical content scattered throughout the writings of St. Thomas Aquinas.

Bourke, Vernon J.: *The Pocket Aquinas*, Washington Square Press, Pocket Books, Inc., New York, 1960, pp. 143–179; on reality and "first philosophy." The excerpts presented in this inexpensive pocket book represent thirty-two of the most important writings of Aquinas.

Clarke, Wayne Norris: "What Is Really Real?" in *Progress in Philosophy*, edited by James A. McWilliams, The Bruce Publishing Company, Milwaukee, 1955, pp. 61–90; on the various meanings of "real" and "being."

Collins, James: *The Existentialists*, Henry Regnery Company, Chicago, 1952; an evaluation of modern existentialism from a Thomistic point of view.

Eslick, Leonard: "What Is the Starting Point of Metaphysics?" *The Modern Schoolman*, vol. 34, pp. 247–263, May, 1957; on the point of departure for a metaphysics grounded in sensible being.

Hawkins, D. J. B.: *Being and Becoming*, Sheed & Ward, Inc., New York, 1954, pp. 105–109; a clarification of the possibles.

Maritain, Jacques: *Existence and the Existent*, translated by L. Galantiere and G. Phelan, Doubleday & Company, Inc., Garden City, N.Y., 1956, pp. 20–55; on the notion of being.

Mauer, Armand: *On the Division and Method of the Sciences*, Pontifical Institute of Mediaeval Studies, Toronto, 1953. This is a translation of questions 5 and 6 of *In Librum Boethii De Trinitate* by Aquinas.

Plato: *Republic,* Book VII. This book contains the famous allegory of
the men in the cave. It is a classic in philosophical literature.

Sullivan, J. W. N.: *The Limitations of Science,* The Viking Press, Inc.,
New York, 1954, pp. 125–150. This selection describes how the
nineteenth-century mentality of science has been succeeded by an
outlook which admits that there are approaches to reality other
than those of the empirical sciences.

Van Melsen, Andrew Gerard: *Science and Technology,* Duquesne University Press, Pittsburgh, 1961, pp. 9–26; on the difference between
philosophy and physical science.

Wild, John: *Introduction to Realistic Philosophy,* Harper & Brothers,
New York, 1948, pp. 9–35; a brief history of realistic philosophy.

II

Changing Existents

The beings of our direct experience are subject to change. Their existence is a changing existence. In this chapter, we shall first present a philosophical analysis of change in general. We shall then consider the two principal types of change: accidental and substantial.

A. CHANGE IN GENERAL

The Fact That Beings Change

The beings, the existents, which we know immediately and directly are constantly changing. A rock loosened by the rains rolls

44

down a mountainside; a tiny seed develops into a mature plant; a kitten opens its eyes and becomes aware of the objects around it; a student by hard study becomes a mathematician, a musician, and even a metaphysician; a burglar changes his way of life and becomes a law-abiding citizen. All these are examples of change with which we are quite familiar and which occur around us every day. That beings change is so evident that the fact is seldom questioned by the average person. The explanation of change, however, is not an obvious matter and requires a difficult philosophical reflection and analysis.

Heraclitus—"All Is Flux"

Some philosophers have been overimpressed by the constant activity and change which confront them wherever they turn. Heraclitus, a Greek philosopher of the sixth and fifth century B.C., held the extreme view that change is the very "nature" [1] of reality: "all things flow and nothing remains (*panta rei kai ouden menei*)." [2] According to Heraclitus, reality· is like a fire which would cease to exist if it ceased to burn. It may also be compared to a river, in which one cannot bathe twice, since the waters flow ever onward. A pupil of Heraclitus, not to be outdone by his master, made the further claim that one could not bathe in the same stream even once.

[1] This statement, of course, is an oversimplification of Heraclitus's position, according to which all being has within it a conflict, or tension, of opposing forces so that dynamism is the very law, if not the very "nature," of being. Many contemporary scholars claim that the flux doctrine of Heraclitus is not a position on the "nature" of being.

[2] This statement contains a partial truth and a valuable philosophical insight. All the things of our experience are in flux. Their very existence is a flux existence; that is, these beings are dynamic, not purely static; they overflow in activity. This does not mean, however, that "to be" is identical with change, or flux. Nevertheless, "to be" is a dynamic act and yields in no way to the dynamism of Heraclitus and Bergson, except that it *de facto* explains the dynamism. Unfortunately, many of our students come away from the Aristotelian-Thomistic analysis of change with the uneasy conviction that somehow "static" act (as they understand it) and "static" potency just do not seem to account for dynamic change, and that Heraclitus and Bergson face the issue more squarely.

If one reads carefully between the lines of the fragments that have come down to us,[3] one finds implicit in Heraclitus's position a virtual identification of reality (of being) with change, or becoming, itself. In such a view, all reality would be pure change; there would be no being, no existent, no thing, which changes; change would be the only reality. And this is the view which the more recent philosophies of flux have taken.[4] In all such philosophies, there is an implicit or explicit denial of being in favor of becoming (change).

Parmenides's Denial of Change

At an opposite pole from Heraclitus is the position of Parmenides of Elea, who flourished at the time of Heraclitus or shortly after him. This Italo-Greek philosopher denied the fact and even the intelligibility of change. His argument, which we present here in a varied form, runs somewhat as follows:

In every change, something becomes, or comes to be; that is to say, something *new* comes forth, or arises, in the change. Now, this something new was either (1) being or (2) nonbeing. There are no other alternatives; there is no middle ground between being and nonbeing.

If this something new already was being, it is not new. If it was nonbeing, it cannot come to be; for from nonbeing, nothing can come forth.[5]

[3] See John Burnet, *Early Greek Philosophy*, 4th ed., A. & C. Black, Ltd , London, 1945, pp. 132–141.

[4] In Bergson's (1859–1941) view, reality is change, flux, or "duration." What we call things, or beings, are simply so many "still pictures" that the mind takes of the fluid real. Our concepts freeze the fluid real into static forms. These concepts are merely intellectual stoppages of the mobile real,' which the scientific mind constructs for itself in its effort to manipulate and control the real. But no matter how many static concepts we form of the flux, the reality slips through our fingers. The mobile real simply cannot be grasped through a succession of immobile concepts. See Bergson, *Creative Evolution, passim*.

William James's (1842–1910) "stream of consciousness" and Alfred North Whitehead's (1861–1947) "process" theory also are recent philosophical offspring of the first great philosophy of flux formulated by Heraclitus.

[5] This principle is true when referred to a becoming without *any* cause

In cither case, change is unintelligible and hence not real. The senses deceive us in portraying reality as changing. The intellect alone, which presents reality as *being*, is to be trusted and must correct the error of the senses. There is no change; all reality is being, and apart from being, there is only nonbeing.[6]

Aristotle's Analysis of Change

The genius of Aristotle (384–322 B.C.) saw a way out of the dilemma proposed by Parmenides without denying the reality of either being or change: *between being* (actual being) *and* (absolute) *nonbeing, there is potential being.* True, there is no middle ground between being[7] and nonbeing, but between being-in-act and nonbeing there is a middle ground, and that middle ground is *being-in-potency.*

Thus, in a change, when something comes-to-be, we do not mean that actual being becomes actual being; for example, a marble statue of Napoleon does not become a marble statue of Napoleon. Nor do we mean that absolute nonbeing becomes being; for from (absolute) nonbeing nothing can come forth. Rather, we mean that being-in-potency[8] becomes being-in-act.[9]

---

whatsoever—both material and efficient. In the philosophy of God, it will be shown that creation is the procession of limited beings from an efficient cause of being, without any material cause.

[6] Another formulation of Parmenides's argument· Change would need to arise either from being or from nonbeing. Now, being cannot become being, since it already is that. On the other hand, nonbeing cannot become being, for from nothing, nothing can come forth (*ex nihilo nil gigni potest*). In either case, change is impossible.

Another formulation: Change involves otherness; that is, a being becomes different (other). Now, other than being is only nonbeing If being became nonbeing, it would no longer be. Nor can being become being, since it already is that. On either alternative, change is not intelligible and hence is not real.

[7] The term here signifies both being-in-act and being-in-potency.

[8] Being-in-potency implies that something exists but that not every capacity in the existent is actualized. It is the condition of being able to acquire a perfection which is not possessed. Being-in-act, on the other hand, implies the possession of the perfection.

[9] Relative nonbeing (namely, being-in-potency) becomes actual being.

Thus, a college sophomore is potentially a philosopher. Existing as a human being he has a *real* capacity, or potency, for philosophy although as yet this capacity is undeveloped, not actualized; he is said to be a philosopher "in potency." In the learning process, the potential philosopher becomes an actual philosopher; the potency, or capacity, for philosophical knowledge is actualized. And in the term of the change, he is actually what he was heretofore only potentially; he is now "in act" to what up to now he was only "in potency."

A stone, on the other hand, does not have the real capacity, the *real potency,* for philosophical knowledge. Consequently, we do not bother to lecture to a stone. It simply cannot become a philosopher; it is not potentially philosophical; it is not a philosopher in potency.

True, in the case of the college sophomore, a nonphilosopher becomes a philosopher; but it is a case of a non*actual* but *potential* philosopher becoming an actual philosopher.[10] The stone also is a nonphilosopher, but it is not even a potential philosopher; hence, it will never be a philosopher in act. It will never pass from potency to act as regards philosophical knowledge.

Continuity in Change. In each and every change, a continuous subject, or substrate of change, is required. There must be a tree which moves with the wind, a human being which grows from boyhood to manhood, a student who becomes philosophical, matter in which substantial transformation occurs. To say there is no subject of change—Heraclitus is reputed to have said this—is an implicit denial of the fact of change.[11]

A subject, or substrate, is required to explain the *continuity* in a change, for change is not a mere substitution of one being for another. Thus, the successive replacement of a small sapling by

---

Nonbeing may be distinguished into absolute nonbeing and potential (nonactual) nonbeing.

[10] Between absolute nonbeing and being-in-act, there is the non-(actual)-being of being-in-(real)-potency.

[11] At the minimum, it is a denial of an element in change without which change is not intelligible.

ever-taller trees might give the illusion of rapid growth but would not constitute a true intrinsic change of the first tree into the last tree.[12] Nor would pouring water out of a glass and replacing it with wine constitute a change of water into wine.

Moreover, change is not an *annihilation-creation* process. Change is not the annihilation of one being and the creation of another being in its place. We should not consider the death of a dog, for example, as a process in which Fido is wiped out, reduced to a zero, or cipher (with the rim knocked off), and chemicals created [13] in his place. In such a "process," the first being would not be changed *into* the other (or others). An annihilation-creation explanation would not account for the *sameness,* or continuity, in change despite the otherness involved in change. Let us consider another example: the same student, who at the beginning of this course had never heard of metaphysics, becomes a metaphysician (at least to some degree); the *same* subject becomes other. The student is not annihilated and a budding metaphysician created in his place; there is true continuity—a sameness amid otherness. This sameness amid otherness must be accounted for in any philosophical explanation of change.

Terminus-from-which and to-which. Every change is *from* something *to* something; that is to say, a change has termini.[14] The leaves in the fall, for example, change from green to brown; water which was liquid turns solid when frozen; I, who was in the next room, am now here.

In the terminus-*from-which* (*a quo*), the subject exists according to one mode of existing; in the terminus-*to-which* (*ad quem*), the subject exists according to another mode of existing.[15]

---

[12] True enough, substitution involves a change (local change) of the things substituted as well as (local) change of the things for which they are substituted.

[13] Creation is not a change in the strict sense, since there is no terminus-from-which. Nothingness is not a true terminus. Nor is there a continuous substrate in creation; there is no true continuity.

[14] Both termini of the change are determinations of the same determinable subject.

[15] Either according to a different primary (substantial) mode, or according

It now *is* different; it exists in a different manner, way, or mode. To change is to become different; to *have* changed is to *be* different.

Potency and Act. In the terminus-from-which (*terminus a quo*), the subject of the change must have a real capacity for the new mode of existing, the new perfection, which it will possess in the terminus-to-which (*terminus ad quem*). This new reality, completion, or perfection, we shall call *act*.[16] The capacity for this perfection we shall call *potency*.[17]

If a being lacks this potency, this real capacity for perfection, it can never undergo the change in which it would receive this new perfection, completion, or "act." A stone, for example, will never become philosophical;[18] it does not possess the real capacity for philosophical knowledge; it is not a philosopher in potency.

On the other hand, a subject which already possesses a perfection, or act, cannot receive, or acquire, that same perfection. In other words, for a being to change, it must be in potency to the new perfection, not in act to that same perfection; it must be deprived of, or lack, that perfection. A man cannot become a man. An adult cannot become an adult. A fully grown tree cannot become fully grown; it already is that. The small and newly transplanted tree, however, has the real capacity for the perfection of being a mighty oak, huge craggy pine, or whatever the case might be: it truly can acquire the perfection which it lacks.

Passage of Subject from Potency to Act. Change itself, however, is not the real potency, or capacity, for "act"; rather, real potency makes change intrinsically possible and intelligible. Nor is change the new perfection, or "act," which is possessed at the terminus-to-

---

to a different secondary (accidental) mode while persisting according to the same primary mode.

[16] Not to be confused with activity, or action. "Act" here is a technical term and translates Aristotle's *entelecheia*.

[17] We shall see that the one principle (potency) is not the other (act); they are really distinct, not as complete beings, but as principles of being.

[18] Nor for that matter will some students become philosophers, though they have the real capacity, since they will not apply themselves sufficiently and persistently to the study of the subject.

which of the change: the building process is not the new house; growth is not the fully developed plant; learning is not the acquired knowledge.

Rather, change is the passing of a subject[19] from potency to act. It is the realizing, or attaining, of a perfection not fully possessed. *Change is the actualization of that which is potential insofar as it is potential;*[20] and when the subject is no longer potential to the act, the change is terminated.

Principle. From this consideration and reflection, it should be manifest that any changing existent precisely as changing is composed of two distinct intrinsic elements, factors, or principles: (1) a principle of determinability, or capacity for receiving perfection —passive[21] *potency;* (2) the new perfection, or determination, which is being realized, or attained—*act.*

Caution—Change Is Concerned with Modes of Being

At this point, it is important to remind ourselves that at present we are not concerned primarily with the act of be-ing (the burden of the first chapter) but with modes of be-ing (of existing). This chapter is a consideration of *modifications* of existence. Change is not a transition from being to nonbeing (annihilation), nor is it a transition from nonbeing to being (creation). Rather, change, becoming, or transformation is an affecting of the manner, or mode,[22] of existing. It is the passage, or transition, from one mode of existing to another mode of existing.[23]

[19] In the next two sections, we shall see that the subject is either substance (in accidental change) or prime matter (in substantial change).

[20] Change, then, is the act of the imperfect (*actus imperfecti*), not the act of the perfect (*actus perfecti*), as are the immanent activities of living beings.

[21] In opposition to *active* potency, or power, which is a capacity for acting, for conferring perfections, and hence is really an act. Our senses, intellect, and will are operative potencies, that is, capacities for operation.

[22] Either of the primary mode (in substantial change) or of a secondary mode (in accidental change). Cf. Louis De Raeymaeker, *The Philosophy of Being,* translated by Edmund H. Ziegelmeyer, S.J., B. Herder Book Co., St. Louis, 1954, pp. 175–176.

[23] Let us not mistake the *mode* of existing for the total existent itself. That would imply a relapse into essentialism.

B.   ACCIDENTAL CHANGE

Two Principal Kinds of Change

Not all changes are of the same type. Some changes are so profound that one being is transformed into a fundamentally different kind of being (or beings). The death of a living being, for example, is a change so radical that in the terminus (to-which) of the change totally different beings exist; the living being has been changed into nonliving beings, into chemicals, and no longer exists. Such changes are changes in the very nature of being; that is, they are changes in the fundamental, or primary, mode of existing.

Other changes are of a less radical kind. A tree may grow a foot taller in the course of a year. Although it really changes, it remains a *tree* (an arboreal existent) and remains *this* individual tree; it is still specifically and individually the same. The act of existing exercised is still of the same specific (substantial) and individual mode; the existent *per*sists, or keeps on existing, according to the same basic, or primary, mode—the arboreal mode of existing.

Let us consider some further examples: I walk into the classroom; I gain 5 pounds; I learn philosophy. In all three instances, I have really changed; I have received a new perfection. Nevertheless, I remain *human* (a man) and remain this human (this man); I do not turn into weight, nor into a classroom, nor into philosophy. I remain specifically (substantially) the same. I keep on exercising existence according to the same primary (or substantial) mode, though I do truly change and exercise existence according to different secondary (or accidental) modes. Changes of this type we shall call *accidental* changes. Such changes are transitions from one nonessential mode of existing to another.

Subject of Accidental Change—Substance

If something is to change accidentally, it must already exist *before* it undergoes the change. Moreover, it must exist *through-out* the change in which the new perfection is received. Lastly, it must *continue* to exist after the new perfection is received, without ceasing to be what it was essentially (specifically); that is to say, it must not cease to exist according to the same primary mode. For example, in order that I may gain 5 pounds in weight, I must exist before the process, exist through the process, and survive the process. The subject which is the substrate of accidental change, and which accounts for the continuity of the unitary, total existent throughout the change, we shall call *substance*.

Accidents—Modifications of Substance

The new determinations, or modifications, received by the being through the change are conceived as "coming to" or "happening to" the substance, and for that reason are called *accidents* (from the Latin word *accidere*, meaning "to happen"). Thus, when a man learns philosophy, he is modified somewhat; the human being is now a philosophical human being; he has passed from potency to act as regards this new knowledge. He is now different (qualitatively) from what he was before, though he remains specifically (substantially) and individually the same. He exercises existence according to a new secondary (accidental) mode while persisting according to the same primary (substantial) mode.

Accidents Said to "Exist in" Substance

Since the new determinations acquired in accidental change do not naturally[24] exist as separate entities but are modifications *of* [25] a subject, they are said to "exist in" a substance. On the other hand, it is said that substance does not need to "exist in" something else. It is that principle by which the unitary, total

[24] In the Eucharist, not only do the accidents of bread and wine exist apart from their natural substance; they exist by acts of be-ing specially created by God for this purpose. See Étienne Gilson, *Elements of Christian Philosophy*, Doubleday & Company, Inc., Garden City, N.Y., 1960, p. 328. The *natural* existence of accidents, however, is to "exist in" a substance in virtue of the existence of that substance.

[25] "An accident is not called 'being' as if it itself had existence, but because by it something is, therefore, it is better called *of* a being (*entis*)" (*Summa Theologiae*, I–II, 110, 2, ad 3ᵐ). It has existence (naturally) only as a modification of a substance by inhering in substance.

existent is capable of existing in itself. It is not the modification of a subject; it is the (determinable) subject of modification; and it is in this sense that substance is sometimes called the "substrate" for accidents.

Substance Not a Static Substrate

We must not think of substance, however, as a dead, inert substrate for accidents, as a sort of metaphysical pincushion into which various accidents are stuck and then removed. This would reduce accidental change to a mere displacement of unchanging parts in an unchanging substrate. Substance would then become "that which remains the same" while the accidents "come and go." [26]

Rather, we must regard substance as a factor, element, or principle[27] of being (and of change). It is that intrinsic principle *by which* the unitary, total existent (John Doe, Fido, Felix, etc.) remains essentially[28] (in the sense of specifically) and individually the same throughout accidental changes. In an accidental change, the unitary, total existent *truly changes*. The accidents do not merely come and go, leaving the being unchanged; rather, the total existent is truly modified. A philosophical man, for example, though he remains essentially (specifically) and individually the same, is truly modified; he is truly different from what he was before. The mighty oak is truly different from the slender sapling planted a century ago. The reformed criminal is really different from the former bank robber.

In all these accidental changes, the potency of the substance has been actualized; there has been a passage from potency to act. Accidents are the intrinsic principles which account for the difference, or otherness, of the total existent as the result of change; substance is the principle which accounts for the sameness of the unitary existent throughout the change.

[26] Such a notion of substance and accidents was justly criticized and rejected by the English empiricists. In any explanation of accidental change based on such a notion of substance, the very dynamism of change would "slip through our fingers."

[27] See De Raeymaeker, *op. cit.*, p. 176.

[28] *Loc cit.*

Accidents Are Distinct from Substance

Although substance and accidents are principles within one and the same being, they are really distinct; the one principle is not the other. The grass is not its color. A dog is not his shape. A man is not his knowledge; he has it. A doctor, a medical man, is a composite of human substance and medical knowledge. The determinable subject (substance) and the determinations of that subject (accidents) are distinct as intrinsic principles by which the unitary existent is human and is medical.

Accidents Are Not Substances within Substance

We must also beware of considering accidents as substances within another substance, as complete beings existing in their own right within another complete being, thus failing to take into account the obvious unity of beings. Rather, accidents (as well as substance) are factors, elements, or *principles* within a being, within an existent.[29] The color of a dog, for example, is an accident, a sensible quality; a canine substance is determined, or modified, by this quality. The reality is an existential unit; the white thing is the canine thing, and the canine thing is the white thing. The dog and his color are not two beings, not two substantial units; rather, we are confronted by a unitary white-canine-existent.

In the unitary existent, the intellect can distinguish between the determinations (in this case, color quality) of a subject and the subject of these determinations, namely, substance. Intellect recognizes that the color is not the dog and that the dog is not his color; intellect knows that the canine existent has the sensible quality of color (an accident).[30]

---

[29] ". . . it is rather called *of* a being (*magis dicitur esse entis*)" (*Summa Theologiae*, I–II, 110, 2, ad 3ᵐ).

[30] By a "formal" abstraction, we can intellectually disengage an accidental modification from its subject and then consider it and discourse about it as if it were a subject in its own right. Thus, we may talk about a man's knowledge, his virtues, his color, weight, etc. We may say, "His *knowledge* is extensive; his *virtues* are heroic." Such a way of speaking, and of considering, is perfectly legitimate and necessary, but one must beware of mistaking the abstract subjects of such predications for concrete substances (that is, unitary existents, subsistents).

Kinds of Accidental Change

Accidental changes are of various kinds. The principal types are quantitative changes, qualitative changes, and relational changes.

A *quantitative* change is one in which a corporeal (material) being increases or decreases. Thus, for a living body to grow taller or shorter, heavier or lighter, fatter or thinner, is a quantitative change. Such changes, of course, are measurable and hence are expressible in number systems and in mathematical constructs.[31] Consequently, they are quite amenable to study and investigation by the empiriological sciences.

A *qualitative* change is an alteration of a subject. A change in color, a change in shape, becoming wiser, more virtuous, more vicious are examples of qualitative change. Unlike quantitative changes, qualitative changes are not necessarily *material* changes.[32] Moreover, many qualitative changes, although they are truly material, are only indirectly measurable and hence are only indirectly amenable to investigation and study by the empiriological sciences,[33] for example, some of the changes involved in the act of sensation (a psychophysical operation).

A *relational* change is the change of one being with reference to something else; for example, one may become an owner (of something else), a debtor or creditor (to someone else), a parent, an agent, a patient, etc. Of special importance (although not the only relational change) is *local* change, or change in place, the acquiring of a relation to another containing body (or bodies). Thus, I would change in place if I should walk into the next room. I would then be within some other containing body or bodies; I would have acquired a new relation.

[31] See Chapter I, Section F.

[32] In the philosophy of man, we shall see that the acquiring of intellectual knowledge involves strictly *immaterial* qualitative change.

[33] It is one thing to say that a science is not interested in studying sensible qualities because they are not readily amenable to empiriometric analysis. It is another thing to claim that they are not real, or are totally subjective. A realist philosopher, whatever his physics or optics may be, knows the reality of sensible qualities; he knows the grass is green.

C. SUBSTANTIAL CHANGE

Fact of Substantial Change

Not all changes are limited to accidental changes.[34] Far more profound than accidental changes are those changes in which a corporeal being is transformed into another, or other, bodily being(s) so that the identity and nature of the original being is lost.[35] In the terminus-to-which of such a change, the original being no longer exists; a being specifically (essentially) different exists instead.

In death, for example, a living, bodily being (an organism) is changed into nonliving beings. On the other hand, a dog who has grown taller and fatter has changed only accidentally; he remains essentially,[36] or substantially, the same; that is to say, he remains dog (canine). However, when the dog has died, new beings (chemicals) exist in its stead; a dead dog is no longer a dog. True, the accidental form, or figure, will remain in the cadaver for a time, but even this is soon lost as disintegration sets in. The dog has been *transformed* into other material beings; one *kind* of being has been changed into a different kind. Such a change, obviously, is not a mere accidental change. Rather, it is the *transition from one essential (specific) mode of existing to another.*

Another instance of substantial change is the assimilation of food by an organism. Food, for many organisms at least, consists principally of nonliving material beings.[37] When assimilated, it

[34] The empiriological sciences, since they are concerned principally with correlating sensible phenomena, do not, and need not, distinguish between accidental and substantial change. To ask whether changes are limited to accidental changes (quantitative, qualitative, relational) is a philosophical, not an empiriological, question.

[35] Note that being is not lost. An act of existing is still exercised though proportioned to a different primary (substantial) mode.

[36] "The mode of substantial being is essence par excellence, and the term 'essence' designates this in the very first place, for the accidental determination is only a modification of the substantial mode of being" (De Raeymaeker, *loc. cit.;* reprinted by permission).   ·

[37] True, there are exceptions to this general rule; for example, in

becomes part of a *living* body (an organism), and in the case of human assimilation, it is even transformed into a bodily being which is capable of thought.[38] What was once food is now part of a being which acts in an essentially (specifically) different way. In such a change, nonliving beings are transformed into living beings, which are substantially different; that is to say, the living beings exist according to a different primary mode. Such a change is not a mere accidental change nor can it be explained as a complex combination of accidental changes.[39]

It is evident, then, that changes from living to nonliving and from nonliving to living are substantial changes.[40] They are transitions from one primary mode of existing to another primary (not mere secondary) mode of existing. We must now endeavor to explain more fully these radical changes, in which an essentially and primarily different being exists at the terminus-to-which of the change.

Prokofiev's musical fairy tale *Peter and the Wolf*, the wolf swallows the duck alive.

[38] The human bodily being is capable of thought, however, not *as bodily* but *as intellectual*. On the other hand, the same intellectual bodily being *as bodily* is subject to the laws of Newtonian mechanics, or to the laws of curvature of Einsteinian space-time. In the philosophy of man, it will be shown that human understanding is an operation independent of the body and its organs (in the order of exercise of operations) although dependent on the senses and their bodily organs for its data.

[39] True, a series of accidental changes is involved in many substantial changes. (The biological sciences give striking evidence for the accidental changes that occur in the assimilative process and in the death of an organism.) Nevertheless, a substantial change is not reducible to any single accidental change or to the sum total of the accidental changes which bring about the substantial change.

[40] Moreover, it is quite possible that transformation of one chemical compound or element into another constitutes a substantial change. (The same, of course, may be true for the "mass to energy" conversions as well) For example, hydrogen and oxygen, which are colorless gases, can be changed into water, a liquid substance having properties radically different from those of hydrogen and oxygen. Since there is some doubt that these differences require substantial change as their adequate explanation, we shall not base our evidence for substantial change on transformations of this kind.

Termini of Substantial Change

We have seen that in accidental change, substance is the principle which explains the continuity in the change. The tree which grows a foot taller remains a tree; it is substantially the same at the end of the change; the total existent *persists* according to the same essential (specific) mode of existing.

In the radical changes which we are now considering, the being existing at the beginning of the change (in the terminus-from-which) goes out of existence; it is changed into another being of a different nature, or essence. The fly which flew into the flame no longer exists; a fundamentally different kind, or species, of being has arisen; instead of the fly, chemicals now exist.

It is clear, then, that at the terminus-to-which of a substantial change, the original existent is not more perfect or less perfect; rather, the original being no longer *is;* some other material being (or beings) now exists instead; a material being (or beings) of a different type, species, or *form* now exercises the act of existing. Existence is still exercised but of a substantially different species, or form.

In brief: the termini (*a quo* and *ad quem*) of a substantial change are two different species, or forms, of material being. These forms, since they primarily determine, or "shape," the very substance, or essence, of the material existents involved in the change, we shall call *substantial* forms.[41]

Continuity in Substantial Change

We must not regard substantial change as the mere substituting of one material being for another. In that case, the original being would not truly change *into* another (or others). In such an explanation, a substantial change would be merely a succession

[41] In opposition to accidental form (especially, that of figure, or shape), which determines, or "shapes," the existent in a secondary way. "The accidental determination is only the accidental modification of the substantial mode of being" (De Raeymaeker, *loc. cit.;* reprinted by permission). Thus, the manikins in display windows are of human form (accidentally) but are substantially plaster of paris. They are fake men, not real (substantial) men.

of beings essentially different. This explanation would not account for the *continuity* in substantial change.[42]

Nor should we think that the original being existing in the terminus-from-which has been utterly annihilated so that absolutely nothing remains. In that case, the new being existing in the terminus-to-which could come into existence only by creation —a coming into existence out of nothing.[43] Again, we should not be able to explain how the first being is changed *into* another (or other) material being(s). Such an account of substantial change would not explain the continuity of the change.

Continuous Substrate of Substantial Change— Prime Matter

To account for the continuity in substantial change, there must be a subject of change, a substrate. This subject is the common element of the change and must be present somehow in both termini of the change. It is the "link" in the process from one term to another. This subject (or principle), which was potential and is now actuated, as regards the new form received in the change, we shall call *matter*—and more precisely, *prime* matter.[44]

[42] In every substantial change, one substance is changed into another substance, or substances. A substantial change implies that something is carried over from the original substance to the new substance. Therefore, in every substantial change, there must be:

1. Some substantial principle that is *common* to the two substances and is carried over through the change. (Otherwise, the new substance would not be produced *out of* the old substance.)

2 Some substantial principle that is *different* in each of the two substances. (Otherwise, there would not be different kinds of things.)

The physicist's principle of conservation of mass and energy (or of mass-energy) is an implicit recognition of the continuity in substantial as well as in accidental change. The physicist as such, however, is not concerned with the difference between substantial and accidental change. When he proposes such questions to himself, as many a physicist does, he is no longer considering these changes as a physicist but as a philosopher.

[43] Creation, we shall see in the philosophy of God, is a coming into existence from nothing (in the sense of material cause) but with dependence on an efficient cause.

[44] It is called *prime*, or primary, matter in opposition to *secondary* matter,

Prime Matter Pure Potency

What is the "nature" of this subject, or substrate, which receives the new substantial form? What "form" does it have of itself? What species, or kind, of material existent is it? Is it, perhaps, an electron, a proton, a neutron, or any of the minute "particles" discovered by physicists (or postulated) to explain material activities on the microcosmic level?

To all these questions (which are really irrelevant), we must reply that of itself, as a principle of the unitary, total existent, prime matter is form*less*. Of itself, it is pure, passive potency for substantial form. As the common determinable substrate, or subject, of substantial trans-*form*-ation, prime matter of itself cannot have any determinate form, or nature. Of itself it is sheer *indeterminate potency* and receives determination from substantial form to constitute the corporeal essence, or nature. Although always determined by some substantial form, it is not of itself any substantial form and remains potency to all (material) forms except that which now actuates it.[45]

Prime Matter vs. Secondary Matter

We shall never encounter prime matter as such in our experience, since prime matter does not exist by itself. Only by an intellectual analysis of substantial change do we know the reality of this elusive principle. The object of our sensory-intellectual experience is "secondary matter"—material beings of a specific form. And we name these beings according to their *form:* canine, feline, murine—dogs, cats, mice. Ordinarily, we do not refer to such beings as "matter." It is more correct to refer to them as mater*ial* beings of a specific formal type.

which signifies material substance of a determinate form. Thus bricks, lumber, cement, etc., are the secondary matter, or materials, which receive the (accidental) form, or figure, of a house. In a wider sense, the squad members are the material, or secondary matter, which receive the coaching (a dynamic accidental form or complex of forms) that makes them a good football team. Thus, we say that a coach must have good "material" with which to build a good team.   .

[45] As potency to all other forms, of which it is *deprived,* matter is the root of corruptibility, of transformability.

Prime Matter, the Root of Corruptibility

Prime matter is neither an electron, nor proton, nor any other particles constructed by physicists in their (provisional and revisional) explanations of the activities and configurations of material beings on the micro scale.[46] It is not something definite, nor qualitative, nor quantitative, with a determinate figure, or shape. Having no determinate form in itself, it is the capacity to receive all material forms except that which here and now actuates (determines) it. Hence, any unitary, total existent to which prime matter belongs as a *principle* of being can be (and sooner or later will be) transformed into other material beings of a different specific form. Prime matter as pure, determinable potency is the root of "corruptibility," that is, of "transformability" into other material beings.

Compared to Plastic Materials

To help us in our consideration of this mysterious principle (though not as a substitute for metaphysical thinking), we may compare prime matter to modeling clay, wax, or any other very plastic material. The clay or wax of itself does not have the shape, figure, or form of Caesar, or of Napoleon, or of any other person. (True, it always has some form, sometimes a merely lumpy form, or shape, though often it comes in cubic form.) It can, however, readily receive the shape, figure, or form (accidental form) of any of these persons. It is quite plastic; that is to say, it is almost purely potential to any one of these accidental forms. Although, it always has some form (accidental form), it remains potential with regard to most other (accidental) forms.[47]

In somewhat similar fashion, prime matter is "plastic" also. It is *pure* potency, not to accidental, but to *substantial* form. Hence, there is a great difference between the potentiality, or

---

[46] See Jacques Maritain, *The Degrees of Knowledge,* translated from fourth French edition under supervision of Gerald B. Phelan, Charles Scribner's Sons, New York, 1959, p. 180, footnotes 1 and 2, for some interesting remarks concerning the "configuration" of material beings on the micro level.

[47] Of course, an extrinsic principle, the modeler, is needed to actuate this potency.

"plasticity," of prime matter and the potentiality of wax. The wax, which is in potency to nearly all shapes (accidental forms), is already a definite form, or species, of material being; it is wax, not gold or bronze. The wax is a material existent of a determinate form; it is already "shaped," or formed, by an intrinsic principle (substantial form) to exist essentially as a waxen, material existent, not as a golden material existent.

When the wax is set on fire, this very plastic material (so plastic to accidental forms) is itself transformed into water vapor, carbon, etc. Underlying this change as continuous substrate is an *absolutely* "plastic" principle—a pure, indeterminate capacity for substantial form. This purely indeterminate and potential principle within material beings is *prime matter*.[48]

Corruption and Generation

The destruction of one thing is the production of another. Let us suppose that the clay or wax, in our example, has the shape, or form, of a sphere and then is formed into a cubic shape. In this case, a waxen sphere is transformed (accidentally) into a waxen cube. In one and the same process, the wax loses its spherical form and receives the cubic form. This comparison may help us to understand the more radical transformation which takes place in substantial change. The death of a dog, for example, involves the production of chemicals. In general, the corruption of one material being is the generation of another, or others (*corruptio unius est generatio alterius*). The destruction of one material being is the production of another (or others).

Corruption and generation are distinguished only by the termini of the change. Thus, when we say that something was corrupted, or destroyed, we are naming a change with respect to the terminus-to-which. When we say that something was generated, or produced, we name the same change, but with respect to the

---

[48] Wax, clay, and other *materials* such as lumber, brick, stones, etc., are the "matter" which receives a structural form, pattern, or design in the various processes of construction of artifacts Since such materials are already of a determinate type, or species, of material being, they are aptly called "secondary" matter in opposition to prime matter.

terminus-from-which. The destruction of one thing is the production of another (or others).

Reduction and Eduction of Form

It may be asked: What happens to the spherical form of the wax when the wax receives the new cubic form? The answer is that the spherical form does not totally and absolutely disappear; it is not reduced to absolute nonbeing nor does it wander off into outer space. The wax which now is *actually* cubic is again *potentially* spherical; it is spherical in potency. The spherical form has been *reduced* to potentiality, or "plasticity," [49] as the new form was *educed*, that is, "drawn forth" from the potency of the wax, which is the continuous substrate of this accidental change.[50] Here, of course, we are dealing with an accidental form—shape, a quality about quantity.

In substantial change, on the other hand, the continuous substrate is prime matter, which of itself is pure potency for substantial, not merely accidental, form. When, for example, a dog dies, the canine substantial (specifying) form is *reduced to the potency of matter,*[51] as the chemical forms are *educed* from the potency of matter. Indeed, the reduction of one form to potency *is* the eduction of the new form (*reductio est eductio*).[52]

SUMMARY

A. Change in General: The beings which we know immediately and directly are constantly changing. Heraclitus was so

[49] Whence it may again be *educed* by the action of an extrinsic principle, an efficient cause, in this case, the modeler.

[50] The extrinsic cause, the modeler, must have this form in mind.

[51] Whence it may eventually be educed again after a series of substantial changes. The chemicals of the dog carcass may be absorbed by the grasses, which in turn may be assimilated by the horse which eats the grass, which in its old age, as not infrequently happens, is "destroyed" and converted into kennel rations, which in turn are assimilated by some (other) canine existent.

[52] The new form arises from the *passive* potency of matter and, as we shall see in a subsequent chapter, from the *active* potency (power) of an extrinsic, efficient cause.

impressed by the fact of change that he implicitly denied the reality of being. Parmenides, on the other hand, noting that all is being, denied the reality of change. Aristotle showed in his analysis of change that change is the passage of a subject from potency to act. Change requires a continuous subject, termini-from-which and to-which, real potency for the new act and actualization of this potency.

B. Accidental Change: Not all changes are equally profound. Changes are of two basic kinds: accidental and substantial. Accidental change is the transition from one nonessential mode of existing to another nonessential mode of existing. The subject of accidental change, which explains the continuity in such a change, is *substance*. The modifications acquired by the substance through the change are the *accidents*. They are said to "exist in" the substance as their subject. We must guard, however, against considering substance as an inert substrate for accidents, which "remains the same" while the accidents "come and go." This would reduce accidental change to a mere displacement of unchanging parts. Nor should accidents be regarded as substances within substances. Rather, they are the determinations of a determinable subject (substance). Accidental changes either are quantitative, are qualitative, or involve a relation to something else.

C. Substantial Change: Substantial change is the transition from one essential mode of existing to another. The death of a living being and the assimilation of food into an organism are evidences of substantial change, that is, changes that cannot be reduced to mere accidental changes. The termini of substantial change are two different substantial, or specifying, forms of material existence. Substantial changes are not the substitution of one material being of a different specific form for another. Nor is substantial change the annihilation of one material being and the creation of another. There is a continuity in substantial change and the principle of continuity is primary matter.

Of itself prime matter is pure potency but does not exist as such; only material beings of a specific (substantial) form exist.

We can get some understanding of substantial form by analogy with plastic materials that can readily receive new accidental forms. The corruption of one material being involves the generation of another. The reduction of one material form to the potency of matter involves the eduction of a new substantial form from the potency of matter (under the influence of an extrinsic principle).

SUGGESTED READINGS

Aristotle: *Basic Works,* edited by Richard McKeon, Random House, Inc., New York, 1941, pp. 745–747, 230–236, 253–257; on change.

Bourke, Vernon J.: *The Pocket Aquinas,* Washington Square Press, Pocket Books, Inc., New York, 1960, pp. 55–56; commentary by Aquinas on Aristotle's analysis of change as presented in the *Physics.*

De Raeymaeker, Louis: *The Philosophy of Being,* translated by E. H. Ziegelmeyer, S. J., B. Herder Book Co., St. Louis, 1954, pp. 170–181; on the structure of substance and accidents as underlying accidental change.

Hawkins, D. J. B.: *Being and Becoming,* Sheed & Ward, Inc., New York, 1954, pp. 97–105; on change.

Koren, Henry J.: *Readings in the Philosophy of Nature,* The Newman Press, Westminster, Md., 1958, pp. 185–190; selected passages from Aristotle and St. Thomas showing how St. Thomas clarifies certain obscurities in Aristotle's exposition.

Van Melsen, Andrew Gerard: *The Philosophy of Nature,* Duquesne University Press, Pittsburgh, 1953, pp. 39–48 (on matter and form); pp. 101–123 (on difficulties concerning substantial change).

Wild, John: *Introduction to Realistic Philosophy,* Harper & Brothers, New York, 1948, pp. 277–295; on change.

III

Participating, Multiple, Limited Existents

In the preceding chapter, we have seen that the beings of our experience are subject to change, both accidental and substantial. We have shown that such changes require intrinsic potential-actual "structure" within being. The present chapter also will be concerned with the "structure" within limited being but will use as a point of departure, not the fact of change, but the fact of participation.

67

A. FACT OF PARTICIPATION

Participation in Existential Order

Although the changing beings of our experience all exist, not all of them exist in the same basic way; their manner of be-ing, their mode of existing, varies. There are many (primary[1] and secondary) *modes* of existing; there are various kinds of be-ing: human, canine, feline, arboreal, aquatic, atomic, electronic, etc.; men exist, dogs exist, cats exist, trees exist, water exists, atoms exist, electrons exist, etc.

All these existents *participate* the act of existing (of be-ing) in fundamentally diverse ways. True, there is a oneness, or unity, amid this great multiplicity; each and every one of the many is an existent, *a* being; that is, it exercises an act of existing proportioned to an essence. Yet no single one of them is exclusively existent, nor is it the totality of existents or the fullness of existing. None of them is THE act of be-ing (*esse*) itself.

The many (of our experience) participate existence, and they participate existence according to various primary, or substantial, modes. In other words, the act of existing is participated according to diverse essences,[2] or natures.

[1] At this juncture, it is not strictly necessary to make a distinction between primary and secondary modes of being. It is necessary, however, to distinguish between *act* of be-ing (existing) and *modes* of be-ing. What concerns us here is the fact that in the beings of our experience, existence is found, not unparticipated, but *participated* according to various modes (primary and secondary).

We should at this point distinguish between specific and individual mode, that is, between specific essence and individual essence. Things *exist* according to an individual mode, of which we cannot form a proper concept; but we do form a proper concept of their specific (common) mode. Obviously, nothing exists according to this purely common mode; for example, there is no common (universal) dog-as-such; there are only individual canines—Fido, Rover, Fifi. As regards our knowledge of the act of existing, we should recall from the first chapter that it is attained, not in a concept, but in an existential judgment.

[2] The term "essence" (nature) most frequently signifies *substantial* essence, that is, the primary mode of existing, the basic whatness, or quiddity,

Participation in Essential (Substantial) Order

Moreover, primary modes of existing, such as the human and canine modes, are found participated in many individuals. Human nature (to be human) is shared by Tom, Dick, Harry, and billions of other human existents: Tom is human; Dick is human; Harry is human. Canine essence is participated by millions of canine existents: Fido is canine; Rover is canine; Fifi is canine.

We must carefully note that Tom is not THE man but merely *a* man; Fido is not THE dog but merely *a* dog. Tom is merely a *participant* in the human mode of existing; Fido is merely a participant in the canine mode of existing. Tom is fully real; nevertheless, he is not the totality of humanity, nor is he exclusively humanity, nor is he the fullness, or plenitude, of humanity. Rather, he is one of many participants of the same primary mode (substantial essence); and the same may be said of Fido.

In brief: primary modes of existing (substantial essences, or natures) are found participated by many individuals of the same specific type.

Participation in Accidental Order

A third and far less radical type of participation remains to be considered. There is participation in secondary modes of be-ing.

---

of the existent; for example, Jones is essentially (substantially) a man (primary mode). The term "essence" is also used sometimes to signify the secondary modes (accidents): we speak sometimes of the essence of this or that accident; whiteness, for example, is essentially a quality. Lastly, "essence" signifies individual essence, the composite of substantial and accidental principles; for example, "That is John Jones (individual essence)." It is in this last sense that the term "essence" is most frequently understood in this chapter.

Moreover, as we have seen, a distinction must be made between specific essence (a universal notion) and individual essence (the substantial essence with all its modifications). ". . . a fundamental structure is necessarily found in all reality which exists only by participation: the correlation, namely, of the existence and the mode of being; and this structure implies always in this mode of being itself a subsidiary correlation, that of the substantial mode and the accidental modifications of this mode . . ." (Louis De Raeymaeker, *The Philosophy of Being*, translated by Edmund H. Ziegelmeyer, S.J , B. Herder Book Co., St. Louis, 1954, p. 334, reprinted by permission).

The many participate in secondary modes (modifications) of be-ing, such as to-be-white, to-be-tall, to-be-wise, etc. Many are white, wise, talking, walking, etc., but none of them is whiteness, wisdom, talking, walking itself.

These secondary modes of existing are not restricted to any one individual existent; for example, Tom is white, but so is Dick. Nor are these modes limited to merely one primary (substantial) mode of existing; for example, some canines are white as well as some humans.

Thus, the secondary modes of existing (accidents) are participated by many existents, some of which differ essentially (substantially) as well as individually; that is to say, they differ according to their basic manner, or primary mode, of existing. In other words, secondary modes of existing (accidents) are participated by many individual existents, even by those of different natures, essences, or species.

B.   PARTICIPATION IMPLIES LIMITATION

Participant "Has" the Perfection, Is Not the Perfection

We have seen that in the beings of our experience there is participation of the act of existing, participation of the primary modes of existing (substantial essences), and participation of secondary modes of existing (accidents).

"Now whatever is participated is determined to the mode of that which participates." [3] Thus, the participated perfection is

---

[3] Aquinas, *Summa Contra Gentiles,* I, 32. We have chosen to follow Geiger's emendation of *participantis* instead of *participati.* See his *La participation dans la philosophie de S. Thomas de Aquin,* Paris, 1942, p. 11, footnote 3.

For a text of St. Thomas which is concerned with *various* orders of participation we quote the following: "To participate is to receive as it were a part, hence, when something receives in a particular way what pertains to another in a universal way, it is said to participate it. And so man is said to participate animal, because he does not have the nature of animal according to its total community; and in the same manner Socrates participates man, and a subject participates accidents, and matter participates

possessed in a "partial" way, in a restricted manner. The participant *is not* the perfection itself; rather, the participant *has* the perfection. Moreover, the participant has the perfection only up to a point, in accordance with its capacity.

This implies that the perfection is *limited*,[4] that there are bounds to the perfection possessed, so that other modes of possessing the perfection are possible. For example, Fido exercises the act of existing according to the canine mode—he is a dog— but does not exist according to the human mode, which is a higher level of existing.[5] Moreover, this individual canine existent (Fido) exists according to the mode of this individual dog and does not possess the perfection of all dogdom; Fido is not dog-as-such. Lastly, this individual canine existent participates in various secondary modes of existing, such as to-be-white. However, he is not whiteness itself. Moreover, this secondary mode of existing is possessed by other canine beings and even by essentially (substantially) different beings such as humans and felines; men, cats, even mice are white.

It is clear, then, that participation in perfection implies

form, since substantial or accidental form, which of itself is common, is determined to this or that subject. And in similar fashion effects are said to participate their cause, and especially when they do not equal the power of their cause . . ." (*In Boeth. de Hebd.,* lect. 2, ed. Mandonnet, "Opuscula Omnia," Paris, 1927, I, pp. 172–173).

[4] " . . the participant is limited inasmuch as that which is participated is not received in the participant according to its complete infinity, but only in a particular way" (*In Lib. de Causis,* lect. 4, ed. Parma, XXI, 725A).

The fact of multiplicity *presupposes* limitation. For many beings to exist, they must differ. If they did not differ, they would be identical, hence, they would not be many In order to differ, however, one must have (or lack) a perfection which the others lack (or have). Hence, all (but one perhaps) are limited.

This argument, though valid for the point it makes about limitation, does not tell us *which* being is limited. We prefer to say that any being which *participates* be-ing—and all the beings of our direct experience do—must be limited, they exist "up to a point." The participant in existence is limited; not so the unparticipated act of existing.

[5] Much less does he exercise existence according to every mode, that is, without any limiting mode.

limitation of that perfection. Our present problem is to explain this limitation.

Plato's Theory of Participation

According to Plato (429–347 B.C.), the individual material beings which we experience are mere participations of a corresponding Idea, or nature, existing in a separate World of Ideas. Fido, for example, is not THE dog, but merely *a* dog—a participant in the universal and immutable nature, essence, or Idea "Dog-as-such." The individual material thing is merely a shadow (although a real shadow) of the *really* real, which is the universal Idea, or archetype, existing in a separate world. There the intellectual soul once lived (before its imprisonment in the body) and experienced the nature in its full perfection.[6] On the occasion of sensory experience of an individual material participant, the soul recalls the unparticipated, pure form, which it once contemplated in the World of Ideas. Whatever perfection the individual material thing possesses consists in its limited and shadowy participation of the absolute nature, or Idea, existing in the world of pure Forms.[7]

To explain the limitation of the many, Plato invoked two intrinsic factors: the finite and the infinite. All things in this shadow world (as distinct from the World of Ideas) are an admixture of two principles: the limit and the unlimited; the shadow realities of our world are a mingling of "nonbeing"[8] with the Idea, or absolute Form.[9]

[6] When through sensation we attain one of the "shadow realities," the intellect recalls the universal archetype, or Idea, which it experienced when it dwelt in the World of Ideas. For Plato, then, intellectual knowledge is "reminiscence."

[7] See *Republic,* Book VII.

[8] The "nonbeing" of Plato, however, is a positive, not a purely negative, principle.

[9] One must avoid the temptation of reading a fully developed Thomistic doctrine of limitation into Plato's theory of participation. For Plato, the limit and the infinite play opposite roles from that of limiting principle and perfecting principle in Thomism. In Plato's view, the limit is the principle of perfection giving form to the boundless, the infinite. In the philosophy of Plotinus, the highest reality, the Good, is the measure and limit

Neoplatonist Theories of Participation

Plato's theory of participation underwent further development and refinement in the hands of Plotinus (205–270) and Proclus (411–485), but it remained for the most part a vague doctrine, since it failed to distinguish clearly the order of reality and the order of thought. The theory, however, contains a basic truth: to explain participation (and multiplicity) of the "one" by the "many," it is necessary to admit some *real principle of limitation* within the limited realities of our experience.

C. LIMITATION BY POTENCY

Synthesis of Two Explanations

It required the genius of St. Thomas Aquinas (1225–1274) to effect a synthesis between the Neoplatonic doctrine of participation (and limitation) and the Aristotelian explanation of change through potential-actual principles. Aristotle had used the theory of potency and act to account for accidental change (in terms of substance and accidents) and substantial change (in terms of matter and form). The Angelic Doctor extended the theory of potency and act to account for *participation* and *limitation,* as well as change.

For St. Thomas, potency became the principle of *limitation* and act became the principle of *perfection.* For St. Thomas, potency and act are real principles within the unitary existent explaining participation and limitation on the levels of accident, substantial essence, and the most fundamental level—the existential order, an order which Aristotle apparently had taken as given and did not bother to explain.

---

of all things; the highest perfection is finite, while relative nonbeing is imperfect to the extent it is infinite, that is, without form or limit (perfection). On this point, see the following article by Wayne Norris Clarke: "Limitation of Act by Potency," *The New Scholasticism,* vol. 24, pp. 177 ff., April, 1952.

Statement of Principle of Limitation

Thus, in the philosophy of Aquinas, *any perfection,* or act
—whether the basic act of existing, essential act (form), or accidental act—which is found *participated,* multiple, and hence *limited,*
forms a *composition* with *limiting potency;* and the act and the
potency are *distinct* as real *principles* (components) of the unitary,
total existent.

This is a preliminary and provisional formulation of a general principle, which we shall derive from a consideration of
perfection and limitation on three levels in limited, corporeal
existents. We shall now consider the three orders from which
this analogously common principle is derived. Later, we shall
again take up this principle to discover its full implications.

D. PERFECTION AND LIMITATION IN EXISTENTIAL ORDER

Participation of Existence

The beings of our direct experience *participate* existence
each in its own particular way; they are beings "by participation."
They exercise existence on different levels: human, canine,
aquatic, electronic, etc. They exist according to various (primary
and secondary) modes.

Primacy of Act of Existing (esse)

The truly revolutionary feature of the doctrine of St. Thomas
was the recognition that "to be" (*esse*), the act of existing, is the
most fundamental perfecting principle in any limited existent.
For example: without the act of existing, a white-human-existent
would not be (1) white or (2) human, because he would not *be*
at all. "To be," to exist, is the "perfection of all perfections, the
act of all acts." [10] Without this radical and basic perfection, no
other perfection is possessed. Without this fundamental perfecting
principle, the unitary, composite existent simply would not *be.*[11]

---

[10] Cf. Aquinas, *De Potentia,* VII, 2, ad 9ᵐ.

[11] In the philosophy of St. Thomas, "to be" is the intrinsic, reality prin-

Essence as Limiting Principle

Limiting the act of existing is essence,[12] the intrinsic principle *by which*[13] a being is what it is and not something else. Essence is the principle[14] which determines the manner, "way," or mode of existing. As intrinsic, real, modal factor it restricts, determines, and limits the act of existing so that it is exercised in a "partial" and not in a "total" way. As limiting principle of the unitary existent, essence is sometimes said to "receive" the act which it limits. Hence, essence is analogous[15] to a container, which restricts and confines its content but is of less import than the content contained.

"What" Factor and "Is" Factor

Essence is that intrinsic factor,[16] or element, in the total ex-

---

ciple of the existent. In Chapter I, we examined other positions on the "nature" of reality and saw that though these positions contained some element of truth, they all failed to reach the basic insight that distinguishes between mode of be-ing and act of be-ing in the singular existent.

[12] Essence here is the individual essence, the composite of quidditative principles. As such it takes in both substance and accidents, both the primary and secondary modes of existing.

[13] Cf. Jacques Maritain, *Degrees of Knowledge,* translated from fourth French edition under supervision of Gerald B. Phelan, Charles Scribner's Sons, New York, 1959, p. 436. It is important to note that essence is not the "total reality which exists" (the subsistent). Rather, essence is an intrinsic principle *by which (principium quo)* the unitary existent is what it is (primarily and secondarily). To equate essence with the supposit is to fall back into essentialism.

[14] Or complexus (composite) of determining principles. Individual essence includes both substantial and accidental principles, all of which are quidditative principles, that is, principles which determine the *mode* of existing.

For an interpretation of essence as an *intrinsic* limiting *mode*, see the article by Gerald B. Phelan, "The Being of Creatures," *Proceedings of the American Catholic Philosophical Association,* vol. 31, p. 124, for 1957. Cf. the following statement by Professor Gilson: "The mode of participation that defines the being at stake is its essence" (*Elements of Christian Philosophy,* Doubleday & Company, Inc., Garden City, N.Y., 1960, p. 191; cf. also p. 194).

[15] Analogy is based on similarities between things. But let us remember that these things are truly *different.*

[16] Essence here refers to individual essence rather than to specific essence,

istent which enables us to answer the question: *What* is it? "To be" (*esse*), on the other hand, is that principle in the unitary existent which enables us to answer that it *is*, that it is real (not merely ideal).

Essence Known in Concept, "Is" in Judgment

The mode of existing, the essence, nature, or "whatness" is grasped by the intellect (according to its specific character) in a proper concept.[17] However, the very existing, or "is-ing," of the existent is known, not in a proper concept,[18] but in a judgment— and more precisely, not in an attributive judgment,[19] but in an *existential* judgment. For example, when confronted by a slithering, serpentine existent, I not only understand *what* it is (the nature, or essence, of the existent) but also know that it *is*, that it exists.

---

which is an abstract, universal nature and hence is not a reality principle. Cf. Maritain, *op. cit.*, p. 435. The term is taken here in a wide sense to include all quidditative (whatness) factors, whether substantial or accidental.

[17] A word of caution is needed here: "essence" in this case is not (merely) essence as primary mode of existing. Essence here is *individual* essence, which cannot be conceived in a proper concept as individual but only according to its specific character. Essence in this context is the totality of the primary and secondary modes of existing as one unified subject (or mode) of existing. What is conceived in a proper concept is the *specific* essence (the primary mode of existing) through the sensible accidents (secondary modes of existing).

[18] We do form an *abstract* concept of the concrete act of existing, which we express by using the abstract term "existence." This, however, is not a proper concept (which is limited to a knowledge of the *essence* of material beings). Rather, it is a mental construct, in which we "essentialize" (in our knowledge) the act of existing, as we must if we are to discourse about it and use it as a subject of predication.

[19] The predicate of an attributive proposition expresses a *mode* of existing, either a substantial or an accidental mode, whether or not something exists according to that mode: for example, "Dinosaurs are reptiles." One must be careful, however, not to overlook the existential status of many propositions which appear at first hand to be merely attributive but are occultly existential: for example, "That (sensible existent) is a snake (primary mode)"; "That snake (sensible existent of determinate, primary mode) is poisonous (secondary mode)."

Related as Potency and Act

Essence is the *capacity* of the existent for existing; and the act of existing fulfills this capacity and is proportioned to it some-what as a content is proportioned to its container.[20] Hence, essence may be called *potency* in the existential order.

"To be," or "is," on the other hand, is the perfecting princi-ple, or *act,* which fulfills that capacity and is restricted by that capacity, so that the composite existent exercises existence ac-cording to a limited mode, or measure. Here we find composition of limiting principle (potency) and perfecting principle (act) in the most fundamental order—the order of existence.

Essence, then, is existential *potency;* it is that principle in a being by which the being is *what* it is. "To be" *(esse)* is existential *act;* it is that principle in an existent by which it *is.* A limited existent is a composite of these real principles, as long as it *is* and as long as it is *what* it is.[21]

Distinct as Real Principles of Being

The act of existing and limiting essence, or nature, are dis-tinct, not as complete beings, but as intrinsic "structural" princi-ples of the unitary, composite existent (the supposit). That princi-ple[22] by which a being is *what* it is, is not the selfsame principle by which it *is* at all. In general, in any limited existent, quidditative

[20] As noted above, this is merely an analogy, since a container (for ex-ample, a beer bottle) and the content (the beer within) do not compose a unitary existent. Thus, a 12-ounce "beer" is a composite of many beings— at least of container and content. A human "be-er," on the other hand, is an existential unit (a subsistent), though composed of act of be-ing and limiting essence.

[21] It should be emphasized that these core principles are not mere mental constructs but *real* intrinsic *principles* constitutive of the unitary, substantial existent (the supposit). They are, for example, more real than electrons, protons, and photons, which may, or may not, be mental constructs formed by the mathematical physicists to explain material, sensible phenomena on the microcosmic level.

[22] Or complexus of principles. Individual essence as determining existence is a composite of substantial and accidental principles. Cf. De Raeymaeker, *op. cit.,* p. 246.

(whatness) principles are not the existential principle; the principles which determine the *mode* of existing (whether primary or secondary modes) are not the principle which accounts for the very *existing* according to such a mode.

Reflected in Our Knowledge. This distinction in the real is reflected in our *knowledge*[23] of any limited existent. In the concept, we grasp what a thing is; in the existential judgment, we affirm that it is. I may, for example, know *what* a whooping crane is and still not know whether one is.[24] On the other hand, I may know what a dodo or dinosaur is and know that none is (exists). Lastly, when confronted by a snake, I know what it is and that one *is;* I recognize my confrontation by an existent exercising the act of existing proportioned to an (individual) serpentine mode, essence, or nature.

Irreducibility of Attributive and Existential Judgments. Concerning any such individual existent of our experience, the judgments "It *is* (exists)" and "It is *this*" (John Jones, Rover, etc.) are *irreducible* to each other, even though these judgments are made about one and the same individual, singular existent and refer to that existent in its concrete unity[25] and not as abstractly known.[26]

[23] Needless to say, it is also reflected in the verbal expression of our knowledge, that is, in existential versus merely attributive propositions.

[24] Some months before this writing, fewer than three dozen of these great birds were known still to exist. Whether, after the many depredations from other animals and hunters on their northward and southward flights, they still *persist* is not known with certainty. Perhaps, as with the passenger pigeons, only the memory of them persists (now and then).

[25] Cf. De Raeymaeker, *op. cit.,* p. 103.

[26] True, we form many abstract, universal concepts of a being's *mode* of existence, but these concepts are reducible to each other. For example, man is known as a substance, a body, an organism, an animal, rational. The higher concepts express the same mode of being as do the lower but express that mode more determinately. Thus, the higher concepts *virtually* contain the lower concepts. Hence, the distinction between these "modes" of being is called a *virtual* distinction. Such distinctions are the work of the mind and do not demand a counterpart in the real, although there must be a *foundation* in the real for these distinctions, which the mind

Concerning any individual existent, the judgments "There is some (sort of) thing" and "It is of this (individual) *sort*" are irreducible.

Now, if knowledge fundamentally is of reality, and truly corresponds to reality,[27] these judgments, of which one expresses the individual mode of being, the other the act of be-ing (existing), must be grounded in a *distinction* between *real* intrinsic principles in the unitary, concrete existent. Otherwise, such judgments (attributive and existential) would be reducible to each other;[28] for example, to judge that something *is* would be to judge it to-be-John-Jones. It follows that limited beings, that is, beings which participate existence, cannot be simple, but must be composite in the very order of being itself.

Composition of Principles of Being. Now, if a being (*ens*), an existential unit (a subsistent), is composed, it cannot be composed of beings. A house is not composed of houses; a house is composed of *parts* which make up the house. Similarly, a composite being is not composed of beings. Rather, it must be composed of intrinsic factors, elements, or *principles* of being; it must be composed of a principle[29] *by which* the unitary existent is what it is—essence —and a principle by which it *is*—the act of existing, "to be" (*esse*).

These principles are related to each other; they are mutually related; they are correlative principles. The essence has no reality except as ordered to the act of existing which it limits. The act of existing, in turn, actuates the essence which limits it. Neither principle has any reality except as a constitutive *principle* of the

---

makes for itself in its effort to present abstractly (and universally) the mode of existing to itself. All these abstract and universal concepts present not the *act* of be-ing, but the *mode* of being (which is individual and singular) more and more determinately. Hence, they are reducible to each other. They do not affirm existence as does the existential judgment.

[27] This is the principle of intelligibility of being. See Chapter I, section F.

[28] Cf. De Raeymaeker, *op. cit.*, p. 145

[29] Or complexus of principles. The individual essence is a unitary composite of substance and accidents. Its substance in turn, we shall see, is a composite of matter and form. All these principles are on the side of quiddity, whatness, nature, essence, measure, or mode, of existing.

unitary existent. The limited being is neither its essence nor its existence; it is the composite of these intrinsic, ontological, "structural" principles. It *is;* and it is *this.*

In brief: the distinction between the act of existing and limiting essence is a *real* distinction; not, however, a real distinction between complete beings, but a distinction between real *principles by which* the unitary existent is and is what it is.[30]

E.   PERFECTION AND LIMITATION IN (SUBSTANTIAL) ESSENTIAL ORDER

Résumé

We have seen that the many beings of our experience are of different basic kinds, or modes. They all exercise the act of be-ing, but none of them *is* the act of be-ing. They exist by participating existence. In fact, a universe of many beings presupposes that the many participate existence according to various limiting modes. Without participation and limitation there simply would not be different, or many, beings.[31] All being would be one.

Multiplicity in the existential order implies participation and limitation of existential act—"to be." We have explained this limitation by composition of the act of existing (as perfecting principle) with essence (as limiting potency).

Participation of (Substantial) Essence[32]

Besides participation in the existential order, we find par-

[30] We shall present further argumentation for this distinction as well as a classification of the various distinctions in section H of this chapter.

[31] All being would be of one kind; or, more precisely, all being would be of no (limiting) kind. Thus, only the pure act of be-ing would exist.

The many must differ. If they do not differ, they are one, not many. In order to differ, one being must have (or lack) a perfection which the other, or others, do not have (or have). Thus, the many, with the exception of one, perhaps, must be limited.

[32] ". . . just as this man participates human nature, so does every created being participate as it were the nature of be-ing (*essendi*) . . ." (*Summa Theologiae*, I, 45, 5, ad 1ᵐ).

It is only in the existential order, however, that all the elements in-

ticipation of the same primary mode of existing in many individuals of the same species. Many beings are essentially (specifically) the same. For example, the human mode of existing is participated by nearly three billion individuals; the canine mode of existing is participated, no doubt, by many millions. Essence,[33] the determining mode of a corporeal existent, is found participated among many individuals.

This participation by many individuals in the same substantial essence (in the same primary mode of existing) implies that such an essence is limited, or restricted, in the individual existent. No individual human existent, for example, exists as the totality of humanity, nor exclusively as humankind, nor as the fullness of humankind. Every individual human existent, whether Tom, Dick, Harry, etc., is a limited *participant* in human nature, or essence.

Substantial Form, Principle of Specification

To account for the specific character of a substantial bodily essence (for example, human rather than canine or feline), there must be an intrinsic principle which determines the level, or grade, of material existence. Since it determines (as it were, "shapes") the basic mode of corporeal existence, it is aptly called *form*. And since it is the *primary* determining ("shaping") factor of the very existence of the total existent, it is aptly called *substantial* form, in opposition to accidental form (for example, figure, or shape), which is a secondary determination of a corporeal

---

volved in the participation structure have ontological status. It is only with reference to the participated act of *existence* that an unparticipated exemplar exists. On the other hand, there is no unparticipated humanity and no unparticipated whiteness. In the order of substantial essence and the accidental order too, there is question of participation in *modes* of existing either primary or secondary. There exists no unparticipated *mode*. One must throughout this chapter keep in mind the highly analogous character of participation in the various orders of existence, essence, and accidents. This point is carefully made in the article by Wayne Norris Clarke, "The Meaning of Participation in St. Thomas," *Proceedings of the American Catholic Philosophical Association*, vol. 26, pp. 156–157, for 1952.

[33] Essence here signifies *substantial* essence.

existent already substantially determined. Substantial form, then, is the intrinsic principle which specifies a material being.

Matter, the Principle of Individuation

Besides a principle of specific determination within the essence, which accounts for the participation by the individual in the species, or essence, there must also be a principle of *individual differences,* accounting for the unique way in which the total existent possesses the specific perfection. This principle is *matter.*

By reason of this principle, every material individual, regardless of its species (form), must be quantitative; that is, it must be extended, have parts outside of parts. Moreover, as an individual it must have its *own* quantity; it must have determinate quantity, determinate dimensions, by virtue of which it can be pointed out and referred to in space. Quantity is an accident that is radicated in matter and flows from matter. (The limits of a being's quantity, however, are determined by substantial form.) Together with its due quantity, matter is the root of individual differences; it is the principle of individuation of corporeal beings which are multiplied within a species.

Matter with its determinate quantity accounts for the fact that a corporeal individual is *this* corporeal existent. Form accounts for the fact that it is a *specific* type of corporeal existent, that it belongs to this species. Form directly determines the existence of the individual existent; by receiving and limiting form, matter explains the individual way in which that essential determination is realized.

Related as Potency and Act

Since substantial form accounts for the "greater or lesser" perfection of the (determinate) capacity of the material essence for existence, it is a perfecting factor—an act. Since matter accounts for the limitation and restriction of this capacity to an individual of the species, matter is a potential factor. Thus, form and matter are related as perfecting act and limiting potency.[34]

[34] Although substantial form is an *actual* principle in the essential order, nevertheless, in conjunction with matter as constituting the composite, sub-

Distinct as Real Principles of Being

Substantial form and matter are really distinct as components of the (substantial) essence of the unitary, total existent: the one principle, form, determines the specification of the composite existent; the other principle, matter (with its due quantity), ultimately accounts for the individuation.

Now, not every quantitative, extended, or *corporeal* being is of the same species, or form. Humans, for example, are corporeal; canines are corporeal; and so are cats and mice. Matter is the principle which explains why they are quantitative, extended, spatiotemporal—in a word, corporeal. But the principle which accounts for the *specification* of these various corporeal beings cannot be identified with matter; otherwise, all corporeal beings would be of the same species, essence, or nature. Obviously they are not. Consequently, the intrinsic principle of specification and the principle of quantification (and of individual differences) must be really distinct principles in the unitary existent—the subsistent, the supposit.[35]

F.   PERFECTION AND LIMITATION IN ACCIDENTAL ORDER

Participation of Accidents[36]

Besides participation in the existential order (of the act of existing), and in the substantial essential order (where the primary mode of existing is participated by many individuals), we discover in the beings of our experience a participation of *sec-*

---

stantial essence, it is a *potential* factor in the existential order; it is potency as regards the act of existing.

[35] By supposit we mean the individual substantial existent with all its accidents.

[36] Again, let us recall the analogous character of participation. Note that in the following classic text on participation, St. Thomas does not say that an unparticipated accident actually exists: ". . . *if* whiteness were self-subsisting, it would be one, since whiteness is multiplied by its recipients" (*Summa Theologiae*, I, 44, 1c).

ondary modes of existing.[37] The same secondary mode of existing is found multiplied in many different individuals. There are, for example, white men, white dogs, white cats, white mice, etc. Whiteness is participated by many beings which differ not only individually but even essentially (substantially).[38] None of these white beings is exclusively white, nor the totality of whiteness, nor the plenitude of whiteness; none is whiteness itself.[39] Every individual, white existent is a limited *participant* in whiteness; a secondary mode of existing is participated by many.

Accidents—Modifications of a Subject

An existent already essentially, or substantially, determined has various nonessential modifications, or determinations; for example, John Jones, who is (primarily) human, is (secondarily) white, tall, fat, wise, etc. Moreover, such an existent acquires further modifications, while remaining substantially (and individually) the same; Jones, for example, becomes mathematical, musical, and even metaphysical. He begins to participate in various secondary modes of existing while remaining essentially the same. These secondary modes of existing, these modifications of an already essentially determined existent, are called accidents.

Accidents are *perfections;* surely to-be-musical, mathematical, philosophical is (metaphysically, at least) more perfect than to be none of these. However, accidents are not the primary, or

[37] Accidents are quidditative, or essential, factors of an existent; that is to say, they are *determinants* of the mode of existing, not the primary but the secondary determinants. True, accidents are not *substantial* essential factors; nevertheless, they are truly whatness principles, which determine not what a thing is substantially, but what color, size, etc., it is. Thus, they are modifications of the substantial mode. Cf. De Raeymaeker, *op. cit.,* p. 334. See also Aquinas, *Summa Contra Gentiles,* III, 7, for the twofold meaning of essence as substantial essence and accidental essence.

[38] The error of racism would in effect raise a secondary mode of existing to the status of a primary mode; it would make an accidental difference an essential (substantial) one.

[39] The only order in which an unparticipated exemplar actually exists is the existential order. In the accidental order, there is question of a *mode* of existing; there is no unparticipated mode. See footnotes 36 and 32 of this chapter.

basic, perfection (to be), nor are they the essential perfection (substantial form); rather, they are modifications of an existent already substantially determined.

Substance—Subject of Modifications

The principle in the unitary, total existent by which it (the subsistent) is modifiable in various ways, and by which it can participate in various modifications while remaining essentially the same, is *substance*. Substance is the subject of the modifications; it receives and limits them. Together with the modifications, it constitutes the modified, unitary existent (the subsistent, or supposit); for example, the mathematician, the musician, the physician, the metaphysician are a composite of human substance and an accidental quality.

Dynamism of Being

Being is dynamic, not purely static. It overflows in activity, which is, as it were, the full flowering of being. Now, activity may be along many lines so that the existent becomes modified in various ways[40] through its own operations. Thus, *one* and the same being may be *many* in its activities; it may participate in various activities. These activities are accidents and are the perfection of the subject in which they "inhere" and which limits them.

Moreover, there is an interaction between beings. One being may act (transiently) on another, modifying it for good or ill. Nevertheless, despite the many activities (either its own or another's) by which a being is modified, the beings of our experience remain essentially stable, at least for a time; that is to say, they remain substantially the same. By reason of substance, the subject of modifications, they retain their primary mode of existing. By reason of this principle, there are a basic stability and *unity*

[40] In living beings, this dynamism is exercised through operative potencies, or powers, which will be studied at length in the philosophy of man. Nonliving beings possess "forces" which are set off, or "triggered," by what the scientist likes to call the "causal" action of other beings. In this sense, all being is dynamic, the living and the nonliving as well.

in these beings which are truly dynamic and become *many* through their own activities and the activities of other beings acting upon them.

Substance and Accidents Related as Potency and Act

Insofar as substance is modifiable, or determinable, it is a *potential* principle; it "receives" and limits the accident.[41] The modifications of the substance, namely, the accidents, are determining factors;[42] as such they perfect the substance; they are perfecting principles—act. Hence, accidents and their substance are related as perfecting act and limiting potency.

Distinct as Real Principles of Being

The subject of modification (substance) and the modifications of the substance are distinct. A mathematician, for example, is not his mathematics; rather, he is mathemati*cal;* he *has* mathematical knowledge. A mathematician participates in mathematical knowledge along with many other men; he is not mathematics itself.

Nor is human *substance* identically mathematical knowledge. The mathematician (as of now) may have existed many years before he developed the intellectual, accidental modification known as mathematics; all that time he was essentially (substantially) human. A mathematician, then, is a composite of human substance and mathematical knowledge; a doctor (a medical man) is a composite of human substance and medical knowledge. It should be clear from this that the substance of an existent is distinct from the new modifications (accidents) acquired.

Moreover, even those accidents which are not acquired, but are present from the inception of existence, are distinct from substance. A white man simply is not his color; he *has* a color.

[41] In the case of a doctor (a medical man), the human substance "receives," or limits, the medical knowledge to this individual, human existent. It is this doctor's knowledge, not that of another doctor or the knowledge of a nonmedical man.

[42] Let us recall that they are not the primary but only the secondary determining principles.

A man is not his intellect or will; he has an intellect and a will. Nor is he his weight; he *has* weight. Substance is not accident; accidents are not substance.[43]

G. ANALOGY OF POTENTIAL–ACTUAL PRINCIPLES

Composition in Three Orders

We have seen that participation, multiplicity, and limitation in three orders are an evident fact. Moreover, we have shown that participation, multiplicity, and limitation in these various orders require a *composition* of intrinsic factors, elements, or principles, in the unitary existent:

1. Of "to be" and essence as regards the existential order
2. Of accidents and substance (composition within essence) as regards the accidental order
3. Of substantial form and prime matter (composition within substance) as regards the substantial order

Similarity amid Differences in Compositions

Although none of these compositions are exactly the same (univocal), there is a common feature in all of them. In every instance, there is a *perfecting* principle, a principle which confers perfection: "to be," accidents, substantial form. In each of these compositions, there is also a *limiting* principle, a principle which "receives" the perfection and restricts the perfecting principle: essence, substance, matter.[44]

[43] An argument for the distinction of substance and accidents will be presented in section H of this chapter.

[44] The composite is neither of its component principles. Thus, the limited existent is neither essence nor existence. Individual nature is neither matter nor substantial form nor its accidents. A modified subject is neither the modification nor the subject; for example, a doctor is neither medical knowledge nor merely human substance; he is a composite of human substance and medical knowledge—a human-substance-knowing-medicine.

Act-Potency Correlation

"To be," accidents, substantial form are *acts*—perfecting principles. Essence, substance, and matter are correlative *potencies*. Thus, "to be" is related to essence, *as* accidents are related to substance, and *as* substantial form is related to prime matter. This may be expressed more clearly as follows:

"To be" : essence *as* accidents : substance
as substantial form : matter

Analogy of Proportionality within Limited Beings

The pairs of intrinsic, constitutive principles are proportionally similar to each other though simply different. This similarity among diverse relations constitutes an analogy of proportionality, not between (limited) beings,[45] but *within* the unitary, total limited existent.

Acts—"to Be," Accidents, Substantial Form. "To be," accidents, and substantial form are truly acts. To rise to an understanding of this truth, we shall first consider *accidents,* since they are more readily understood as act than are the more profound actualizing principles, namely, substantial form and the act par excellence, "to be."

Let us begin by considering the shape, or figure, given to wax by a sculptor. This shape, or figure, is a perfecting principle, a "bettering" factor. Without this accidental form (a quality about quantity) the wax would remain a more or less shapeless mass. That there is a waxen Napoleon or a waxen Caesar instead of a waxen cube—the stuff sometimes comes in cubic containers—is due to the figure imparted to the wax. This accidental form, therefore, is a perfecting factor, an actualizing principle, or *act;* the same may be said of any accident, that is, of any secondary determination of being.

In a more profound and radical way, the *substantial form* is a perfecting principle; it specifies a nature, or substantial essence.

[45] See Chapter I, section G.

In the case of the wax, it makes the material being in question to be *specific*, to be waxen, instead of wooden or golden; it "shapes," or determines, the very existence of the total existent. As such, the substantial form is an actualizing principle, a perfecting principle, or *act*.

In an even more fundamental way, the very *existing* of a being is a perfecting principle. Although Hamlet seems to have doubted the issue, we all know that "to be" is better than "not to be." One simply cannot be mathematical, musical, metaphysical (all accidental perfections), or be human (substantial, specific perfection) unless one does *be* (exist). The very existing of the unitary, composite existent is its basic perfecting principle, the most fundamental actualizing factor, or *act*. Indeed, it is the "act of all acts, the perfection of all perfections." All other acts are merely determinations of it.

Potencies—Matter, Substance; Essence. To rise to a knowledge of limiting principles as potencies, we may begin with a crude example from the world of accidental units (more than one being united somehow)—a container and its content. A 12-ounce "beer" is a composite of perfecting content and limiting container. The container limits and confines the content. The limiting factor of this accidental composite unit is the capacity, or potency, of the container.

Returning to substantial units (one subsistent), we can now more readily understand that accidental perfections are limited by their subject (substance). Various qualities, such as knowledge, color, shape, etc., are limited by the capacity of their subject. Thus, the knowledge of a man, of a dog, and of a worm varies in proportion to the limiting capacity, or potency, of the subject. (A philosophical worm, that is, a worm knowing philosophy, would be an oddity indeed.) The limiting principle in such cases is the capacity, or potency, for the accidents. *Substance* is that potency.

Substantial form, which is a perfecting principle in the order of essence, is restricted by matter (with its due quantity), which is the principle of individual differences. Matter (with its due quantity) is a potency for the specifying substantial form and limits the form to this individual. Thus, no man is man-in-general but is a man "with this flesh and these bones"—an individual, human existent, not humanity as such. The limiting principle is the capacity, or potency, for this individual specifying principle (substantial form). *Matter* (with its determinate quantity) is that potency.

In the most fundamental order, the order of existence, essence (what something is, the mode of existing) is a limiting principle.[46] It is the capacity, or potency, for existing. Now, no being can exist above its capacity; a feline existent, for example, cannot exist as a dog, nor can a canine existent exist as a man. The limiting principle is the capacity, or potency, for existing. *Essence* is that potency.

Differences in Compositions. Although the intrinsic potential-actual compositions, or "structures," within an existent are (proportionally) similar to each other, they nevertheless have important differences.

Existence, accidents, and substantial form are all *acts,* but they are not act in the same manner. Existence is the actualizing principle of the total, unitary existent (the subsistent) making it *be.* Substantial form determines it to be *what* it is primarily. Accidents determine it to be *what* it is secondarily. For example: substantial form determines Fido to be canine; accidental forms determine him to be brown, long-eared, etc.

On the other hand, essence, prime matter, and substance are *potencies,* but they are not potency in the same way. Prime matter is *in*determinate potency for substantial form. Essence is determinate potency for existence. Substance is a determinate primary mode of existing potential to secondary modifications.

Moreover, an act in one order may be potency *in another order.* Thus, substantial form, which is act in the substantial order, in conjunction with matter as constitutive principles of

---

[46] Or a complexus of principles. Essence contains many quidditative principles, both substance and accidents. Material substance in turn is a composite of matter and substantial form.

the substance is potency to accidents. The composite of substance and accidents (acts), which is the individual essence, in turn is potency to existence. Existence, however, as basic, or primary, act is in potency to nothing. It is the "act of all acts."

Substantial form and accidents (accidental, or secondary, forms) are acts which *determine;* that is, they cause the existent to be of some specific kind or to exist according to some modification. Existence, however, is an act which does not determine a being; it makes it *be.*

We may conclude this section with a general remark: The relation between the components of being is always proportionally similar to the relation between other potential-actual components. Nevertheless, this relation is always different. Hence, this potency-act correlation is rightly said to be analogous; and the analogy is one of *proportionality,* not between beings, but *within* being.

H. REAL DISTINCTION BETWEEN POTENTIAL–ACTUAL PRINCIPLES

What is the distinction between the various potential-actual, correlative principles within a limited being? To answer this question, we must give a division of the diverse kinds of distinctions. We must distinguish distinctions. In general, we may say that those things are distinct, of which one is not the other; *distinction* is the negation of identity. Now, distinction can be of various kinds.

Mental Distinction

Distinctions may be discovered by the mind, or they may merely be made by the mind; that is to say, distinctions may occur in reality independently of the mind, or they may be the work of the mind itself in its effort to acquire more and more determinate "views" of the reality.[47]

Virtual Distinction. One and the same unitary existent can be grasped by the intellect (according to the being's essence) by

[47] Somewhat as a star image we see in a telescope becomes more and more definite as the focus is sharpened.

various concepts. For example: the specific essence of man can be grasped as (1) a substance; (2) a body (corporeal substance); (3) organism (living body); (4) animal (sentient organism); (5) man (rational animal). Although in this instance there is only one unitary existent, one reality, the intellect forms five *distinct concepts* of the (substantial) essence of this same existent. Here we have a distinction of concepts, of ideas, but not a distinction in the real.[48]

The successive, higher concepts express more and more determinately the (substantial) essence of the existent. The more general concept (the lower concept) contains *indeterminately* the intelligible content of the higher; thus, substance *can* be bodily (or not), a body can be living (or not), a living body, or organism, can be sentient (or not), an animal can be rational (or not).

The higher and more determinate concept, in turn, contains the lower *virtually;* thus, the concept "man" (rational animal) presents man as having the perfections presented in the lower concepts: animal, organism, body, substance.[49] Hence, such a distinction is aptly called a *virtual* distinction.

Other Kinds of Mental Distinctions. There are other kinds of mental distinctions, but we need not consider them here.[50] What

---

[48] Nevertheless, a distinction in the real is the *foundation* for the mental distinction. matter is not form. Matter as indeterminate principle can be actualized by various forms of increasing perfection.

[49] The reason, of course, is that man's mode of existing *virtually* contains the lower modes; he has the powers (and activities) of beings existing according to these lower modes, although he is not any of these lower beings *actually.* Thus, man has sensitive activity, but he is not a brute; he has vegetative activity, but he is not a cabbage; he has chemical activities (and structure), but he is not chemicals; he has atomic activity (and structure), but he is not atoms; he even has electronic activity (a man is a fairly good conductor of electricity and can be electrocuted), but he is not electrons. The higher being may have the activity (and structures) of lower beings; thus, the higher being is *virtually,* not actually, the lower beings.

[50] The virtual distinction sometimes is called a *major* mental (logical) distinction in opposition to the *minor* mental distinction, such as that between "being" and its transcendental properties (one, true, good), which

is of supreme importance, however, is to be able to distinguish between mental distinctions and real distinctions. What is the criterion, or norm, which will enable us to recognize that a distinction is *made* by the mind?

Norm for Mental Distinction—Direct Predication. In the example we gave of a virtual distinction, the various concepts formed by the mind can be predicated *directly* of one and the same subject. One and the same subject, man, is a substance, a body, an organism, an animal, rational.[51] Such a direct predication of many concepts (or terms) of a common subject expresses the *real identity* of the object(s) of these various concepts. This distinction, then, is made by the mind itself in its effort to know more and more determinately the essence of the being known. Such a distinction, obviously, is not a real distinction, even though, as in this case, there may be a foundation for the distinction (which the mind makes) in the real.

Real Distinction

There are distinctions in the real independent of the work of the mind.[52] These distinctions are not made by the mind; they are *discovered* by the mind. And whether our minds discover these distinctions or not, these distinctions remain the same.

---

make explicit what "being" only implies. These properties will be examined in Chapter VII.

Another distinction should be discussed, namely, the *purely verbal* distinction. This is merely a distinction of words; for example, the distinction between "man" and "rational animal" is merely verbal. Although one may form the same concept twice so that there are two distinct mental operations, nevertheless, the intelligible content is expressible equally well by using the word "man" or the words "rational animal."

[51] A more precise formulation which respects the *essential* status of the predication: The human mode of existing is substantial, bodily, organic, sentient, rational.

[52] The mind, however, in its activity recognizes this distinction either by forming distinct concepts or by conceiving *and* judging (existentially). Thus, real distinctions are also "mental." On the other hand, mental distinctions are *only* mental. However, it is only in and through distinct knowledge acts that we can attain the distinctions in the real.

Real Distinction between Complete Beings. Some real distinctions are distinctions between complete beings, that is, between unitary existents, and are immediately perceived as such. For example: this man and that man, this man and that dog, this dog and that dog are immediately perceived to be *really* distinct; the one simply is not the other. Hence, we do not directly predicate the one of the other.

Moreover, they are really distinct as *complete beings,* not as parts, elements, or principles of a being. The one does not depend on the other to exist; although Fido may be man's best friend, a man can exist without him.

Furthermore, what is true of these individual existents (John and Fido) is true of all the beings that participate in the same nature. Human beings, wherever and whenever we find them, simply *are not* canine beings, for men are rational while dogs are not. And canine beings (although in some cases they are better-treated than human beings) are simply not human beings. To paraphrase a famous remark, which brought much opprobrium upon its author: Dogs are but brutes, albeit very attractive brutes. Men and dogs are *really* distinct as *complete* beings.

Real Distinction between Principles of Being. What is the distinction between the various potential-actual factors in a unitary existent (the subsistent)? What is the distinction between the act of existing and limiting essence, between specifying substantial form and individuating matter, between modifying accidents and the substantial subject of modifications?

The Thomistic contention is that the distinction between the intrinsic, constitutive principles of the unitary, total existent is (1) a *real* distinction, not a mere distinction of concepts, or ideas; (2) a real distinction, not between complete beings, but between correlative *principles* within the being, within the unitary, total existent (the supposit).

The opposition to this distinction by some philosophers is occasioned largely by their failure to understand the kind of distinction involved and sometimes to an overzealous exposition by its upholders, which would make the distinction one between two "things" (*res et res*) rather than a distinction between co-related, "structural" principles within one existent.

Principles of Being

If a unitary existent, or being, is composite, it cannot be composed of beings,[53] but only of "parts," or principles, of being. A house is not composed of houses; it is composed of parts of a house. Similarly, a composite being is not composed of beings; it can be composed only of "parts," factors, elements—*principles* of being. If individual beings are composite—and we have given the evidence for this composition—the composition cannot be one of many beings. Such an explanation of composition within being would disregard the obvious *unity* of beings; one being simply is not many beings.

Constitutive principles of being do not exist in themselves; they have no reality apart from the being of which they are the principles; they are not separate existents (subsistents). Rather, they are intrinsic principles by which the unitary existent *is*, and is *what* it is (primarily and secondarily). Thus, by reason of substantial form, the total existent is of a definite species; by reason of matter (with its due quantity), the "entire" being is individuated; by reason of accidents the existent is modified; and by reason of the act of existing, it *is*.

These principles, although they may be called "parts," since they make up the whole being, are not *quantitative* parts, or integral parts—like arms, legs, ears, etc. Substance and accidents,

---

[53] From two beings in act, one being in act cannot result. This is a crucial principle in Thomism. "For many cannot become one absolutely unless they be related as act and potency. Those things which are in act, are united only insofar as they form a collection or aggregation, which are not one absolutely" (*Summa Contra Gentiles*, I, 18).

One must, for example, guard against explaining the parts of an organism as if these parts were substantial units in themselves. Organisms are not mere aggregations; they are simply (absolutely) one. The multiplicity of their parts must not be explained in such a way that the obvious unity of the whole (which produced and maintains the parts) is made unintelligible. The primary reality here is not the part. Nor is the organism the mere sum total of parts.

primary matter and substantial form are *essential* parts, or principles, constituting the essence. Essence and the act of existing are principles constituting the existent. What we observe is the existing thing, the subsistent, but by intellectual reflection we know that the principle by which the thing is *what* it is and the principle by which it *is* are not the same.

Specific Arguments for Distinctions between Principles of Being

It will be helpful at this point to summarize the arguments already presented separately for the real distinction of potential-actual principles in the three orders of existence, essence, and accident.

Essence and Act of Existing. We can know *what* a thing (or who someone) is and still not know whether it *is*. I can know, for example, who John Jones is and still not know whether he still is (lives). However, when confronted by a real existent, we not only know what it is (at least in an indeterminate way), but we also judge that it *is* (exists). The difference between merely conceptual knowledge, on the one hand, and the conceptual-judgmental knowledge of the existent, on the other, must be grounded in distinct, real factors in the existent itself—essence and the act of existing. Otherwise, whenever we formed the concept of what a thing is, we would necessarily judge that it is.

Moreover, concerning any individual existent, the judgment that "it is" and the judgment that "it is this" *cannot be reduced* to each other. The judgments "There *is* some (sort of) thing" and "It is of this (individual) *sort*" are not one and the same. In other words, the attributive judgments concerning the mode of existing (whether primary or secondary mode) and the existential judgment concerning the fact of existing are *irreducible.*

Now, if knowledge is of being (the principle of intelligibility), the distinction between these judgments must be grounded in a distinction within the existent itself—a principle explaining the exercise of existence and a principle (or complexus of principles) explaining the mode of existing.

Matter and Form. It is evident that material beings are not all of the same specific nature. If matter and form were really identical, all corporeal being would be restricted to one nature, or species.

Moreover, there are *many* beings of the same nature, of the same specific type. This is not intelligible unless the principle of specification (substantial form) is "received" in a distinct principle of individuation (matter) to constitute the individual essence. Hence, matter and form must be really distinct.

Substance and Accidents. The modifications of a subject and the subject of modifications must be really distinct. The determinations of a subject, namely, the accidents, and the subject of these determinations, namely, substance, are not identical.

Moreover, there are *many* participants in the same accidental perfection. Again, this is not intelligible unless the principle of accidental perfection is "received" in a distinct principle—substance.

General Argument—Indirect Predication of a Common Subject

The real distinction between principles of a being precisely *as principles* is reflected in the way we predicate these principles of a common subject, as "parts" of a whole. We do not say, for example, that a doctor *is* medical knowledge, *is* human nature. Rather, we say a doctor *has* medical knowledge (as one constitutive principle), *has* a human nature, or substance (as another intrinsic principle). In like manner, we do not say that a limited existent *is* existence, *is* essence. Rather, we say a limited being *has* existence (as one constitutive principle), *has* essence (as another intrinsic principle). Thus, existence and essence are predicated *indirectly* of the common subject (the limited existent).[54]

[54] The limited existent is not a third thing distinct from essence (the mode of be-ing) and the act of existing. Neither, on the other hand, is the limited existent identically its essence (nor existence); rather, it exists according to *one* mode, according to one "thing principle."

Indirect Predication of Quantitative Parts. The significance of indirect predication is more obvious to us when there is question of
the quantitative parts of an organism.[55] We do not say, for example, that man *is* his right arm, that man *is* his left arm. Such *direct*
predication would signify an identity of the part with the whole.
Rather, we say, "Man *has* a right arm; man *has* a left arm."

An indirect predication of this sort signifies (1) a *real* distinction (2) between *parts* of a common subject. The full significance
of this predication is somewhat as follows: man's right arm is not
his left arm; man, the common subject, is a composite of (at least)
two distinct parts—a right arm and a left arm.

Keeping in mind the analogous nature of such predications,
we may now consider how principles of being are predicated indirectly of their common subject.

Indirect Predication of Principles of Being. A limited existent *has*
existence (as basic perfecting factor) and *has* an essence (as basic
limiting factor). This predication signifies: a *real* distinction—the
act of existing is not the limiting essence; a real distinction between *principles* of being—the principles belong to the common
subject as intrinsic components.

Moreover, an individual, determinate substance (essence) *has*
a specifying form and *has* individuating matter. Again, the predication signifies a real distinction between constitutive principles of
a common subject, the composite substance.

Finally, the accidentally modified subject *has* as one com-

[55] An organism is not the mere sum total of its parts, as a mechanical
unit (for example, an automobile) is the sum total of its parts. An organism
evolves its parts and maintains its parts; moreover, it evolves its own kind
of parts (elephants grow trunks, crabs grow claws, turtles grow shells, etc.).
The reason for growing one kind of anatomical structure rather than another is the "way" the being is "structured" metaphysically. A material being
of a specific formal type will act in accordance with its specific nature;
among these activities is the growing and maintaining of an anatomical
structure. Then, too, a being may even lose some of its anatomical parts (a
foot, hand, arm, leg) and still remain substantially the same. While losing
parts of its anatomical structure (an accidental quality about quantity), it
still retains its basic ontological, or metaphysical, structure.

ponent principle the subject of modifications (substance) and *has* as other principles the modifications of that subject—the accidents. Such a predication signifies a distinction between real principles in the modified subject.

Principles of Being Are Correlative

". . . Act and potency are spoken of in relation to each other. . . ." [56] All the reality of a limiting potency is an order, or relation, to the act which it limits. In turn, the reality of a limited act is a relation to the potency which limits it.[57] In this way, potential-actual principles of being are mutually related—co-related;[58] that is to say, they are correlative principles within being.

Beings by Analogy of Proportion

Existence, "to be," is the act of acts, the basic intrinsic actualizing principle. In any limited being, the potential-actual principles (with the exception of existence itself) are related, or proportioned, to the act of existing, which they determine in some way. By reason of this relation, or proportion, all these principles pertain to being, and in this sense may be called "being," not in the strict and proper sense, but by an *analogy of proportion*. We must remember, however, that "being" in the proper sense signifies the unitary, total existent, the subsistent. It is only within a subsistent as its intrinsic, "structural" principles that the potency-act correlations have any reality.

[56] *Summa Contra Gentiles*, I, 22.
[57] Not every act, however, is ordered to a potency. If a being's essence is pure form (an angelic nature), such a form, which is essential act, is not ordered to potency. Nor is the act of existing in a being which is pure existential act ordered to potency.
[58] This relation, or correlation, is often called a *transcendental* relation. Unless one respects the *correlative* character of potential-actual principles, one is apt to consider them as little substances within the subsistent (as beings within a being), a position which does violence to the obvious unity of beings. In our experience, we encounter individual beings (subsistents). Their participation of perfection in three orders requires intrinsic, ontological, structural principles. These principles, however, are not the object of experience. They are intelligible necessities we discover in being to explain participation, multiplicity, and limitation of being.

Moreover, this proportion, or relation, to existence *differs* in the various potency-act correlations. Essence, as potency, is directly related to existence, its act. Within essence, substance (potency) is related to accidents (act), and through the composite essence both principles are indirectly related to existence. Within material substance, matter (as pure potency) is related to substantial form (its act), thus composing the substance, which together with its accidents is related to existence.

Existence, however, as basic act is not proportioned, or related, to a higher act. It is the act to which all other acts (and potencies) are related within the existent; it is the act to which they pertain. In virtue of this pertinence, relation, or proportion, the other acts (and their potencies) are being, and are called such, by an analogy of *proportion*. They are acts and potencies only by reason of their proportion to the act of existing, "to be" (*esse*), the supreme act.

Symbolic Diagram of Potency-Act Correlations

Metaphysical thinking requires that we free our considerations of reality from all sensible imagery. It demands that we view being purely as *intelligible,* not as imaginable, or as sensible. Metaphysical knowledge must terminate neither in the external senses nor in the imagination, but in the *intellect alone.*[59] Nevertheless, even metaphysical knowledge has its roots in sensory (sensory-intellectual) experience. Hence, it may be helpful to attempt to illustrate the various potential-actual correlations within limited material being by a diagram. Let us not forget, however, the symbolic character of all such diagrams. They are only aids, not substitutes, for metaphysical thinking.

In this diagram, the fundamental act, "to be," is placed at the bottom. The accidents, through which we know the substantial essence of the being and the fact of be-ing, are placed at the top. The juxtaposed arrows pointing in opposite directions indicate a potency-act co-relation.

[59] *In Boeth. de Trin.,* VI, art. 2.

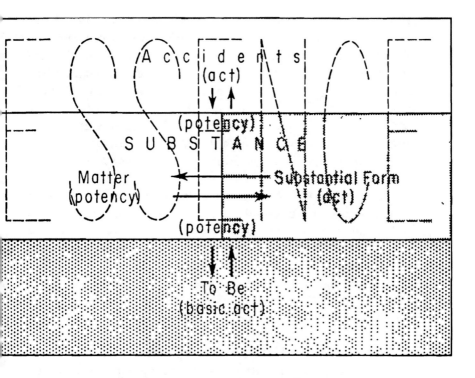

I. ACT AND POTENCY ENCOMPASS BEING

Ultimate Terms of Empiriological Sciences

The experimental, empirical, or empiriological sciences do not claim to study beings as they are in themselves. That is the task of philosophy. Rather, these sciences study (material) beings through their *sensible appearances* (phenomena) and insofar as they are measurable in some way.[60]

Nor are the *findings* of empiriological sciences necessarily ex-

[60] Within the flux of sensible phenomena, these sciences attempt to discover inseparable antecedent-consequent correlations with a view to predicting and controlling future phenomena. The explanation of the phenomena and their nexus need not be an ontological explanation. Thus, these sciences proceed in a positivistic way. Cf. Jacques Maritain, *Philosophy of Nature*, Philosophical Library, Inc., New York, 1951, pp 45-72.

pressed in terms of the things themselves which are studied. Some findings are expressed in *numbers* which have a value and meaning in relation to certain sensible standards of measurement existing either in a national or international bureau of standards: for example, so many inches, feet, meters, grams, pounds, liters, gallons, etc. Other findings are expressed in *mathematical constructs,* such as horsepower units, calories, BTUs, ergs, dynes, angstrom units, a place in the periodic table, etc. Thus, a man is found to be a 6-footer; that is, he is found to be extended six times the extension of the foot standard. Or, a man is said to eat 3,000 calories per day. As a matter of fact, he does not eat calories, but meat, potatoes, bread, etc. The number expresses the energy the food contains in terms of, and in relation to, an extrinsic standard, the mathematicized caloric unit.

We see, then, that the empiriological sciences express many of their findings concerning sensible, material beings in terms of something else, which in turn may need further explanation. Such explanations are not ultimate explanations, nor need they be.

Ultimate Terms of Thomistic Philosophy

Philosophy, on the other hand, must endeavor to give an explanation of all beings in *ultimate* terms,[61] that is, in terms which cannot be reduced to further terms. For the philosophy of St. Thomas Aquinas (and for Aristotle as well), the ultimate terms are *act* and *potency.* Our knowledge of all being is expressible in these terms.[62]

Reality Is Either Changeable or Unchangeable

Whatever exists is either changeable or unchangeable; there is no middle ground. If changeable, it is a composite of act and potency for further act.[63] If unchangeable, it must be pure act.

---

[61] "Term" in this context means not only the oral, or written, expression of a notion, or knowledge, but also the knowledge itself.

[62] The reason, of course, is that all being is truly composed of potential-actual principles or is Pure Act itself. Our knowledge is of being.

[63] Moreover, changing being precisely *as changing* is composed of potency and act, since change is the actualization of that which is potential insofar as it is potential.

Thus, the terms "potency" and "act" can be used to express our knowledge of all reality insofar as it is subject to change or not. Such a unified world view was accessible to Aristotle, who (for the most part, at least) seems to have taken the very be-ing, or existence, of changing beings as given.[64]

Perfection (Act) Is Either Limited or Unlimited

St. Thomas Aquinas used the terms "potency" and "act," not only to explain being insofar as it changes, but also to encompass reality from the viewpoint of its perfection and limitation, its multiplicity and participation, even in the order of existence.

Any participated and multiple perfection is limited and forms a composition with limiting potency. On the other hand, any perfection which is simple must be unlimited (in its own order), unique, and unparticipated.[65]

Thus, all being and its intrinsic structure and modifications are expressible in terms of act and potency.

Every Existent Either Participates Existence or Is Existence

The most profound expression of being is in terms of *existential* act and *existential* potency. Every being (*ens*) either participates the act of be-ing or is the act of be-ing itself. Every existent is either limited or unlimited. If limited, it is a composite of the act of existing and limiting essence. If unlimited, it must be the Act of Existing itself.

Aside from limited and unlimited existents, apart from participants of be-ing and the unparticipated Pure Act of Be-ing, nothing exists or can exist.[66] It is in this sense that act and potency

[64] The problem, why limited beings should be at all, seems to have escaped Aristotle.

[65] Thus, according to St. Thomas, an angel, since its nature is pure form, is unlimited in the order of essence, is unique (is the entire species), and is unparticipated in that order, although it does participate existence.

[66] One might object that besides "being" change also exists. Strictly speaking, however, only beings exist although these (limited) beings do truly change. Moreover, even change is expressible in terms of potency and act; it is the act of a being in potency insofar as it is in potency.

encompass being. All being is expressible in terms of potency and act.

SUMMARY

A. Fact of Participation: The act of existing is found participated in many primary modes. Primary modes of existing (substantial essences) are participated by many individuals. Secondary modes of existing (accidents) are participated by many individuals, of which some are even essentially different.

B. Participation Implies Limitation: The participant *has* the perfection, is not the perfection itself. It has the perfection in accordance with its capacity, that is, in a limited way. In Plato's theory of participation, the individual "shadow" realities are an admixture of "nonbeing" with the Idea, or absolute Form. The Neoplatonists developed and refined this theory.

C. Limitation by Potency: The doctrine of St. Thomas Aquinas is an original synthesis of the Neoplatonic doctrine concerning participation and the Aristotelian doctrine of potency and act regarding change. Principle: Any act which is found participated, multiple, and hence limited, forms a *composition* with limiting potency, and the act and potency are distinct principles of the unitary, total existent.

D. Perfection and Limitation in Existential Order: "To be" (*esse*), the basic perfection, is found participated according to many primary modes. Essence limits the act of existing. The (specific) essence of a being is grasped in a concept, the act of existing is affirmed in an (existential) judgment. Essence and existence are related as limiting potency and perfecting act. They are distinct as real principles within being as is manifested by the irreducibility of existential and attributive judgments about the same existent.

E. Perfection and Limitation in (Substantial) Essential Order: Primary modes of existing (substantial essences) are participated by many individuals. The principle of specification in such beings is substantial form; the principle of individuation is matter (with its due quantity). Matter and form are related as potency and act. They are distinct as real principles of being.

F. Perfection and Limitation in Accidental Order: Secondary modes of existing (accidents) are participated by many individuals even essentially distinct. These modifications of a subject are the accidents; the subject of the modifications is substance. Being is dynamic; one and the same being is many in its activities. The activities are accidents of a subject (substance). Substance and accidents are related as potency and act. They are distinct as real principles of being.

G. Analogy of Potential-Actual Principles: The composition of potential-actual principles in three orders is similar yet different, that is, analogous. The act-potency correlations are analogous by an analogy of proportionality within being. To be, substantial form, accidents are acts, perfecting principles; matter, substance, essence are potencies, limiting principles. The actual principles differ in the way they are actual principles; the potential principles differ in the manner in which they are potencies.

H. Real Distinction between Potential-Actual Principles: In general, distinctions may be merely mental or they may also be real. The most important mental distinction is the virtual distinction, and the norm for identifying this distinction is direct predication. Real distinctions are either between complete beings or between parts or principles of one being. The distinction between essence-existence, matter-form, substance-accidents is a real distinction and this is shown by specific arguments. That these distinctions are real distinctions between *principles* of being is manifested by their indirect predication of a common subject. Principles of being are mutually related; they are correlative. They are beings by analogy; the analogy is that of proportion to the act of existing.

I. Act and Potency Encompass Being: The ultimate terms which express the findings and correlations of the empiriological sciences are numbers (in relation to standards of measurement) and mathematicized constructs. The ultimate terms of Thomistic philosophy are act and potency. Reality is either changeable or unchangeable. Perfection is either limited or unlimited. Every being either participates existence or is Existence itself.

SUGGESTED READINGS

Clarke, Wayne Norris: "The Meaning of Participation in St. Thomas," *Proceedings of the American Catholic Philosophical Association,* vol. 26, pp. 147–157, for 1952.

————: "The Limitation of Act by Potency: Aristotelianism or Neo-Platonism?" *The New Scholasticism,* vol. 26, pp. 167–194, April, 1952.

De Raeymaeker, Louis: *The Philosophy of Being,* translated by E. H. Ziegelmeyer, B. Herder Book Co., St. Louis, 1954, pp. 29–31, 327–334; on participation and "structure" in limited beings.

Phelan, Gerald B.: "The Being of Creatures," *Proceedings of the American Catholic Philosophical Association,* vol. 31, pp. 124 ff., for 1957; an interpretation of essence as intrinsic limiting mode.

Plato: *Republic,* Book VII; on participation.

Van Roo, William A.: "Act and Potency," *The Modern Schoolman,* vol. 18, pp. 1–5, November, 1940; on potential-actual composition within limited material being.

IV

Efficient Causes

In the last two chapters, we were concerned largely with the *intrinsic* principles of limited beings and of the changes that occur in them. In this and the following two chapters, we shall be discussing the *extrinsic* principles of limited being and of change. We shall be concerned with efficient, final, and exemplary causes.

A. CAUSE vs. OCCASION, CONDITION, ANTECEDENT

Cause, a Term of Many Meanings

Even before we formally begin the study of philosophy, we often make some sort of inquiry into the causes of things and of

107

the changes that occur in them. However, the prephilosophical mind is apt to use the term "cause" with reference to many meanings to which the philosopher would not attach the term at all. We may, for example, hear people say that darkness is the cause of burglaries, that good cooking causes good digestion, that slavery caused the Civil War, that a rise in temperature to 108 degrees Fahrenheit was the cause of a man's death, that a drop in temperature to 32 degrees and below was the cause of the freezing of water, etc. In philosophy, however, the term "cause" has a restricted and technical meaning. In our study of the causes, one of our principal tasks will be to distinguish causes in the strict and proper sense of the term from the other meanings often attached to it. We must distinguish cause from occasion, condition, and antecedent.

Occasion

It might be statistically verified that many more burglaries are committed on dark nights than on moonlit nights. The darkness might then be called a "cause" of the burglaries. But when we consider the matter more carefully, we see at once that the darkness did not bring about, or effect, the burglaries. The actual burglarizing was by the burglars themselves; they effected, or brought it about. The darkness did not have a *positive influence* on the burglarizing process; it did not "flow into" the effect; it merely gave the opportunity to carry out the process secretly and to make a safe getaway. (Burglaries, however, can be committed by skilled practitioners of the trade even in broad daylight.) The occasion does not act; it does not exercise action; it merely furnishes a favorable opportunity for action. Hence, an occasion is not a true (efficient[1]) cause.

Condition

Good cooking is connected in some way with good digestion, and sometimes people will say that good cooking is responsible for

[1] Nor is it a material, formal, or final cause. We shall see in this and in the following chapter that there are various kinds of causes. What the prephilosophic mind most readily recognizes as a cause is usually an *efficient* cause.

good digestion, that it is the "cause" of good digestion. Now, it is true enough that most civilized people cannot digest some foods unless they are well-cooked. Nevertheless, the cooking does not digest the food; it merely removes obstacles to the digestion of the food. Thus, it is not an (efficient) cause but merely a condition. A condition merely removes obstacles that would keep an (efficient) cause from acting. A condition does not have a positive and direct influence on the effect.[2]

Antecedent

In the empiriological sciences, an antecedent phenomenon and its inseparable consequent (or concomitant) are often said to be related as "cause and effect." For example, a temperature of 108 degrees Fahrenheit in a man for any appreciable period of time is almost invariably followed by the man's death. The high temperature is then said to be the cause of death.

Now, it is true that a very high temperature is seldom separable from death in the case of a human organism; such an antecedent phenomenon has its inseparable consequent.[3] Nevertheless, when we consider the positive factors at work, which contributed to the man's death, we come to realize that it was actually the microorganisms boring from within which did the man in. The high temperature, perhaps, manifested the causal influence of these microorganisms. The temperature itself (for the scientist, a reading on a measuring device) did not have a positive *influence* on the effect; it did not enter into, or "flow into," the effect.[4]

[2] Other examples: The opening of a container filled with canned goods is required as a condition for us to eat its contents. The cap of a telescope must be removed (by an efficient cause) for us to focus the instrument on a star target. Gas must be compressed in a cylinder head and a spark applied for it to explode. In all these instances, it should be noted that the placing of the necessary conditions implies the efficient causality of some agents, though these agents are not the causes of the actions we have in mind—the eating, the focusing, the exploding of the gases.

[3] Scientific "causes" often are conditions that must be placed to unleash the natural dynamism of material beings. For example, a lighted fuse "causes" the dynamite to explode. Or, on a larger scale, a plutonium bomb acting as a fuse "causes" a hydrogen-bomb "explosion."

[4] We see, then, that scientific causes (antecedents of inseparable conse-

To use another example: a patient may recover from an infectious disease after taking his favorite quack remedy. He might then say that the patent medicine was the "cause" of his cure, since the cure took place *after* taking this "remedy." (*Post hoc, ergo propter hoc.*) The true causative agents, however, were the antibiotics administered by the doctor, which by their causal action destroyed the invading microorganisms.

Proper Cause[5]

A cause in the strict, or proper, sense is *simultaneous* with its effect, not merely antecedent to the effect. A house, for example, is being built while and as long as the builder builds. True, the cause is prior, or antecedent, to the effect as the principle, or source, from which the effect flows. This priority, however, is not a priority of time, but of *nature;* the effect does truly flow from the cause as its (prior in nature) principle; the cause is prior as principle.

Cause and effect, then, are contemporaneous. Thus, the wood is being sawed only while the carpenter is actually sawing it. The table is being made only while the carpenter is busy making it. When he stops working at five o'clock, he is no longer an actual table maker but only a table maker by profession. It is incorrect, therefore, to say that he *is* the cause of the table (behind which

---

quents or inseparable concomitants) are not necessarily causes in the philosophical sense. Nevertheless, the discovery and correlation of scientific causes and effects is a very worthwhile endeavor and is of great value in predicting and controlling phenomena, one of the principal aims of the scientist. These "causes," however, must never be confused with philosophical causes.

[5] Also to be distinguished from proper causes are (some) *reasons.* True, every cause is a reason, but not every reason is a cause, especially a bad reason. A (good) reason is anything that enlightens the mind as an explanation. Unlike a cause, a reason need not be real. In logic we learn that the premises are the reason for the conclusion. We assent to the conclusion *because* of the premises; the knowledge of the premises "causes" the knowledge of the conclusion. Moreover, in the philosophy of God, we shall see that God, the Uncaused Cause, is His own reason for existence (since He is Existence), but is not His own cause.

the teacher is now seated). Rather, he *was*—the good man died many years ago—the cause of the *making*[6] of the table.

More important, however, than simultaneity of proper cause and proper effect is the *positive influence* that a cause (in the strict sense) has on the existence of the effect. A proper cause affects *existence,* either in its mode (cause of change) or in its act (creative cause). This will become more apparent in our treatment of the various causes. Also the diverse *modes* of influence of each of the various types of causes will become clear.[7] In this chapter, we shall discuss efficient causes.

B.   EFFICIENT CAUSES OF CHANGE

Problem Regarding Changing Being

Change, we have seen, is the passage of a subject from potency to act. Cold water, for example, which was potentially hot, becomes actually hot when heated. Such a change is an *accidental* change, and the subject of the change is substance, which, in this case, receives a new qualitative determination, or act.

In a *substantial* change, the subject is prime matter, which passes from potency to act as regards a new substantial form as the old form is reduced to potency of matter. Thus, the corruption of the dog is the generation of minerals; the reduction of the canine form to potency of matter is simultaneous with the eduction of the new forms from the passive potency of matter.

In both kinds of change, whether substantial or accidental, a subject passes from *potency to act;* a potential subject is actualized.

Intrinsic composition of potency and act, we have seen, renders such changes *intrinsically* intelligible. However, a further explanation is needed. Why should the cold water become hot at

---

[6] He is not now nor ever was the cause of the be-ing (existing) of the table. He caused it to come-to-be; he merely changed something already existing.

[7] We shall take up this point again after we have studied the different kinds of causes. See Chapter V, section H.

all? Why should matter lose the canine form and receive the form of chemicals? In brief: granting that change is intrinsically intelligible by composition of act and potency for further act, why should changes occur at all? Why, for example, does the cold water not remain cold? In precise terms, our problem is this: When a subject passes from potency to act, *whence the new act?*

Every Change Requires Extrinsic Principle

It is a fact of direct observation that changes do occur, that beings do change. Moreover, we often directly observe something bringing about, or effecting, the change. We may, for example, observe a carpenter transforming a pile of wood (a wooden pile) into a wooden table. We directly observe not only the change which takes place but also the extrinsic principle bringing about the change.

In other instances, however, we may observe a change but cannot observe what is bringing about the change. We may, for example, observe an object catching fire and be unable to discover what is setting the object on fire. We may notice that the temperature of a room is rising and still be unable to observe what is bringing about the change in temperature. Nevertheless, we do know that something *is* bringing about, or effecting, this change.

Moreover, we know that not only this or that change, but that every change, is brought about. As metaphysicians, we are interested not in merely observing this or that individual changing being and whatever brings about its changes; rather, we are concerned with explaining why *every* change must be brought about, whether we observe what is bringing about the change or not.

Nothing Moves Itself from Potency to Act

By a consideration of changing beings, whether their changes be substantial or accidental, we realize that in *any* change, a subject is moved from potency to act, that a potency is being actualized. Now, nothing can reduce itself from potency to act. The cold water, for example, cannot heat itself; it depends on an extrinsic principle, the fire, for its being-heated. Nor, in a substantial change, does matter give itself the new substantial form; rather, it is moved from potency to act by extrinsic generative agents.[8] To be moved from potency to act, a subject depends upon the influence of some extrinsic principle; it is under the influence of something acting upon it—an agent, or *efficient* cause.

Dependence on Efficient Cause in Act

Why cannot a subject reduce *itself* from potency to act? Why cannot the fire heat itself? Why cannot matter move itself to the new form? The answer is that the subject would be *in potency and in act* with regard to the same perfection at the same time. To receive the perfection, the subject would need to be in potency and not have the perfection. To confer the perfection, the subject would need to possess the perfection and be in act. Such a supposition is an unintelligible contradiction: the subject would both have and not have the same perfection at the same time.

Consequently, we must hold the opposite proposition: *Nothing is reduced from potency to act except by an extrinsic principle;* and, since there is question here of an extrinsic principle which confers perfection, this extrinsic principle, or *agent,* must possess the perfection; that is to say, it must be *in act.* For example, that which is actually hot can heat; actual cats can generate kittens. This extrinsic principle, which actuates the potency, we shall call an *efficient cause* (of change).

C.   EFFICIENT CAUSE OF BE–ING

Problem Regarding Limited Existents

A more fundamental problem than the problem why limited beings *change,* is the problem why they *are.* Why should limited beings *exist at all?*[9] This problem is so basic and radical (in the

---

[8] In the case of animal generation, this is accomplished by the animal parents, who are in act with regard to a specific form and cause the eduction of the new form from the potency of matter as the old form (or forms) are reduced to the potency of matter.

[9] The problem applies to each individual limited being and to the sum

etymological sense of the word) that it is often overlooked and certainly has been overlooked even by philosophers of considerable intellectual penetration, who have taken existence as given.

We have explained in the preceding chapter that the many participants in existence, the many limited beings of our experience, require intrinsic composition of the act of existing (*esse*) and limiting essence. They exist in *diverse ways* by reason of their intrinsic, limiting essences, or determining modes. It is only in virtue of these different, limiting modes that *many* can exist. Otherwise, all reality would be of one mode, or kind.

A further problem now arises: Granted that there are *many* beings by virtue of different limiting essences, why should any of these mere participants in existence exist at all? Any existent exercising the act of be-ing according to a restricting and limiting essence, so that it exists only "up to a point," should rather *not exist*. Shot through with limitation and negation of perfection, it should rather *not be*. And yet it *is;* it exists.

"To Be" Is Not Their Essence

We must locate our problems very precisely. To exist, to be, is not a problem; that something is does not give us pause. But that a *limited* being should exist, that a mere *participant* of be-ing should exist, this should give us pause; its very existing should not be taken for granted.[10]

To state the problem another way: A limited being is not *the* being,[11] but merely *a* being, a participant in the act of be-ing.

---

total of them even though they might *forever* exist. Why should beings which merely participate existence *be* at all?

[10] Not only professional philosophers but also many students seem to take existence for granted—for "granite," as one student expressed it—that is, as solidly established. Here we are *questioning* our "solidity" in being. Contemporary existentialism, despite its many errors, has done Thomism a great service, by calling attention to the precariousness of existence, especially of our own human existence. It has helped us to get back to a sense of wonder that we *are* and continue to be.

[11] A being in which act of be-ing is its very essence is its own explanation for existence. It *is* (exists) purely and absolutely, without adulteration of limitation. Existence is what it *is*, consequently, the very intelligibility for its existing is found within this Existent itself.

Now, beings which merely *participate* the act of be-ing are not intelligible as existing in their own right; they are not existentially autonomous.[12] And yet they *exist*. Why?

In such beings, what they are does not explain, or account for, that they are. And yet they *are*. Certainly, the essence (the limiting mode) does not explain the very existing of the unitary, total existent, for essence, although a positive factor, is merely the capacity for existing, the limiting and restricting "recipient" of existence; it is the determining, intrinsic, mode principle of the total existent. As such, the essence does not explain that the existent should *be*.

Limited Being Exists Contingently

The limited existent is not the act of existing; rather it *has*, or participates, existence according to the capacity of its essence. Such a being does not necessarily exist; it merely happens to exist; it exists *contingently*. Such a being can *not*-be; it need not *be*. Now, why should a thing which need *not* be BE? Why should it exist at all?

Our problem, then, resolves itself to this: In any existent which is not existence, but has existence, *whence* existence? Why should a mere participant in be-ing BE rather than not-be? Why should a limited existent, or the entire complex of limited existents,[13] exist at all?

Dependence on Extrinsic Principle

Once we have clearly seen the problem concerning limited existents, or participants in existence, the following principle will become quite obvious: Whatever is not existence, but has existence, *has* it from an *extrinsic principle*, from an efficient cause of existence. Whatever participates the act of be-ing according to a limiting mode depends upon an extrinsic source for its very

[12] One trained in the terminology of the law might say that such beings are not intelligible as existing *suo jure* (in their own right).

[13] This problem arises even on the supposition that the entire complex of limited beings has forever existed. Not one of them, nor all of them, would be intelligible as existing in its own right.

reality as an existent.[14] No limited existent can make itself be.

We cannot appeal to the essence to explain the very existing of the total existent, for essence is merely the restricting, determining mode of the existent. It explains what it is, the manner, or way of existing, but it does not account for the very *existing* of the unitary existent.

Moreover, in order to confer the act of existing, the essence would need to have it. In order to receive existence, the essence would necessarily lack it. Thus, the existent would be prior to itself; it would be and not be. Now, this is a contradiction. It follows that the essence cannot confer existence on the existent.

It is clear, then, that every limited existent, every participant in existence, exists with *dependence* on an extrinsic principle of existence, on an efficient cause of be-ing. Without the *here and now* influence of such a cause, it simply would not be what it is, but, more fundamentally, it would not be at all. In brief: limited beings exist *by derivation*.

D. GENERAL PRINCIPLE OF EFFICIENT CAUSALITY

Summary

The two truths we have formulated concerning the origin of change in limited beings and the origin of limited beings themselves may be summarized in one general proposition: *Every effect depends* (here and now) *upon an efficient cause.* In this proposition, the term "effect" means either one of two things: (1) any change, whether substantial or accidental, which may occur in limited existents; (2) the limited existents themselves considered precisely as existing.[15]

---

[14] Cf. *Summa Theologiae*, I, 44, 1, ad 1.

[15] In this context, the term "effect" is not tautological as is often charged. Students should refrain from defining effect as "that which is produced by a cause" and then defining cause as "that which produces an effect." Such definitions are merely tautological and tell us nothing new. They remind us of the definition of a Republican as a "GOP member," who in turn is defined as a "Republican."

The causal proposition[16] implies that every changing being precisely as changing is related by a relation of *dependence* to an extrinsic principle in act, an efficient cause, from which the change proceeds. Moreover—and this is the more profound meaning— the principle implies that every limited existent (every being by participation) is related by a relation of dependence to an extrinsic principle upon which it depends here and now *to exist*.

A Universal and Necessary Principle

This law of dependence on an extrinsic principle, or source, is *universal;* that is, it holds true for each and every effect. There are no exceptions to this law. The reason is that the principle is based on a consideration of the very intelligibility of changing beings (regarded as changing) and limited beings (considered as existing): *no* subject can reduce itself from potency to act; *nothing* which merely participates existence can account for its own existing. A denial of the principle of efficient causality owing to some alleged exception would simply involve one in a hopeless contradiction.

The principle is also *necessary*. This means that effects do not merely happen to be caused; rather, they *must* be caused; it cannot be otherwise. For, without a relation of dependence to an extrinsic principle, an efficient cause, the effect would not be: no being can be *changing* without dependence on an extrinsic principle of change; nor can limited beings *exist* without depending on an extrinsic principle from which they derive existence.

The universality and necessity[17] of the principle of efficient causality is arrived at by an intellectual consideration, such as we have given, of changing, limited beings. Its universality and necessity (and certitude) does not rest merely on an experience of this or that *individual* causation, even though our knowledge of this principle is ultimately derived from individual causations.

[16] The causal proposition is restricted here to efficient causality It is not limited, however, to this kind of causality.

[17] We may add that the principle is also absolutely certain. Our intellect is determined so that it gives assent to it as soon as we understand the meaning of the principle; the contradictory is then known to be impossible.

Rather, one must *intellectually* grasp the necessary dependence of changing beings (as changing) and participants in existence (as participating) on an extrinsic principle, or source, before one can mentally and verbally formulate this law.[18] Thus, the principle of efficient causality expresses an intelligible necessity we find in changing, participating existents.

> Although relation to a cause does not enter into the definition of the being (*ens*) which is caused, nevertheless, it follows as a result of what belongs to its intelligibility (*ratio*). For from the fact that something is a being (*ens*) by participation, it follows that it is caused by another. Hence, a being of this kind cannot be, unless it be caused. . . .[19]

E.   INFLUENCE OF EFFICIENT CAUSE

Causal Influence

A cause has a positive *influence* on the existence or the coming-into-existence (the be-ing or becoming) of something. Thus, in the production of a marble statue of Napoleon by a sculptor, there are various causal factors:

1. The marble (material cause), out of which the statue is made, accounts for the fact that it will be this *individual* statue.
2. The figure, or shape (formal cause), imparted to the marble accounts for its being a statue of Napoleon rather than a statue of Caesar; it accounts for the type, or *species*.
3. The sculptor (efficient cause) by his *action* imparts the (accidental) form to the (secondary) matter.

All the causal factors have a positive *influence* on the effect: matter by individuating the effect, form by specifying, the efficient

[18] See Étienne Gilson, *Elements of Christian Philosophy*, Doubleday & Company, Inc., Garden City, N.Y., 1960, p. 296, footnote 34; see also pp. 69–70 of this same work.
[19] *Summa Theologiae*, I, 44, 1, ad 1ᵐ.

cause by *exercising its action*. The last phrase must be carefully explained.

Agent and Patient in Transient Action

Every efficient causation involves an agent and a patient. For example, in the action through which cold water becomes heated, the agent is the fire, which is actually hot; the patient is the cold water, which is potentially hot. The agent in act acts upon the patient, which is in potency. It is the patient which passes from potency to act, not the agent. Hence, the action is *in the patient*. In our example, the heating action is in the water; it is the water (the patient), which becomes heated.

The action is conceived as if it passed from the agent across to the patient, and for this reason, action of this type is called *transient action*.[20] Such an action (transient action) is the perfection of a distinct patient, not of the agent.

Action-Passion

The passage from potency to act within the patient insofar as this change proceeds *from the agent* is called (transient) *action*. The same passage from potency to act in the patient, insofar as it *modifies the patient* is called *passion* (being-acted-upon). Thus, we speak of heating and being heated, pushing and being pushed, teaching and being taught.[21]

Action and passion, however, are not one and the same reality, even though they are grounded in one and the same passage from potency to act. Surely, heating is not the same as being heated, striking is not the same as being struck, teaching is not the same as being taught.[22] The difference between action and

[20] In opposition to the immanent activity of living beings, which "remains in" the agent, in the sense that it is the perfection of the agent itself, not of a distinct patient.

[21] Note that agent and patient are distinct. It is one thing which does the heating; it is another which is heated. One man pushes; the other is pushed. The teacher teaches; the students are being taught.

[22] One must pay tuition for being taught. One is paid (modestly) for teaching.

passion comes from the two relations involved: (1) *as from* the agent; (2) *as in* the patient. The passage from potency to act in the patient plus the relation *as proceeding from* the agent consitutes *action.* The same passage from potency to act *as modifying* the patient constitutes *passion.*

Action—the Communication of Perfection

When an agent exercises its action upon a patient, it *communicates* the perfection to which it is in act; that is to say, it moves the patient from potency to act as regards that same perfection. Thus, a heating agent communicates heat to the body which is being heated; a body in a state of motion communicates motion to another body; the teacher communicates what he actually knows to the students who are being taught.[23]

Agent as Agent Is Unchanged

Now, an agent can act only insofar as it is in *act:* a radiator can heat the surrounding air only insofar as it is actually hot; a teacher can communicate only what he actually knows. Moreover, the more an agent is in act, the more it can be an agent.[24]

A being can change, however, only insofar as it is in *potency.* Since an agent precisely as agent must be in act, it follows that an agent in acting is *unchanged.* Thus, it communicates its perfection *without losing* the perfection. By actuating the potency

---

[23] The teaching and being-taught process is here selected to exemplify the communication of a perfection which obviously is not lost by the agent. As an example, it has many defects, since teaching and being taught are primarily complex *immanent* activities, although they do involve much transient action. A teacher must "bombard" the students; he must set the air in motion to communicate his knowledge. He must "beat the air." The air beats back. The teacher feels "beat" at the end of the class, not because he has been drained of the knowledge he has communicated to his students, but because the elements of material causation involved in the teaching process make him *patient* as well as agent.

[24] For example, the hotter the radiator, the more it can heat; the more the teacher knows, the more he can communicate to his students (other things being equal), he cannot communicate what he does not know. Nothing gives what it does not have (*nemo dat quod non habet*).

of the patient, the agent does not necessarily lose its own perfection.

We must be careful not to conceive the exercise of action as a mere local transfer of perfection, as a sort of displacement of act from agent to patient; that would be to conceive action in a crude materialistic, and even mechanistic, way. A teacher, for example, while teaching his students communicates the knowledge to which he is in act; he can communicate only what he actually knows; he cannot teach what he does not know. In the teaching process, the students pass from potency to act as regards the new knowledge; they are being taught; their potency for knowledge is being actualized. The causality involved here surely is not a mere local transfer of perfection, as if knowledge flowed from the mind of the teacher into the minds of the students. If that were true, the teacher at the end of the term would be minus the knowledge communicated and might be in need of a replenishing, or refueling.[25] As a matter of fact, the teacher by presenting the matter anew is apt to understand it all the more clearly and may even receive new insights. By actualizing, or helping to actualize, the intellectual potencies of his students, he does not thereby lose the knowledge to which he is in act; rather, he *communicates* (diffuses) his knowledge without losing it.

Material Action Involves Reaction

It is often objected that the actions we know best (material transient actions, such as pushing, pulling, striking, etc.) involve a transfer, or loss of energy, a loss of perfection. We must bear in mind, however, that in *material* action, the agent is also acted upon; the agent is *patient* as well as agent.[26] For example, when a man pushes a wheelbarrow, the wheelbarrow pushes back; when one billiard ball strikes another, the other strikes back. Such actions have their opposite, and opposed, reaction. Hence, the

[25] Some students seem to be under the impression that summer schools for teachers fill precisely this need.

[26] Not, however, in the same respect. Nothing can be simultaneously agent and patient in the same respect, since it would need to be in act and in potency at the same time as regards the same perfection.

agents, the efficient causes, of these actions are "worn out" while acting, though not *as* acting (as agents). In such actions, it is in virtue of being a *patient* that the agent loses perfection, in this case, energy, as the agent communicates perfection.

Agent Need Not Be a Patient

Although the agents of our direct knowledge are all *patients* as well as agents when they exercise their action, nevertheless, to act is not to be acted upon. An agent need not be acted upon simply to be an agent. It is not the nature of transient action as such that it involve an opposite and opposed reaction; that is due to the (limited) *kind* of transient action involved—material, transient action.[27] Moreover, and this is the precise point at issue, an agent is not an agent insofar as it is acted upon (moved from potency to act) but precisely because it is *in act;* and insofar as it is in act it is unchanged.

Transient vs. Immanent Action

The activity we have been studying in this chapter, transient action, is the perfection, not of the agent, but of a distinct patient. We shall see in the philosophy of man that the vital operations of living beings are not transient, but *immanent.* This means that they are the perfection of the agent[28] itself which acts. Thus, our intellectual, sensitive, and vegetative operations are the perfection of the agent (the active principle) which acts, not the perfection of a distinct patient. For example, when I view the Grand Canyon,

[27] Here we are disengaging "transient action" and "agent" from the material conditions with which the causation of our direct experience is enmeshed, without, however, excluding such conditions from causation. This is done by a judgment of "separation" (a negative judgment which presupposes positive knowledge). Similar judgments were used to "separate" being from the limiting conditions especially of matter and essence. See Chapter I, section C.

[28] Instead of "agent," it is better to use the term "active principle" of immanent actions, since there is no distinct patient in immanent actions. The term "agent" is used more frequently with reference to the principle of transient action.

it is I who am perfected, or bettered, by the experience, not the object looked at, which remains unchanged. Nor is my activity the mere passive reception of an impression from the object viewed.[29] That would reduce this sensory-intellectual experience to the transient action (within me, the patient) of a stimulating object. Rather, I actively live the thing cognitively. Such an operation is not the act of a being in *potency* (transient action); it is the act of a being, or power, *in act* (*actus perfecti*); it is self-operation but not self-motion from potency to act. Immanent activity and transient action must not be confused.[30]

F. UNIVOCAL AND ANALOGOUS EFFICIENT CAUSES

Univocal Efficient Causes

Since an agent acts insofar as it is in act, the actuation in the patient will be similar to the agent's perfection. Thus, a heating agent, for example, a hot radiator, will heat the surrounding cold air; in animal generation, the parents, who are of a definite species, or form, will produce offspring of the same species, or form (unless other lines of causation intervene); like generates like. This truth is often expressed in the formula: Every agent acts in a manner similar to itself (*Omne agens agit sibi simile*).

A corollary of this truth is that from the actions of a being (and the result in which the action terminates), we can know

[29] True, human knowledge presupposes the transient action of sensible beings upon our sense organs (of which the sense potencies are the quasi form), thus reducing our cognitive powers from potency to specific act. This, however, is only the "preparation" for the immanent operation of sensing; it is not the act of knowledge itself.

[30] Identification of activity with motion (passage from potency to act) makes it impossible to explain the self-motion (activity) of living beings. The immanent activity of living beings is not a passage from potency to act; it is the act of a being (or power) in act. However, it may presuppose actuation of a potency. Moreover, it may perfect the being as a whole.

the nature of the being. The mode of activity manifests the mode of existing. For example, when we become aware of a heating process, we know that some heating agent is at work. From the nature of the offspring, we know the nature of the animal parents, both their specific nature[31] and to some extent their individual nature. The reason is that the perfections of the effect must be contained likewise in the efficient cause. Such causes and effects, it is clear, are of the same nature. A cause of this sort is called a *univocal cause*.

Analogous Efficient Causes

However, when the effect proceeds from an *intellectual* efficient cause,[32] the effects may be of various kinds. True, human generative causes (parents) generate offspring of the same species. In such a causation, the efficient cause and effect are of the same form; such a causation is univocal.

Human causality, however, is not limited to the univocal causality of generation. Human beings, besides reproducing their own kind, can produce all manner of effects: pieces of furniture, paintings, statues, novels, buildings, speeches, etc. These effects resemble their cause, not in the substantial order—surely a house does not resemble a man—but are similar to the thought, or idea, of them existing in the mind of their producer, an intellectual efficient cause. Thus, the assembled bricks, wood, and glass of a house have the stamp of man's intellect upon them. The house, however, does not bear a similarity to man in the same way in which human offspring are like their parents.

Since the cause in such cases, although somewhat similar to the effect, is strictly speaking different from the effect, we may aptly call such causes *analogous*.[33]

---

[31] At least in a general or descriptive way. True, we do not know their specific natures in their very specificity.

[32] Or from a sentient knowing cause of a higher order, for example, a beaver, who knows how to build dams and beaver houses, how to fell trees, etc.

[33] St. Thomas regularly uses the term "equivocal cause" in this precise sense.

Knowledge of Efficient Causes from Effects

A knowledge of the very existing of an effect leads to a knowledge of the *existence* of an efficient cause.[34] The reason is that cause (in the proper sense) and effect are contemporaneous, and the effect depends here and now on the existing cause. For example, by knowing that a room is becoming heated, I can conclude that something *is* actually heating it. However, a knowledge of the *essence,* or nature, of the effect does not always lead to an exhaustive and comprehensive knowledge of the nature of the efficient cause which produced (or is producing) the effect. The reason is that a higher cause can produce the effects of lower causes (or at least some of them), but its causality is not exhausted by the production of the lower effects.[35]

Not all effects are produced by univocal causes. Many are produced by analogous causes. Consequently, the perfection of the effect does not necessarily manifest the full perfection of the (efficient) cause. A beaver dam, for example, shows me that a cognitive agent of a high order has been at work, and usually the agent at work was a beaver. Let us suppose that a reasonable facsimile of such a dam has been put together by a human agent. In such a case, a knowledge of the effect would not give a comprehensive knowledge of the nature of the cause, since this cause is capable of producing effects of a higher order.

G. ACTIVITY FOLLOWS UPON BE–ING

Mode of Activity Manifests Mode of Existing

In general, we know what a thing *is* through what it *does;* we know the mode of existing (be-ing) through the mode of activity; a being's manner of acting manifests its manner of existing. Thus, we can recognize a human existent through the specifically human operation of thought, as manifested through

[34] Precisely as causing.

[35] The higher cause contains the perfection of the lower causes, if not formally, at least *virtually,* that is, in an equivalent manner.

speech. Barking manifests a canine existent; mewing, a feline existent.[36]

We must note well, however, that it is not through the *lowest* operation that we know the mode of an existent, its nature, or specific essence. We know, for example, what man is specifically, not through his sensitive, vegetative, chemical, atomic, and electronic activities; for he has these activities in common with the brutes, the plants, the compounds, and atomic particles,[37] although he is not any of these *actually*. Rather, we know the nature, or essence, of a human existent (or any other existent) through its *highest* operations, which in the case of man is intellectual operation.[38]

Order of Discovery and Ontological Order

The human intellect, in the order of *discovery*, proceeds from a knowledge of the mode of activity to a knowledge of the mode of existing. The *metaphysical* order, however, is the reverse of the order of discovery, the order of knowledge. True enough, the mode of acting *manifests* the mode of existing; as a thing acts, so it is. We know the kind of thing it is from the way it acts. But it is precisely because a thing *is*, or exists, that it can act. And the more perfectly it exists, the more perfectly it can act.[39] Because something barks, I *know* that it is a dog. Because Fido *is* a dog, he barks. He is not a dog because he barks.

[36] Barking and mewing, however, do not necessarily manifest a specifically distinct nature, as does rational speech. We do not claim to know the specific natures of brute animals in their specificity. Often we must content ourselves with a definition through several common accidents.

[37] One might add that man has (analogously) the structure of the lower beings also, but that none of these structures are his basic, metaphysical structure. For example, man has vertebrate structure, cellular structure, biochemical structure, molecular and even atomic structure.

[38] One may legitimately say that man is *virtually* a brute, plant, chemicals, atoms, subatomic particles, mass-energy, etc., in the sense that the unitary, human existent has their activities (and structure) in an analogous way.

[39] Nonbeing cannot act at all. Only beings can act.

Mode of Existing Determines Mode of Activity

It is evident, then, that the mode, or manner, of existing determines the mode of activity. Because things are in a certain way, they tend to act that way. Beings act in accordance with what they are; they act in accordance with their nature, their mode of existing.[40] No (limited) being escapes this determination of action, this law of its nature. Activity follows upon be-ing (*agere sequitur esse*); as a thing is, so does it act.[41]

H.   INSTRUMENTAL EFFICIENT CAUSES

Problem

The paintbrushes wielded by Michelangelo produced the Sistine Chapel murals. The violin in the hands of a Menuhin re-creates the Beethoven concerto. A pen, or other writing instrument, produces a great poem. How can these various *instruments* produce an effect more perfect than themselves?

Instrument Is Joined to Principal Cause

Obviously, the best of paintbrushes in the hands of a Sunday painter would never have produced the Sistine masterpiece. Similarly, the most expensive Stradivarius in the hands of an amateur would never render the Beethoven concerto. Although the instrument does truly produce the effect as a real cause, it depends in some way on another cause to produce it. And since the effect is proportioned, or assimilated, more to the other cause than to the instrument, we shall call this (other) cause the *principal* cause. Thus, Michelangelo, Menuhin, and the poet, in the ex-

[40] See Henri Renard, S.J., and Martin O. Vaske, S.J., *Philosophy of Man*, The Bruce Publishing Company, Milwaukee, 1956, p. 299. See also Gilson, *Elements of Christian Philosophy*, p. 241; Louis De Raeymaeker, *The Philosophy of Being*, translated by Edmund H. Ziegelmeyer, S.J., B. Herder Book Co., St. Louis, 1954, p. 273.

[41] Activity is the expression of the dynamism of the act of be-ing; it is the budding forth, a sort of overflow, of existence.

amples given, are principal causes; that is to say, they act by their own power. The *instrumental* cause, on the other hand, acts only insofar as it is moved by the principal cause.[42]

Proper and Instrumental Power

When a principal cause produces an effect through an instrument, there is only one action, but in the instrument we can distinguish two really distinct powers: the power *proper* to it and the *instrumental* power it has insofar as it is conjoined to, and elevated by, the principal cause. It is proper, for example, to an axe to be a cutting instrument; one cannot very well write with it or paint with it.[43] But that it should cut logs into the right shape for a log cabin belongs to it insofar as it is under the influence of an intellectual cause and is elevated for a time by a power imparted to it from the principal cause. This power is called the instrumental power. It is by virtue of instrumental power that the instrument is able to produce an effect above the perfection of its own form; in this way, the paintbrush is able to produce the great mural.

Instrumental Use

Natural forces may be used *instrumentally* to bring about an effect intended by the principal cause. A lumberjack, for example, instead of grubbing up the stump of a tree by the direct use of simple instruments, such as an axe and a shovel, may use the natural power of dynamite to blow the stump sky-high. In such cases, the powerful activity of a *natural* agent is directed along an intended line by the principal cause.[44]

[42] True, the principal cause (if it is a limited being) is also moved to act, but it is the principle, or source, of its own activity; it has its active power, not transiently, but habitually and permanently (*per modum habitus*).

[43] Its usefulness as an instrument is restricted by the type of instrument it is. Some instruments can be used in a wide variety of ways owing to the way they are structured; for example, a monkey wrench will fit a large variety of nuts equally well (or unwell). Other instruments can be used in only one way (or in a limited number of ways); for example, a lawn mower can be used to cut grass and for very little else.

Even human *free* agents may be used instrumentally to bring about a desired action, whether it be morally good or evil. A gangster overlord may use a well-paid henchman to assassinate a rival gang lord. Although the first gang lord does not actually pull the trigger of the murder weapon (the direct instrumental cause), nevertheless the murder is attributed primarily to him as principal *moral* cause. The reason is that the instrument depends on the principal cause for a true causal influence. The same, of course, is true also of actions performed in a good "cause" under the instigation of a great political or religious leader.

Simple vs. Complex Instruments

Some instruments, such as a knife, axe, or paintbrush, are relatively *simple,* but can be used to bring about a great variety of effects, depending largely on the skill, or technique, of the principal cause which makes use of them.

Other instruments are quite *complex* and are adapted to a specialized function; for example, a lawn mower will cut grass very well, but one cannot carve a wooden statue with it. The complexity of such instruments is usually proportioned to the specialization of function, and the perfection of its function often depends directly on this complexity of structure.[45]

Effect Is Proportioned to Principal Cause

Since the instrument does not act except by virtue of the causal influence of the principal cause, the effect is said to be proportioned, or assimilated, to the principal cause. A great artist

[44] Note that the natural agents, for example, dynamite, are efficient causes in their own right. They are not mere instruments. The principal cause places a condition which releases the natural dynamism of the natural agent. Consider the use of freezing water to fracture a glass jar. Consider also the use of dam-building beavers to check erosion in a mountain valley.

[45] Some complex instruments, however, can produce a vast variety of effects. Modern electronic computers, for example, are quite flexible in function. A large pipe organ is more flexible in function than a relatively simple instrument such as a violin or cello. The perfection of such complex instruments is proportionate not only to the skill and technique of the principle cause, but also to the perfection of the instrument itself.

can still produce a reasonably good painting with poor-quality brushes; a great violinist can render a great concerto on a cheap instrument; a good lumberjack can fell a tree with a dull axe. However, without the power of the principal cause, not even the best instruments can produce an effect above the perfection of their own form. Indeed, they cannot produce any instrumental effect at all.[46]

As regards the proportion of the effect to the principal cause, a distinction must be made between simple and complex instruments. When there is question of simple instruments (knife, paintbrush, axe, etc.), the effect is proportioned almost completely to the principal cause. However, in the case of complex instruments (electronic computers, large pipe organs, automation machinery), the perfection of the effect, although still somewhat proportioned to the principal cause, depends more and more on the perfection of the instrument itself.[47]

Thus, the lyric tone of Casals's cello is due largely to Casals (though he must have a reasonably well-toned instrument); the majestic roll of a mighty pipe organ is due largely to a multitude of well-voiced pipes (though admittedly a reasonably good organist must be at the console).

Instrumental Power Is Transitory

The instrumental power by which the instrument produces an effect above its own form is communicated from the principal cause, not as a permanent and complete reality, but as a *transitory* influence (as a motion). The paintbrush, for example, is capable of producing a beautiful painting only as long as it is conjoined to the principal cause, the artist. The influence of the principal cause is gone as soon as the artist lays down his brush; the brush is then capable of nothing in the line of artistic production.

The influence of the principal cause does not terminate in

[46] This is true of instruments precisely *as instruments,* but insofar as they are existents, they may conceivably become agents.

[47] The perfection of the instrument depends on the structure, or design, built into the instrument by an intellectual efficient cause.

a complete form, or act, but in an imperfect act; thus, the influence of the principal cause does not remain as a permanent possession (*per modum habitus*) but passes immediately. Moreover, the influence of the principal cause, as it were, "passes through" the instrument and terminates in the patient; it does not terminate in the instrument.

SUMMARY

A. Cause vs. Occasion, Condition, Antecedent: A cause in the philosophical sense must be distinguished from occasion, condition, and antecedent. An *occasion* merely furnishes a favorable opportunity for the cause to act. A *condition* removes obstacles that would prevent a cause from acting. A mere *antecedent* precedes the effect in time. None of these has a positive and direct influence on the existence or coming-into-existence of the effect, as does a cause. A *proper* cause and its effect are simultaneous.

B. Efficient Causes of Change: Problem regarding changing being: When a subject passes from potency to act, whence the new act? Nothing reduces itself from potency to act; change depends on an extrinsic principle, an efficient cause, in act.

C. Efficient Cause of Be-ing: Problem regarding limited existents: Why should beings which merely participate existence be at all? In such beings, to be is not their essence; they exist contingently, not necessarily. Such beings depend on an extrinsic principle, an efficient cause, to exist; they exist by derivation.

D. General Principle of Efficient Causality: Every effect depends here and now upon an efficient cause. "Effect" here means (1) the changes that occur in limited beings, (2) the limited beings themselves. The principle is universal; that is, there are no exceptions. The principle is necessary; that is, it cannot be otherwise. The principle expresses an intelligible necessity we find in changing, participating existents.

E. Influence of Efficient Cause: The efficient cause has its influence on the becoming or be-ing of the effect by exercise of action. In every efficient causation, there is an agent in act, a patient in potency, and transient action in the patient. The passage from potency to act (in the patient) *as from* the agent constitutes (transient) action. The same passage from potency to act *as in* (as modifying) the patient constitutes passion. Action is the communication of perfection from agent to patient without loss of the perfection on the part of the agent. The agent, precisely as agent, since it is in act, is unchanged. Material action, however, involves an opposed reaction; the agent in such actions is also patient, and hence is subject to change. However, it is not the nature of action as such that it involve reaction; that is to say, an agent need not also be patient. The operations of the living beings are immanent, not transient; such actions are the perfection of the agent itself, not of a distinct patient.

F. Univocal and Analogous Efficient Causes: In univocal causation, agent and effect are of the same specific perfection. The perfections of the effect are contained in the same way in the agent as in the patient. In analogous causation, effect and efficient cause are simply different though somewhat the same, in that the effect resembles the idea in the mind of an intellectual cause. A knowledge of the nature of the effect does not always lead to a comprehensive knowledge of the nature of the cause, since not all causes are univocal.

G. Activity Follows upon Be-ing: The mode of activity manifests the mode of existing. In the order of discovery, the intellect proceeds from a knowledge of the mode of activity to a knowledge of the mode of existing. The ontological order, however, is the reverse of this: the mode of existing determines the mode of activity. As a thing is, so does it act.

H. Instrumental Efficient Causes: Problem: How can an instrument produce an effect above its own perfection? The instrument is joined to a principal cause. Conjoined to this cause, the instrument has, besides the instrumental power proper to it, an instrumental power insofar as it is elevated by the principal cause. The instrumental power is transitory; it does not remain as a permanent possession.

SUGGESTED READINGS

Aristotle: *Basic Works,* edited by Richard McKeon, Random House, Inc., New York, 1941, pp. 752–754; on principles and causes.

Bourke, Vernon J.: *The Pocket Aquinas,* Washington Square Press, Pocket Books, Inc., New York, 1960, pp. 67–77; commentary by Aquinas on Aristotle's exposition of the four causes.

Hawkins, D. J. B.: *Being and Becoming,* Sheed & Ward, Inc., New York, 1954, pp. 137–149; on causality in Aristotle and Hume.

La Plante, O. J.: "The Traditional View of Efficient Causality," *Proceedings of the American Catholic Philosophical Association,* vol. 14, pp. 1–12, for 1938.

Maritain, Jacques: *A Preface to Metaphysics,* Sheed & Ward, Inc., New York, 1939, lecture 7.

Meehan, F. X.: *Efficient Causality in Aristotle and St. Thomas,* The Catholic University of America Press, Washington, D.C., 1940.

V

Final and Exemplary
Causes

In the preceding chapter, we examined one of the *extrinsic* principles of changing, limited being, namely, the efficient cause. We saw that the efficient cause has its causal influence by exercise of action. In the present chapter, we shall inquire into the nature of another extrinsic principle—the end, or goal, of action. We shall also examine the exemplary cause and its mode of influence on intellectual agents. Finally, we shall make some remarks about causes in general.

134

A.   DETERMINATION OF ACTION (FINALITY)

Problem

A block of marble in a sculptor's studio will not receive the form of Napoleon except by the action of a sculptor. He is the efficient cause of the transformation of the marble block into a marble Napoleon. While the sculptor chisels away at the marble, he does not act in an aimless way (unless, perhaps, he be a member of the "actionist" school). Rather, he acts along a definite line. Were we to ask him, "Why are you belaboring that rock?" or "What do you have in mind?" or "What do you intend to make out of that block?" he might answer in a huff, "Nothing—nothing—nothing at all." But we would know that he was evading our question.

When an agent acts, whether transiently or immanently, it acts this way rather than that; it acts definitely, *determinately*. The agent acts rather than *not* and acts along a definite line. It does not act indefinitely, indeterminately. Whence this *determination* of action (1) to act at all; (2) to act in a specific way?

Self-determination of Human Agents

Human agents are able to determine their own (human) activities.[1] They can intellectually hold in consciousness various goals, or ends, compare them, and allow themselves to be attracted into action by one of them in preference to the others. Human agents in their human acts make up their mind, or decide: to act or not to act; to act one way rather than another. The indeterminacy of the agent is removed by *self-determination*, by "free choice." Thus, a man may freely determine to build a doghouse rather than a doll house (transient actions); or he may determine himself to study metaphysics rather than mathematics, or to contemplate the sunset (immanent actions); or he may determine himself not to act at all along any of these lines.

---

[1] This statement must be restricted to what are called *human acts*—those acts in which man acts precisely as man, namely, the acts which proceed from the deliberate will. See *Summa Theologiae*, I–II, 1, 1c.

Determination of Action in Animals

Brutes also seem to hold an end, or goal, in consciousness:[2] a bird, for example, will seek twigs with which to build its nest; a robin will hunt worms to feed itself or its young. Obviously, there is some knowledge of a goal, or end to be attained, and the tendency, or seeking, follows upon this knowledge. Unlike man's knowledge, however, this knowledge is merely on the *sense* level, and there is no comparison, in the strict sense, of various proposed ends, or goals. The determination, or selection, of goals, or ends, is not in the animal's power. It cannot *not* seek the sensible goods presented in sense knowledge.[3] The animal is determined to seek to act along this line whenever the proportionate sense knowledge arises.

Determination of Action in Plants and Minerals

Plants also act determinately, but the determination is in no way due to (their) knowledge; for the plant simply does not know. Thus, the tiny sapling, which knows nothing about selective assimilation of chemicals from the ground, tends to grow into a mighty oak. When we plant a small tree, we implicitly recognize this tendency, or determination, to act along a definite line toward a definite goal, which is present in the plant even though the plant is incapable of knowledge.

Similarly, in the world of chemical compounds, of elements, atoms, and subatomic particles, action is determinate and definite.[4] An electron, for example, is said to revolve around a nu-

[2] We cannot enter into the consciousness of brutes. Nor can they communicate with us by using arbitrary signs, such as words. Nevertheless, they often act the way we do when we have knowledge and tendency toward something.

[3] Whether present in direct sensation or in imagination, as in the case of the animal which forages for food.

[4] The Heisenberg principle of "uncertainty," or "indeterminacy," does not seem to be a denial of determinacy of action, but a denial of certainty of observation, prediction, and manipulation of microcosmic events. Moreover, the principle (primarily at least) seems to be concerned with the measurable *phenomena* of action, not with the proper *causes* of the phenomena. See A Van Melsen, *The Philosophy of Nature,* Duquesne University Press, Pittsburgh, 1953, p. 214 ff.

cleus; thus, it is said to tend to act (and actually acts) in a determinate way. It does not act like a proton or neutron or photon. Hydrogen does not act like carbon; helium does not act like uranium. Nevertheless, their action, though different, is definite, determinate. Whence this determinacy of action?

Principle of Final Causality

The fact of determinate action is clear and evident from an observation of agents acting. However, why these agents should act at all, rather than not act, why they should act one way rather than another, is not explained except by the influence of some principle which moves, or attracts, them into action along a determinate line. This causal principle of action is the end, goal, or *final* cause. Without the influence of a causal principle in the order of finality, the agent would not act.

> Were an agent not to act for a definite effect, all effects would be indifferent to it. Now, that which is indifferent to many effects does not produce one rather than another. Wherefore, from that which is indifferent to either of two effects, no effect results, unless it be determined by something to one of them. . . . Therefore, every agent tends to some definite effect, which is called its end.[5]

The argument is a reduction to absurdity (*reductio ad absurdum*). By denying that an agent acts for a definite end, we deny that the agent acts. Now, an agent which does not act is not an agent—a contradiction in terms. It is clear, then, that every agent must act determinately; that is, it must act for a definite end, whether the action be transient or immanent.

The same type of argument applies to action itself: action which is not directed to a definite end is not action—a clear contradiction.

We see, then, that the principle of final causality is *universal*. There are no exceptions to the principle, because it expresses what is true of agents precisely as agents. It is also a *necessary*

[5] *Summa Contra Gentiles*, III, 2.

principle: agents (whether free or not) necessarily act for some end; they cannot act otherwise.

B. INTENTIONAL ORDER

End Moves Agent

The end is the effect to be produced or to be attained. The end attracts, or moves, the agent to act, rather than not to act, to act this way rather than that; the end finalizes the agent's activity. Now, the end must exist somehow in order to move the agent into action. Certainly, it does not exist in the *real* order. For example, the eating of ice cream, which is my goal of activity after this class, does not yet exist in the real order; surely, I am not spooning the tasty stuff into my mouth here and now. And yet the end must exist in some way in order to move the agent to action. True enough, the ice cream does exist, but the existence (and contemplation) of ice cream is not precisely the end; rather, the end is the eating of ice cream (ice cream to be eaten).

Since the end does not exist in the *real* order (the order of attainment), it must "exist" in the order of *intention*. The end exists "tendentially," as a "being intended." Before a body falls to the ground, it has tendency to fall. Before a slender sapling grows into a mighty oak, it has tendency to grow and to grow that way. The end, then, by being intended, determines the agent to act; by being the object of inclination, it finalizes the activity of the agent.

Various Orders of Intention

This is all quite obvious in free choices, in which man determines his own ends.[6] Here the intentional order is an *intellectual* intentional order. Various goals, or ends, can be proposed, various courses of action presented, in intellectual consciousness.

---

[6] We are concerned here with immediate, or proximate, ends. Man does not determine his primary, or ultimate, end. He necessarily and naturally seeks happiness.

After comparing these ends, we allow ourselves to be freely attracted by one rather than another; or we can choose not to act at all. The end is intellectually known and freely intended; it "exists" in the sense that it is an intellectually known object of free tendency.

In the case of animals acting for a definite end, the intentional order is on the *sensitive* level. The animal cannot propose various goals as alternatives, nor can it compare the various goals, or even examine a single goal for its goodness and limitation. The end is sensibly known and desired necessarily, not freely. The end here "exists" in the sense that it is a sensibly known object of nonfree tendency.

In the case of plants and minerals, the end is merely sought. It is not known; and yet there is determinate (though nonconscious) "intention" of an end. The action is goal-directed; an end is being sought; the end exists as a "being intended." The plant or mineral does truly *tend* to an end.

C. MODE OF INFLUENCE

By Being Intended

The end, the cause in the order of finality, has a positive influence on the action of the agent. However, its influence must be distinguished carefully from the influence of the other causes. The final cause does not exist in the real order (the order of attainment); hence, it cannot act; its influence, therefore, is not the influence of an efficient cause. Nor does it directly specify the effect; that is the role of the formal cause. Rather, the end, the final cause, has its influence by *being intended,* sought, or desired.

If the agent is intellectual, the final cause, or *purpose,* has its influence by being *intellectually known* and *freely desired.* If the agent is merely sensitive (an animal), the final cause has its influence by being *sensibly known* and *necessarily* desired. If the agent is not cognitive, as in the case of plants and the chemical world, the final cause (the goal of activity) has its influence by merely *being desired,* that is, by merely being the object of tendency, or inclination.

First in Intention

The final cause is often called the *end,* a term which connotes that in which the action of the agent terminates (ends). It is that which is ultimately achieved by action (whether something produced or possessed); hence, it is aptly called the *final* cause, a term which connotes something last.

As a causal principle of action, however, the end, goal, or purpose (in general, the final cause) is *primary,* or first, in its influence.[7] Without intending an end, the agent will not act. Without the action of an agent (efficient cause), matter will not receive form: prime matter will not receive substantial form, nor will secondary matter (substance or substances) receive new accidental form. The end, then, is rightly said to be *first* in intention though *last* in attainment (*primus in intentione, ultimus in executione*).

Cause of Causes

In any causation, therefore, the end is of fundamental influence. In the words of the Angelic Doctor, "The end is the cause of causes, because it is the cause of causality in all causes."[8]

D. APPETITE, TENDENCY, FINALITY

Appetite

The inclination of an agent to an end is called variously: tendency, appetite, drive,[9] finality. Such inclination is always consequent upon (determined by) some form, whether intellectually known form, a sensibly known form, or simply the substantial form of the nature.

[7] Cf. *Summa Theologiae,* I–II, 1, 2c.
[8] *De Principiis Naturae* (*in medio*).
[9] An unfortunate term, since it often connotes *efficient* causality rather than final causality.

Intellectual, Sense, and Natural Appetites

The free inclination in man (to limited goods, or ends) consequent upon intellectually apprehended good is the *intellectual* appetite, or *will*.

The necessary inclination in an animal consequent upon sense knowledge of a sensible good is called *sense* appetite. (The passions, or emotions, are the operations of sense appetite. Sense love and hate are the basic emotions.)

The necessary inclination in any being (even sensitive and intellectual beings) consequent upon the substantial form which specifies its nature is called *natural* appetite.[10] Thus, an electron naturally tends to circulate around a nucleus; a plant by its very nature tends to grow; an animal naturally strives to develop itself as an animal; man naturally (not freely) seeks happiness.[11]

Nature

The natural appetite of a being (whether mineral, plant, animal, or man) is not distinct from the nature of the being. Rather, natural appetite is the primary, or basic, orientation of an existent in the line of activity (which is a sort of overflowing of the act of be-ing); it is the nature itself viewed as basic determinant of the mode of activity.

Essence, or nature, determines the act of be-ing to a certain manner, or mode. Things *exist* according to the capacity of their nature. Moreover, they *act* in accordance with this same capacity. For activity is the dynamism of the act of be-ing determined by the essence, or nature. Insofar as we view this intrinsic determining principle as a determinant of existence, we call it *essence;* when viewed as primary determinant of activity (the full flowering of existence), we call it *nature.* It is clear, then, that nature

[10] It is important to note at this point that the notion of appetite and the appetites themselves are *analogous.* Appetite is always inclination to good, but this inclination is never the same.

[11] Unlike other corporeal beings, man can come to a knowledge of his natural appetite, of his necessary and natural desire for happiness in the possession of absolute good, which is the basis and ground for his free choice of means.

is nothing else than the essence[12] of an existent viewed as a principle of operation whereby the total existent tends necessarily to a primary, or ultimate, end.

E. FINALITY OF NATURE PRESUPPOSES INTENTIONAL ORDER [13]

Finality of Individual Actions

Agents in their individual actions act determinately; that is, they act for definite ends, which move them to act by being intended. Moreover, these ends are prior to the effect, not in the real order, but in the order of intention. Furthermore, there are various orders of intention and various types of tendency. All this has already been considered in this chapter.

Finality of Natures

We must now ask ourselves this question: Does the determinate inclination, tendency, or finality of a *nature* to one primary end, or complexus of ends, presuppose intentional order? Does, for example, the natural inclination of a canine existent along one line of finality (as opposed to that of beings feline in nature) presuppose an extrinsic, intentional order?

Obviously, natural tendency to a primary (ultimate) end is *determinate,* whether known by the being which has this tendency or not. Even in the case of man, who is free as regards immediate, proximate ends, there is a *natural* and necessary inclination, or finality, toward an ultimate end, whether he ever reflects upon this finality or not. This primary, or natural, tendency is present even before the awakening of intellect and the first apprehensions of sense. Even in his unconscious states, an individual human has a *human* nature; that is, he has a determinate finality of nature to the completion and fulfillment of a human existent, not the actualization of a canine existent.[14]

---

[12] Essence here means *substantial* essence, not accidental essence.

[13] A more precise title: Finality of a being *according* to its nature requires intentional order.

[14] Moreover, even though a man might wish to be canine, he cannot

How are we to explain determinate, natural finality along one essential, or specific, line rather than along another? This question will again arise in the next chapter.

Extrinsic Intentional Order

Our provisional answer must be somewhat as follows: Just as all *individual* actions are prefigured in tendency, or intentional order, so also the determinate finality of a *nature* to a general complexus of actions along one line is prefigured in intentional order, even though the beings possessing this finality have no knowledge of it.

Plants, for example, tend to grow and evolve into fully developed plants. There is know-how in them; but the knowledge is not theirs. Although their actions manifest intellectual direction to end, the directing intellect is not their own. In some way, they must depend on an *extrinsic,* intellectual, intentional order for their determinate natural finality to end.[15]

Now, the end must be known *as end* (universally), to which means are ordered. The means must be known *as means* (universally) ordered to the end. Also, the proportion, or relation (of suitability), of means to end must be known. All this requires *intellectual* (not merely sense) intentional order.

Necessity of Nature an Insufficient Explanation

Many determinist and mechanist philosophers of the last century[16] thought that internal necessity, or "nature," was a suf-

---

change his nature. Natural finality is not free. He might then consider himself "stuck" with a human nature—a radical "beatnikism" indeed. Such a person would manifest the most radical ingratitude: a rejection of his lofty mode of being, and even of the basic perfection of be-ing.

[15] ". . . the operation of nature, which is toward a determinate end, presupposes an intellect which furnishes an end for the nature and orders the nature to that end. For this reason, every work of nature is said to be the work of intelligence" (*Summa Contra Gentiles,* III, 1).

[16] These philosophers mistakenly thought they saw in Newtonian mechanics and Darwin's evolutionary theory a philosophical generalization concerning the nature of reality and activity. Thus, they were asking the sciences of phenomena to play the role of philosophy, a part they are not qualified to play.

ficient explanation of the determinate tendencies in beings. They failed to consider a more profound question: Whence this internal necessity? Whence this determination of nature? The natural necessity along one line of finality rather than along another is a sort of intellectual impression. It presupposes an extrinsic intellect which imparts this impression, this finality to end.

F. CHANCE EVENTS

What is to be said of "chance" events, of accidental happenings, such as the unexpected finding of a treasure by a man digging a well or the unforeseen and unintended collision of two automobiles? How are we to explain the "chance" meeting of a young man and young lady whom a matchmaking mother has sent upon an errand? Or the more celebrated "accidental" meeting of Dido and Aeneas as related by Virgil in the *Aeneid?* Are such occurrences produced by efficient causes intending a definite end, or are they due, not to determinate causes, but to something called "chance"?

Absolute Determinism—a Mechanistic Universe[17]

Some philosophers, especially of the last century, denied all chance occurrences, and held that effects proceed rigorously and inexorably from their causes. To such thinkers, in any closed system (whether a test tube or the entire corporeal universe), various causes are at work, and they will inevitably produce their effects. Like a clock wound up, which can only run down, the determinate causes in the universe can only produce their determined effects in accordance with their internal necessity, or nature. Such a universe can only "unwind" in accordance with the spring tension put into it by a master clockmaker (and clock winder).[18]

[17] We do not claim that this position was ever held by any philosopher in its purity.

[18] In such a universe, there would be no strict finality, no real striving for goals. Everything would be due to an "impulsion from the past," not to an "attraction to the future."

Moreover, in this position, a person who can discover all the causes at work in such a closed system can predict whatever these causes will bring about to the very crack of doom. True, there may be certain gaps in our knowledge of these causes, at the present stage of scientific development, but the scientific ideal of knowledge through causes ("antecedents" of "consequents") may someday be realized. Then we shall be able to predict whatever these determinate causes will do and, perhaps, manipulate these causes to bring about what we wish and will (though the latter acts of wishing and willing are already determined).

Absolute Indeterminism—a Chance Universe[19]

Other thinkers are overimpressed by the chance events that occur: the freaks, sports, and mutants of biological development, the unpredictability of behavior in many things from human beings and the weather to electrons and other subatomic particles. To such thinkers, the law of "cause and effect" (which usually means inseparable antecedent and consequents) is too often "more honored in the breach than the observance." Hence, to strive for scientific knowledge, which claims to be a knowledge through causes, is to pursue an unattainable goal.

According to this position, the universe and the things in it are not subject to necessary law, to cause-effect relationships. Rather, it is a sort of freewheeling universe, in which anything and everything goes; like the weather, the entire universe is unpredictable. Causes are not in control of events; chance, often freakish and outrageous chance, seems to be in control. We should not seek for causes behind chance events, for the simple reason that chance events have no causes; they just happen.

An Ordered Universe with Chance Effects

The two positions already presented are, of course, extreme pure positions. There is a large middle ground between them. Obviously, causes are in control for the most part in this universe;

[19] Nor do we claim that anyone holds this as a pure position. Even the celebrated Heisenberg principle of indeterminacy is usually limited by its upholders to the phenomena of the microcosmic world.

things do tend to act in accordance with the demands of their nature: the little trees we plant do tend to grow, and many of them reach adult stage; an object released in free space near the earth does fall to the ground; water at 32 degrees will freeze, expand, and fracture the surrounding inelastic container. For the most part, at least, definite and determined causes are in control; or, at least, antecedents have their inseparable consequents.

Chance events, however, do occur, whether they be fortunate (as the finding of the treasure) or unfortunate (as the collision of the two automobiles). Treasures are found by chance. Accidents happen even in the best-regulated families, we say. Do such chance occurrences have a cause?

Meeting of Two or More Causes

When we consider the matter carefully, it becomes evident that not only does a chance event have a cause, it has *more* than one cause. The chance event is the result of the *meeting,* or intersection, of two or more lines of efficient causation. We have examples of this almost every day on our busy streets. The driver of one automobile sets in operation a line of determinate and finalized efficient causes. (Ordinarily, the intended effect is achieved; his destination is reached.) The driver of another automobile sets in operation another line of efficient causes. Both lines of causation meet, or intersect, literally at the intersection. The intended (and ordinarily achieved) ends are not achieved by either agent. Instead, a third and unforeseen effect occurs: both autos wind up on the curb badly wrecked; their drivers wind up in the hospital, a destination neither of them intended or foresaw.

Such an event is called a chance event, an accidental happening. Does it have a cause? It should be obvious now that such an event has *at least* two causes, whose causations meet. The chance event is the resultant of the causation of the two causes. It was not, however, intended or foreseen; that is to say, the *meeting* of the two lines of causation was not intended or foreseen by either agent. Chance, then, implies the absence of a cause regulating the intersection of two or more determinate causal lines.

An observer, however, who could see both lines of causation

(for example, a man watching the intersection from a corner window several stories above street level), might anticipate, or foresee, the meeting of the two causal lines. Nevertheless, he would still rightly refer to the collision as an "accident," a "chance" effect. The reason is that he did not intend or control the meeting of the two causal lines. He did not "plan" the accident; he did not regulate the two determinate causal lines involved. (And the same must be said for the two drivers.)

Intended Intersection of Causes

On the other hand, what may look like a chance effect to two human agents involved in a resultant causation, may really have been planned by a third agent; that is to say, a third agent may purposively set two causal lines in operation, intending and foreseeing (with greater or less certainty) their meeting and the resultant effect. Thus, some "accidents" are planned.[20] Such was the "accidental" meeting arranged by the matchmaking parent between her daughter and the young man of her (the mother's) choice. However, from the standpoint of the two lines of efficient causation involved, the event still remains a chance event; that is to say, the event happens without being intended by either of the two causal lines.

Matter, the Principle of Indeterminacy

Every agent produces its like (*omne agens agit sibi simile*), and by knowing the agents at work, we can ordinarily know the effect that is being produced. Thus, a heating agent will generate heat; cats will generate cats; fruit flies will generate fruit flies. However, in all material causation, there is a certain *indeterminacy* owing to the fact that matter, although always under a determinate form, is still in potency to all other material forms. And when two lines of causation intersect in this indeterminate

[20] Moreover, once we discover the two or more lines of causation whose intersection produced the fortunate "chance" event, we can reproduce the "happy accident" at will. Thus, an organist tries to remember the particular stop combination (accidentally set up) which produced the pleasing sonic effect.

substrate, the form which terminates the change may be that of *neither* agent, but a new form which up to now has never been educed from the passive potency of matter.[21] Thus, sports and mutants may arise in a generative process, when other lines of causation (such as X rays and radioactive agents) besides the animal parents have an influence on the total process.

Matter, it must be remembered, is in potency to all forms (except that which now informs it), including those forms which up to now have never actuated matter. There can and will be new things under the sun.

In brief: we live in an ordered universe, in which for the most part determinate causes are in charge; nevertheless, chance effects do occur; such effects are truly caused; indeed, they are the resultant of more than one cause meeting in indeterminate matter; such an intersection of causes can be intended, foreseen, and set in operation by a third agent.[22]

G.   EXEMPLARY CAUSE

Product Imitates Idea

When an intellectual agent acts, it produces an effect which imitates more or less perfectly what the agent had in mind. Thus, when an artist produces a painting, the finished product will imitate more or less perfectly the artistic conception he had in mind and will imitate remotely the external model or objects from which this knowledge may have been derived.[23] The idea,

---

[21] We must bear in mind, however, that causations of this kind are not divorced from the influence of the primary efficient (and final) cause. The primary cause will be studied in the next chapter.

[22] From considerations in the next chapter, it will become clear that limited causes and their causal meetings cannot escape the finality imparted to them by the Primary Cause. Hence, from the standpoint of the Primary Cause, there are no chance effects.

[23] In the case of great art, this "idea" is not a mere faithful conception of external reality, but an original insight arising from the "creative" depths of the human spirit. Thus, new architectural forms, new musical forms, new modes of painting are not a mere "imitation" of nature; rather, they

or conception, of the effect to be produced is called an *exemplary* cause. In the words of St. Thomas, it is "a form in imitation of which something comes into existence from the intention of an agent that determines an end for itself." [24]

Causal Influence through Efficient Cause

This idea (*eidos* in Greek), or form, in the mind of an intellectual agent has a real influence on the *production* of the effect; for the agent acts in accordance with this knowledge. True, the conception, or idea, in the intellect is not always achieved in the materials as the intellectual agent might have wished. This is often due either to defect in materials (for example, poor-quality marble), or to defective tools (instrumental causes), or to a lack of good technique. Nevertheless, no matter how good one's materials, tools, or manual technique may be, the artistic conception, or form, in the mind is of primary importance in any production. The materials will not receive a new form except through the action of the agent, and this action takes the *form,* or direction, given by the idea in the mind. In other words, the idea (exemplar) gives the specification to the action of the agent.

The causal influence of the exemplar, therefore, is had not directly, but through the *mediation* of the *efficient* cause.[25] Unless the intellectual being acts (efficiently causes), even the most lofty artistic conception, or idea, will not have a shred of influence on the production of an effect.

An Extrinsic Formal Cause

Since the specifying influence of the exemplar directly affects only the *action* of the agent and does not *intrinsically* enter into the constitution of the product, the exemplar is often called

---

are analogously a "creation." The human intellect is not merely conformative to reality; it is truly *formative* of new reality See Jacques Maritain, *Creative Intuition in Art and Poetry,* Pantheon Books, New York, 1953, pp. 71–159.

[21] Aquinas, *De Veritate,* III, 1c.

[25] Exemplary causality must not be overemphasized to the exclusion of efficient causality. Knowledge that does not specify productive activity is not an exemplary cause.

an extrinsic formal cause. However, the perfection of the form enshrined in the materials mirrors the perfection of the form, or idea, which was in the mind and gave direction, or specification, to the productive effort. The exemplar, or model, then, may be said to be *imitated* in the effect; the production is modeled upon it.

Objectively Same as Final Cause

Objectively the exemplar is the same as the final cause, or end, since it is that form which is known and desired, thus moving the agent into action. However, from the standpoint of the agent, the mode of influence varies: the final cause has its influence by being intended; the exemplary cause has its influence *by being imitated;* that is to say, the exemplar specifies the action of the agent so that this action (in external matter) terminates in a form which imitates more or less perfectly the form, or idea, in the mind of the intellectual efficient cause.

Many Exemplates—One Exemplar

When there is question of many productions of one and the same form, the (formal) unity of the many is a clear manifestation of one exemplar. Thus, many cabinets of the same form, or pattern, point to the same design, which originated in one mind. We shall see in the next chapter that the unity of the many participants in be-ing manifests one exemplar of the many.

H.   CAUSES IN GENERAL

Definition of Cause

After the careful and detailed consideration we have made of effect and cause, we should no longer confuse them with antecedent-consequent correlations (the "cause-effect" of the scientist), or with the occasions and conditions which are so often called "causes" by the prephilosophical mind. It should now be obvious that a cause in the proper sense is a *principle* which has a positive *influence* on the existence or coming-into-existence (the be-ing or becoming) of something else.

Mode of Influence Varies

Although the causes all have a positive and direct influence, nevertheless the mode of influence differs for each of the various kinds of causes. (Hence, the motion of cause and causes themselves are analogous.)

Influence on Becoming. Let us consider the various modes of causal influence on *becoming,* for example, on the production of an artifact. In the production of an artifact, let us say a statue of Napoleon, the material cause (the marble) *individuates* the effect; it accounts for the production of this *individual* marble Napoleon; another marble Napoleon would require another block of marble, a different set of materials. The formal cause (in this case an accidental form) *specifies* the effect, accounting for the production of a marble Napoleon instead of a marble Caesar, to which the material was also in potency. The efficient cause, the sculptor, by his sculpturing *action* brings about the production of the effect—the transformation of a marble block into a marble Napoleon. The end, or goal, of the action has its influence by *being intended;* it moves the agent to the production of this specific and individual effect; throughout his sculpturing action something determinate is being intended. The exemplar (the internal conception) has its influence by *being imitated* in the effect; that is to say, it directly specifies the action of the efficient cause, so that the term of the production imitates the idea in the mind (and remotely imitates the external exemplar, or model).

Influence on Existence. We may also consider the various modes of causal influence on a more profound level, the level of *existence.* In a limited existent, matter (with its due quantity) causes the unitary existent to be *individual;* substantial form causes it to be *specific;* the ultimate end is naturally *intended;* the efficient cause makes the total existent *be.*

Thus, matter (with its due quantity) causes me to be *this* human; rational form causes me to be specifically *human;* happiness is natural, *intended* by me as primary, or ultimate, goal; an extrinsic efficient cause by its action causes me *to be;* as a participant in be-ing, I am modeled upon a primary exemplar (which is also my efficient cause). For a complete understanding of this, however, we must await the next chapter.

Cause Is a Principle

One last clarification must be made. A cause is said to be a principle. Now a *principle* is that from which anything in any way proceeds, or flows. A principle is a source of some kind. Thus, Lake Itasca is the source, or principle, of the Mississippi River; parents are the source, or generative principles, of their offspring; a cabinetmaker at work is the source, or principle, of the construction of the cabinet; the knowledge that "where there's smoke, there's fire" may be the principle, or source, of the knowledge that red, raging flames are consuming one's house.

Principles of Knowledge and Reality Principles. A principle of *knowledge* is some first, or primary, knowledge from which other knowledge proceeds.[26] Thus, conclusions flow from their premises, which are the principles of the conclusion.

A *reality* principle, or real principle, is that from which reality proceeds, whether *being* or the imperfect reality of *change.* It is a source from which something either *is* or *becomes.*

Intrinsic and Extrinsic Real Principles. Matter and form are *intrinsic* real principles of the essence of an existent: matter accounts for the individuation of the essence; form determines the total existent to be of this specific essence. The efficient cause and the final (and exemplary) cause are *extrinsic* real principles. It is from the "being intended" of an end that the efficient cause acts at all and along a specific line. It is from the action of the efficient cause that the becoming (change) or being proceeds.

The efficient causes which we directly observe are themselves dependent on extrinsic principles from which they proceed; they are "principled" principles. The next chapter will be concerned with the *primary* principle both of becoming and of be-ing.

[26] The first principles of one science may be the established conclusions of another science. Eventually, we must come to *absolutely* first principles.

SUMMARY

A. Determination of Action (Finality):   Problem: Whence determination of action? Human agents determine their own (free) actions. Determination of action in brutes is consequent upon sense knowledge. In plants and minerals, action is determined by their natures alone. Principle of finality: every agent acts for an end.

B. Intentional Order: The end moves the agent by being the object of inclination; it does not exist in the real order. By being the object of tendency, or inclination, it finalizes the activity of the agent. There are various orders of intention: intellectual, sense, and the merely natural.

C. Mode of Influence: Since the final cause, or end, does not exist in the real order, it does not act. Rather, it has its influence by being intended: by being intellectually known and freely intended in the case of human free agents; by being sensibly known and necessarily desired in the case of animals; by being merely intended, and in no way known, in lower beings. The end is first in intention but last in attainment. It is the cause of causes, since it is the cause of causality in all the causes.

D. Appetite, Tendency, Finality: Appetite is inclination to an end consequent upon (determined by) form, whether intellectually known form, sensibly known form, or simply the substantial form of the nature of the being. Natural appetite is the primary orientation of a being in the line of activity. Essence viewed as determining this primary, dynamic orientation is called "nature."

E. Finality of Nature Presupposes Intentional Order: Not only does finality in individual actions presuppose intentional order; also, the finality of a nature to a primary end or complexus of ends presupposes intentional order. This intentional order is extrinsic and ultimately intellectual.

F. Chance Events: According to Absolute Determinism, effects proceed inexorably from their determined causes; there are no chance effects. According to Absolute Indeterminism, all events are due to chance; there are no determinate causes producing determined effects, nor should we search for them. The middle position: this is an ordered universe, in which for the most part determined causes are in control; but chance effects do occur. A chance event is the result of the meeting of two or more lines of causation, thus producing an unintended and unforeseen effect. A third agent, however, may deliberately intend and foresee the meeting of the two causal lines. The indeterminacy in material causation, which allows for chance effects, is due to prime matter.

G. Exemplary Cause: The exemplar is the idea of the effect to be produced existing in the mind of an intellectual efficient cause. It has its influence by specifying the action of the efficient cause so that the form in which the causation terminates imitates the form of the exemplar. Hence, it is often called an extrinsic formal cause. Objectively, it is the same as the final cause, but its mode of influence is different.

H. Causes in General: A cause is a principle which has a positive influence on the be-ing or becoming of something else. This influence is had by individuating (material cause), by specifying (formal cause), by exercising action (efficient cause), by being intended (final cause), by being imitated (exemplary cause). A *principle* is something primary from which something else either is, becomes, or is known. There are principles of *knowledge* and real principles (principles of being). Real principles are either *intrinsic* or *extrinsic.*

SUGGESTED READINGS

Aristotle: *Basic Works,* edited by Richard McKeon, Random House, Inc., New York, 1941, pp. 243–247 (on chance); pp. 249–252 (on necessity and determinism).

De Raeymaeker, Louis: *The Philosophy of Being*, trans. by E. H. Zie-gelmeyer, S. J., B. Herder Book Co., St. Louis, 1954, pp. 270–281; on final and exemplary causality.

Maritain, Jacques: *A Preface to Metaphysics*, Sheed & Ward, Inc., New York, 1939, lectures 5 and 6.

Pace, E. A.: "The Teleology of St. Thomas," *The New Scholasticism*, vol. 1, pp. 213–231, July, 1927.

Van Melsen, Andrew Gerard: *The Philosophy of Nature*, Duquesne University Press, Pittsburgh, 1953, pp. 217–234; on determinism, scientific causality, predictability, probability, and random events.

Wild, John: *Introduction to Realistic Philosophy*, Harper & Brothers, New York, 1948, pp. 307–315; on chance, determinism, and in-determinism.

VI

The Primary Cause

In the preceding chapters, we have given an explanation of participating, changing existents in terms of *intrinsic* potential-actual principles (Chapters II and III) and *extrinsic* causal principles—the efficient, final and exemplary causes (Chapters IV and V). Now, the causes of our direct experience are *caused* causes. In this chapter, we shall be concerned with the *Uncaused* Cause. We shall briefly examine the general structure of the arguments by which we rise from a knowledge of the changing, participating existents which confront us in experience, to a knowledge that an Uncaused Cause exists, which is the Pure Unparticipated Act of Existing. An adequate development of these arguments, however, must await a course in natural theology, or philosophy of God.

156

A. KNOWLEDGE OF CAUSES
   THROUGH EFFECTS

Proper Cause and Effect Are Contemporaneous

We have seen in an earlier chapter, that "cause" as frequently understood is merely an occasion, condition, or antecedent. A cause in the strict, or proper, sense, however, exists as a cause only while having its influence on the effect. Thus, a builder is an actual (not merely habitual) builder only while the house is being built.

True, even a proper cause is prior to the effect, but this priority is one of *nature,* not of time; the cause is prior in this sense, that it is the principle from which the effect proceeds and on which it depends; it is prior *as principle.*[1] The effect depends on an existing cause exercising its causal influence here and now; and when the cause no longer exercises this influence, the effect no longer exists. Thus, a pencil is suspended in the air only so long as I suspend it: it depends on me here and now for its being suspended. When I no longer hold it up, or release it, it is no longer suspended in mid-air and falls to the ground. The effect *proceeds* from the cause and proceeds *here and now.*

Knowledge of the Existing of a Cause

Because of the simultaneity of cause and effect and the dependence of the effect on the cause, we can rise from a knowledge of the existence of an effect to the knowledge of the here-and-now

---

[1] The effect can be considered as regards (1) its coming-into-existence (*in fieri*) and (2) its very existence (*in facto esse*). Without a proper cause of becoming, the effect cannot come-to-be. Without a proper cause of existence, it cannot be existing. Now, the (secondary) cause of becoming is not the cause of existence. The (secondary) cause of becoming only causes the effect to be *this* or *that;* it does not cause the effect *to be* simply. Hence, the effect can exist even without the influence of the (secondary) cause. Thus, a house exists without any here-and-now causal influence from its builder, the cause of the *becoming* of the house. However, the very *existing* of the house still remains a problem and needs an explanation. (The accidental form, house, is caused by the substantial existents which make up the house. The substantial existence of these beings in turn is caused here and now by the Cause of limited be-ing.)

existence[2] of the cause. I may, for example, observe something catching fire and not observe anything setting it on fire; and yet I know that some existing cause is at work.

True, the effect does not necessarily tell us everything about the perfection of its cause (unless the cause turns out to be univocal), but it does impart the knowledge that the *cause exists* (precisely as a cause).

Knowledge of the Perfection of the Cause

Moreover, the existing effect tells us that the (efficient) cause in some manner possesses the perfection of the effect, since it is communicating this perfection. When the temperature of a volume of water is raised 10 degrees, I know that there *is* a cause at work raising the temperature. Moreover, I know that the heating agent has the energy needed to produce this rise in temperature, and perhaps more, but I do not know necessarily whether the heating agent is a gas flame, an electric current, or radioactive agents. I know, however, that the cause contains the perfection of the effect (if not formally as found in the effect) at least in an equivalent way, that is to say, at least *virtually*.[3]

---

[2] True, we can also rise to a knowledge that there *was* a cause from a knowledge of the term of the change, or becoming. For example, by looking at a wooden table (made out of a wooden pile), I know that there must *have been* a proper cause exercising its causality in the past, but I do not know whether that *quondam* agent still exists. The carpenter was the efficient cause of the becoming of the table, of the wooden pile becoming a wooden table He is not, however, a proper cause of the table *now,* either of the becoming or the be-ing of the table. Indeed, the good man retired many years ago and has since passed to his reward.

In this chapter, we are attempting to prove, not that there must *have been,* but that there must *be,* a Primary Cause.

[3] This means that the agent need not be of the same specific perfection as the effect, although it must be of a higher, not a lower, species. In former times, a 20-dollar gold piece had the perfection of a silver dollar (and more) although it was not silver itself; it had the buying power of the silver piece (and more); it was *virtually* a silver dollar.

B. NO INFINITE SERIES OF EXISTENTIALLY SUBORDINATED PROPER CAUSES

Caused Causes

We observe that many causes are themselves caused; that is to say, they are *caused* causes. The caboose of a freight train is moved locally by the boxcar to which it is coupled, but the boxcar in turn is moved by another boxcar, and so on down the line to the locomotive, which is the "primary" cause of the local movement in this system. However, the local movement of the locomotive in turn is caused by the exploding steam or diesel fuel in the cylinder heads.[4] Can a series of subordinated causes, of *caused* causes, be carried to infinity? Would such an infinite regress in causes explain an effect? Before we answer this question, we must distinguish carefully between an *incidentally related (per accidens)* series of subordinated causes and a series of *existentially subordinated (per se)* proper causes.

Series of Incidentally Related Causes

To explain the existence of a kitten which is biting my finger here and now, I do not need to invoke the long line of parent cats, grandparent cats, etc., nor the long line of biological species preceding them. The kitten can *exist* and can *act* upon me independently of any influence from the parent cats, grandparent cats, etc., who, perhaps, are no more. The parent and grandparent cats (if still existing) are only *incidentally* related to the kitten's act of biting, in the sense that they *were* the generative causes of the kitten (or of a generative cause of the kitten). Their existence and activity, however, is not necessary for the here-and-now existence and biting activity of the kitten. Thus, the parent, grandparent, etc., cats are *not proper* causes of either the biting activity or the existence of the kitten. Only incidentally (*per accidens*) can they

---

[4] Thus, our problem (the ultimate extrinsic explanation of change) begins all over again.

be called causes; they can be called causes in this sense that they *were* once upon a time generative causes of the next generation of cats before ceasing to exist.[5]

In a series of such "causes," there is no reason why the series cannot be extended backward to infinity provided there is plenty of "time." And on the supposition that the corporeal universe has an indefinite past extending ever farther back,[6] it is difficult to give a reason why such a series could not extend to infinity.[7]

[5] That these incidentally subordinated causes did exercise causality at some time in the past is a necessary condition (*conditio sine qua non*) for the action of the last, or present, cause (in this case, the kitten biting my finger). But their causation does not here and now bear upon the very action of the last cause.

[6] We must not bootleg truths from Revelation concerning the temporal origin of the corporeal universe. Some may be startled by the words of St. Thomas on this point: ". . . That the world did not always exist, is held by faith alone; it cannot be proved demonstratively. . . . The reason is that the newness of this world cannot be demonstrated from the world itself. For the principle of demonstrative argument is the essence of a thing. However, everything considered according to its species abstracts from the here and the now; and for this reason it is said that universals are everywhere and always. Hence, it cannot be demonstrated that man, or the heavens, or a stone did not always exist. . . . That the world began is an object of faith; it cannot be proved demonstratively nor ascertained in any way (*non scibile*). And it is useful to consider this, lest anyone, presuming to prove demonstratively what is of faith, should bring forth arguments which are not cogent; for, this would give unbelievers the occasion to ridicule, thinking that for such reasons we believe the things that are of faith" (*Summa Theologiae*, I, 46, 2c).

Compare the following statements on the origin of the corporeal universe made by a famous British astronomer, A C. B. Lovell, director of the Jodrell Bank experimental station: "The evolutionary theory [Lemaître's] places the creation of matter at a definite moment in the remote past beyond human investigation. . . . In the contemporary theories of continuous creation [Hoyle, Bondi] the processes of formation should still be occurring all around us, and are therefore open to human investigation . . ." (*The Individual and the Universe*, Harper & Brothers, New York, 1958, pp. 102–104).

[7] At the most, arguments based on the impossibility of such an infinite historical series would prove that there must *have been* a first cause. It should be stressed that a historical series of *limited* causes, regardless of their number, is an inadequate explanation of the real effects which we experience. In such a series, there is no explanation why any of these causes should *be* or be causing.

Series of Existentially Subordinated Proper Causes

A series of existentially subordinated *proper* caused causes, on the other hand, cannot be extended to infinity. As in the links of a suspended chain, there is an interdependence of causality in such a series; each cause in the series *depends* here and now on all the prior (in nature) causes for its very causality. Moreover, all the causes in the series must exist *simultaneously.*

If such a series of subordinated proper causes extended to infinity, this would imply the existence of an *actual* infinite number of causes. Now, an actual infinite number (of beings) is a contradiction, since one can always add to a number. Hence, the supposition which involves this contradictory consequence must be false.

A more basic reason for the impossibility of an infinite series of subordinated proper causes is the fact that in such a series there would be *no primary*[8] cause from which the others would derive their causal influence. There would be no primary cause causing, hence no intermediate causes causing, hence no immediate (or last) cause causing, hence no effect being caused.[9] Since by "effect" we mean either the changes that occur in limited beings, or the limited beings themselves, we would have to deny both the changes that occur in limited beings and the very existence of limited beings.

Existence of Primary Cause. Since we cannot deny the obvious data of our experience—limited beings and the changes that occur in them; and since we cannot deny that effects demand the *existence* of proper causes; and since the series of proper caused causes[10]

[8] We shall not use the term "first" cause, because this term ordinarily connotes a temporal priority. The term "primary" does not necessarily have this connotation and aptly connotes priority of *nature.*

[9] To explain the causality of the immediate cause by an appeal to an infinite series of caused (proper) causes, multiplies to "actual infinity" the number of inadequately explained causes. It merely increases the problem of explanation.

[10] The impossibility of such a series is not restricted to efficient causes. It is equally unintelligible to appeal to an infinite series of subordinated proper final and exemplary causes.

cannot be carried to infinity, we are forced to admit that such a series must have a terminus, that there is (exists) here and now a *primary* cause, from which the other causes derive their causal influence and very be-ing, and from which the present effects ultimately derive *here and now*. This, in brief, is the argument for the existence of a primary *efficient* cause, which we shall now present at greater length. Other arguments with different points of departure will prove the existence of a primary cause in the order of finality and a primary exemplary cause.

C.   EXISTENCE OF PRIMARY EFFICIENT CAUSE

Argument from Fact of Change in Limited Beings

We shall present the argument for the existence of a primary efficient cause with two different points of departure: (1) the changes that occur in limited existents; (2) the very existence of these limited beings themselves. In both cases, our argument will begin with sensible reality, that is, with objects of sensory-intellectual experience.

Fact of Change in Limited Beings. It is an obvious fact of direct sensory-intellectual experience that the limited beings which surround us are subject to change, to substantial as well as accidental change. There is a reduction of subjects from potency to act, either substance receiving new accidental form or matter receiving new substantial form. Limited beings are moved from potency to act.

Principle of Efficient Causality Regarding Change. Now nothing is changed except by the influence of an extrinsic principle of change. Nothing is reduced from potency to act except by an extrinsic principle, an agent, in act. Motion from potency to act requires a mover.

No Infinite Series of Interdependent Principles of Change. But an infinite series of interdependent, extrinsic principles of change is not intelligible. An extrinsic principle itself moved from potency to act depends in turn on another extrinsic principle in act. Such a regress, however, cannot be carried to infinity. An infinite series of moved movers is not intelligible, for in such a series there would be no Primary Mover, hence no intermediate movers, hence no immediate (or last) mover, and hence no motion, no change (whether accidental or substantial).

Therefore, There Must Exist a Primary Principle of Change, itself unchanged: a primary principle in act accounting for all passage from potency to act; a primary principle in act, which accounts for all actualization; a Primary Mover unmoved. For, if this principle of change were itself reduced from potency to act, it would depend on a prior (in nature) principle. Hence, this principle would not be the *primary* principle, and change would still remain unexplained.

Hence, This Primary Principle of Change Must Be Unchanged, Pure Act, Unmoved. And this principle we call God.[11]

Argument from Existence of Limited Beings

Fact of Existence of Limited Beings. The beings of our experience are of many different kinds. They participate the act of existing; hence, they are limited; consequently, they are composed of the act of be-ing and limiting essence. They are not existence itself. They do exist, but they exist with limitation—permeated, so to speak, with negation of perfection. Existence is not their essence; they merely participate in existence; they *have* existence; and they have it merely "up to a point."

Principle of Efficient Causality Regarding Limited Beings. Now whatever is not existence, but merely *has* it (participates existence) according to a limiting mode,[12] here and now has it from an ex-

---

[11] From this Primary Act all change (the realization of new act) derives here and now, although (usually) through secondary causes.

[12] ". . . everything which is according to any mode whatsoever is from God (*omne quod quocumque modo est a Deo esse*)" (*Summa Theologiae,* I,

trinsic principle. Any being in which the act of existing is not the very essence exists by derivation. Any being which is composed of the act of be-ing and limiting essence depends on an extrinsic principle simply to exist. It is not intelligible as existing in its own right; it is not existentially autonomous; it merely happens to exist.

No Infinite Series of Interdependent Principles of Existence. An infinite series of beings in which one being here and now *has* existence from another, which in turn derives existence from another, etc., is simply not intelligible. For, in such a series, there would be no primary being communicating existence, hence no intermediate beings receiving existence to be communicated, hence no last being communicating existence, hence no being receiving existence.[13]

Therefore, There Must Exist (here and now) *a Primary Being*[14] from which all other beings derive, or receive, existence. This being itself does not *have* (derive) existence; otherwise, it would not be *primary*, and limited beings would not as yet be accounted for as existing.

Hence, This Primary Being Must Be Existence Itself; that is to say, the act of existing is not distinct from its essence. It does not |exist according to a limiting mode, essence, or nature; rather, its

---

44c). "*Omne enim ens, quocumque modo sit, oportet quod derivetur a primo ente . . .*" (*Ibid.,* I-II, 79, 2c).

[13] As a matter of fact, there is no series whatsoever of finite beings communicating the act of existing. No finite being can cause existence; it cannot cause anything to be, but only to become. This point will be discussed in the last section of this chapter.

[14] This Being is called "Primary," not as connoting temporal priority, but as connoting the priority of the one principle of all other reality. ". . . in virtue of its contingency, even an eternal world would require a creator. . . . The act of creation must be thought of, not as a mere calling of the world into being for the first time, but also as an act which continues to maintain it in being" (G. A. Wetter, *Dialectical Materialism,* translated by Peter Heath, Frederick A. Praeger, Inc., New York, 1958, p. 442).

mode of existing is a "modeless mode." It exists unrestricted, unlimited; it is the pure unadulterated act of Be-ing itself. And this
Being we call God.

D. EXISTENCE OF PRIMARY FINAL CAUSE

Fact of Natural Things Tending toward End

The beings of our experience have a natural, or necessary,
tendency to a determined end. Electrons by their very nature tend
to circulate around a nucleus; a grass seedling naturally tends to
grow into an adult plant; the slender sapling necessarily tends to
grow into a mighty oak; a kitten in accordance with its nature
tends to develop into a cat; man naturally seeks happiness; his
intellect (an accidental nature) by its natural bent seeks truth, his
will seeks the good. The limited existents which we directly and
immediately know are naturally and necessarily inclined to determined ends, which they fundamentally seek in some way in all
their actions. Limited beings are naturally inclined to definite
ends (or complexus of ends) by some sort of intrinsic impression,
somewhat as an arrow is inclined (violently, not naturally) to its
target by the archer.[15]

Principle of Finality[16]

Now the finality, or natural inclination, of a limited existent
to a definite end presupposes an extrinsic intellect, which knows
the end of the being existing according to that nature and, as it
were, impresses the inclination to that end in the being. In other
words, an extrinsic intellectual being inclines this being naturally
to an end by giving it existence according to a definite nature.[17]

[15] This is stated merely as an example. We are not arguing from analogy
but from the fact of natural finality.

[16] See Chapter V, section E.

[17] Activity follows upon existence (*agere sequitur esse*). A limited being
exists according to a determining essence. It acts in accordance with the kind
of existence it receives. Essence viewed as determinant of activity is called
nature.

The reason'why an extrinsic intellectual being is needed is that the end is in the *intentional* order. This principle holds not only for individual ends of individual actions, but holds true also for the natural end of a being as a whole. (It even holds for man, who can freely determine himself to immediate ends, but cannot freely incline himself to his primary, or ultimate, end, which he naturally and necessarily seeks.) Intentional order is required to explain natural tendency.

Moreover, this intentional order must be *intellectual,* since the end must be known as end (universally), the means must be known as means (universally) and must be ordered to the end. For this intellect is required.

Lastly, the intellect which foreknows the natural ends must be *extrinsic* to the beings which receive natural tendency.

No Infinite Series of Proper Causes in Order of Finality

Now, if the extrinsic intellect which foreknows the end of a limited being (and which imparts the natural tendency) is itself limited, such an intellect in turn is naturally inclined to a distinct end, to which the intellect is in potency.[18] Again we must appeal to an extrinsic, prior (in nature) intellect, which knows the end of the finite intellect (truth) and gives this intellect its finality to end.

But we cannot carry to infinity this line of intellects ordering other limited intellects to end. An infinite regress of finalized, intellectual finalizers is not intelligible. Such a series would explain neither the finality of any limited intellect toward truth nor the natural finality in nonintellectual beings to their appointed ends.

Therefore, There Must Exist a Primary Intellect

It follows that there must exist a primary intellect, the primary principle in the order of finality, which knows the ends of all other beings and inclines them to their distinct ends by imparting to them their natural inclination. If this primary intellec-

[18] The ultimate reason is that such an intellectual being is not the act of be-ing itself but a composite of the act of existing and limiting essence.

tual being were itself inclined to a distinct end,[19] it would depend upon a prior (in nature), extrinsic intellect for its natural tendency to the end, to which it would be in potency. Hence, it would not be the primary, ordering, intellectual being, and natural finality would remain unexplained.

Hence, This Primary Intellect Must Be Its Own End

We must conclude that this primary intellect is its own end. And since end implies goodness, this primary intellect does not participate in goodness but is *Goodness* itself, which all other things seek by natural finality; it is the first principle in the order of finality. Since it cannot be in potency to its end (truth), it must be Truth itself; it must be pure, existential act—the subsisting intellect. And this Being we call God.

E. EXISTENCE OF PRIMARY EXEMPLAR [20]

Another argument[21] proceeds from the diverse *grades of existing* to the unparticipated act of existing itself. The argument, how-

[19] Again, the ultimate reason would be that it is composed of the act of be-ing and limiting essence.

[20] We use the term "Primary Exemplar" because we are concerned, not with an exemplar of an essential or accidental *mode* of existing in a Platonistic sense—unparticipated *modes* do not exist—but with the basic exemplar, the exemplar of limited beings (the Unparticipated Exemplar of the participants in be-ing).

It should be noted that only in the existential order does the unparticipated perfection have ontological status. The reason ultimately is that it is an exemplar, not of a *mode* of existing (whether essential or accidental), but of the act of *existing*. See Chapter III, footnote 32.

[21] "The fourth way is taken from the degrees found in things. For we find in things something more or less good, true, and noble. . . . But more and less are said about diverse things inasmuch as they approach in diverse ways to that which exists maximally. . . . Therefore, there is something which is most true, and the best, and most noble, and consequently that which is maximally being. . . . But that which is said to be maximally such in a genus is the cause of all that belong to that genus. . . . Therefore, there is something which is for all beings the cause of their existing, and goodness, and every perfection whatsoever. And this we call God" (*Summa Theologiae,* I, 2. 3*c*).

ever, does not explicitly, at least, appeal to the impossibility of an infinite series of proper caused causes, as do the arguments proving the existence of a primary efficient and final cause.

Fact of Participation

The beings of our experience exist according to diverse primary grades: electronic, aquatic, arboreal, canine, human, etc. This means that they are more or less perfect precisely as existents; they *exist* on lower or higher levels; they *participate* the act of existing according to the diverse capacities of their essence.

Principle of Exemplarity

But the act of be-ing in limited existents is higher or lower, more perfect or less perfect, "more or less," not insofar as it recedes from nonbeing, but insofar as it approaches the pure act of be-ing. The act of existing on many diverse levels in limited existents is intelligible only in relation to the pure act of existing,[22] which is *imitated* more or less perfectly in limited existents, and from which they *derive* their own act of existing.[23]

Therefore, There Must Exist the Pure Act of Be-ing

It follows that there must exist the pure act of be-ing, the One Exemplar of the many beings existing by participation, which also is their *efficient* cause communicating to them existence in accordance with the capacity of their essences. And this Being we call God.

We must beware lest we interpret this argument in a Plato-

---

[22] "It is necessary that all things which are diversified according to diverse perfection of existence (*essendi*), so that they exist more perfectly or less perfectly, be caused by one primary being which exists most perfectly. And for this reason, Plato said that unity must come before all multitude. . . . And Aristotle said . . . that which is maximally being . . . is the cause of every being . . ." (*Ibid.*, I, 44, 1c).

[23] This argument should not be divorced from efficient causality, since the influence of the exemplar is *indirect* by specifying the efficient causation. The point of the argument is that the exemplates (participants in existence) manifest the pure perfection of their exemplar (the unparticipated act of be-ing), Who (efficiently) causes them to exist.

nistic sense. We are using as our point of departure, not the *idea* of a being—in that case the argument would terminate in an idea —but real beings which participate the act of be-ing. The proof rises from participated acts of existing to the unparticipated act of existing, which is the exemplary *and efficient* cause of gradated existents.[24]

F. ANALOGY OF PARTICIPATION BETWEEN CREATURES AND GOD

God Is the Act of Existing (*Ipsum Esse Subsistens*)

We have shown that there must exist a Primary Efficient, Final, and Exemplary Cause, and that this First Real Principle, Whom we call God, is the very act of existing itself. "To be" is God's very essence; to exist is His nature; "what" God is *is* is Itself.

Let us state this in another way: Having shown that there must exist a Primary Principle from which all limited existents and their changes derive, we now ask ourselves "what" this prin-ciple is, its mode, or manner, of existing, in order to distinguish it from other beings.

We distinguish the beings we know best (corporeal beings) by grasping their primary mode, or manner, of be-ing—their essence, nature, or whatness. When we come to God, however, and ask "what" He is, we must say that is is what He is—Pure, Un-adulterated, Unqualified, Unconditioned, Absolute Act of Exist-ing (*Ipsum Esse Subsistens*). In the case of God, the "what," essence, or nature is not a restricting and limiting determination, or mode, of existing; the act of existing itself is *what* God is.[25] What we in accordance with our imperfect way of knowing regard

[24] The reader is warned that demonstration of the existence of God as *pure existential act* is much more complicated than might appear from the brief sketch of the proofs presented here. A fuller development of these proofs will be forthcoming in the philosophy of God.

[25] God does not "have" an essence, in the sense of a *limiting* essence. See Louis De Raeymaeker, *The Philosophy of Being*, translated by Edmund H. Ziegelmeyer, S J., B. Herder Book Co., St. Louis, 1954, p. 308.

as essence, or nature, in the case of God, is nothing other than the pure act of Be-ing (*Esse*). God absolutely IS (*simpliciter est*).[26] His *Esse* is a modeless *Esse*.

Creatures Have an Act of Existing

The limited corporeal beings, the creatures, however, in which our knowledge of the existence of the Primary Principle has its source, *have* existence; they *participate* the act of existing. This means that they exist in a "partial," or qualified, manner. Hence, they are really distinct from God, Who exists without qualifications, in a modeless manner, or "in every manner" (*omnimodo*). Nevertheless, these corporeal beings do have a community with God in this, that they do *exist:* act of be-ing (not God's Act of Be-ing, of course) is realized in them, though always according to the capacity of their limiting essence, or nature.

Analogy of Participation, or Eminence

God, then, is the Unparticipated Act of Be-ing (the Subsistent Act of Be-ing); creatures merely participate the act of be-ing. God *is* Existence; creatures merely *have* existence.

Hence, when we affirm that God *is* (exists), the word "is" signifies an act of existing unlimited by a *distinct* nature, or essence. When we affirm that creatures *are* (exist), the verb signifies an act of existing "received in" a limiting essence, which it actuates. This analogy between participated acts of be-ing and the Unparticipated Act of Be-ing is fittingly called the analogy of *participation*, from the standpoint of creatures, since creatures participate existence. It may also be called the analogy of *eminence*, since God is supereminently the act of be-ing, which creatures participate.

Not the Analogy of Proper Proportionality

This analogy between the Be-ing of God and the be-ing of creatures should be carefully distinguished from the analogy of proper proportionality between limited existents, which we have already discussed briefly in the first chapter. All limited beings,

᠌ Cf. Étienne Gilson, *Elements of Christian Philosophy*, Doubleday & Company, Inc., Garden City, N.Y., 1960, p. 233.

though different from one another, have a community, or similarity, in that each of them exercises an act of *existing* proportioned to a *distinct* essence, which limits and differentiates the act of existing. The act of existing is never twice the same, nor is the essence ever twice the same, but there is always a proportion, or relation, of these two real and really distinct principles to each other in every limited existent.

In God, on the other hand, there are not two really distinct factors. In God, the act of be-ing is not proportioned to a distinct and limiting essence.[27] "To be" is His very essence. He is analogously (eminently, not numerically) the act of be-ing which creatures participate according to the diverse capacities of their essence.

Thus, there is a true *community*, or similarity, between God and creatures. And yet this community is by no means a monistic or pantheistic oneness. The Unlimited Unparticipated, Absolute Being simply *is not* the limited, the participated, the qualified. God, like the creature, *is*, but He is *absolutely*. Creatures are merely angelic, human, canine, aquatic, electronic, or according to some other limiting mode.

G. SECONDARY CAUSES ARE TRUE CAUSES

Primary Cause Is Cause of All Other Reality

We have proved the existence of a Primary Reality, from which every other reality proceeds (here and now). Limited *existents* exist with dependence on this principle, which is the Pure Act of Existing Itself; they proceed from this principle; they exist by derivation.

Moreover, the various *changes*, the various transitions from potency to act, which limited beings cause in other limited beings, have their ultimate source in this same Primary Principle. There is no passage from potency to act, no achievement of new perfection, except in dependence (here and now) on the Primary Prin-

---

[27] Although according to our imperfect way of knowing God, we consider it as if it were thus proportioned.

ciple, which is Pure Existential Act. The Primary Cause is the cause even of the causality of limited beings and grounds their causality; He causes them both to be and to act.

Malebranche and Occasionalism

Some philosophers have been overimpressed by the all-pervading causality of the Primary Cause, even to the extent of denying that limited beings (creatures) are true causes. According to this position, the so-called actions of creatures are merely *occasions* for God's action. This doctrine, which is known as "occasionalism," found its most famous exponent in Nicolas Malebranche (1638–1715). A careful consideration of the relation of the Primary and secondary causes is needed to answer the difficulties presented by this position.[28]

Causality Is either of Be-ing or of Becoming

To show that limited beings (creatures) are true causes, though they are themselves caused, we must distinguish between the two basic kinds of efficient causality. All causation has for its term either a limited *being* or a *change* in limited being which terminates in a substantially or accidentally different being.

Finite Beings Can Cause Only Becoming

Creatures, however, can cause only becoming; they cannot cause something *to be*. They can make something already existing different; they cannot make it exist. As caused causes, they can act only upon preexisting subjects and can transform them either accidentally or substantially. Thus, a man can change the appearance of his dog by cutting the dog's hair or he can dispatch him to dog Valhalla.

Limited beings, however, cannot cause the *existing* of any limited thing; for the limited act of existing is a universal effect. Now, a universal effect demands a *universal* cause. Any cause ca-

---

[28] The problem is primarily concerned with efficient causality, but there is no reason why these thinkers should not also deny final causality to creatures.

pable of producing a universal effect must be capable of producing it in every case. The limited existent which we suppose as cause of existence should, then, be able to cause this universal effect of limited existence in *every* case, including its own case.

Now, it is simply not intelligible that any existent should cause itself to be.[29] In order to receive existence, it would need to *not* exist. In order to confer existence, it would need to *exist*. The same existent, then, would be and not be; it would be prior (in nature) to itself. Now, this is a clear contradiction. Hence, the supposition on which it rests is false. It follows that limited beings cannot cause existence.

Finite Beings Are True Causes

Although the very causality of finite beings is caused, so that they are secondary causes, nevertheless, they are *truly* efficient causes. Moreover, they are *principal* causes and not mere instruments, as will be shown.

If creatures were not true causes of their actions, we could *never know the natures* of things, and hence could never have scientific knowledge (*scientia*), which is based on a knowledge of the natures of things.[30] For we know what things are through what they do; we know the natures of beings through the activities which they efficiently *cause*. To deny that we can know the natures of beings implies that we must stop in our efforts to achieve scientific knowledge.

Moreover, limited beings would exist *without any purpose,* since the Primary Cause alone would act. Since the Primary Cause would be producing all activities directly, the very existence of limited beings would be to no avail.

Lastly, it is a fact of direct experience that we do *cause our own activities*. We are aware, for example, that we make our own choices, our own acts of will, and that nothing makes these choices for us.

[29] Not even God causes Himself to exist. He is the Act of Existing itself and does not need an extrinsic cause to explain that He is.

[30] *Summa Contra Gentiles,* III, 69.

Argument

It follows from all this that limited beings are true causes of becoming. For, causality is either of be-ing or of becoming. Finite beings are true causes. But they cannot cause be-ing. Hence, they are true causes only of becoming. They can cause change in existing beings; they cannot cause beings to exist.

Finite Beings Are Not Mere Instruments

Although the causality of limited beings is itself caused, so that they are secondary causes, nevertheless, they are not necessarily limited to being mere instruments. An *instrumental* cause acts only in virtue of a power communicated to it in a transitory and incomplete way, present in it somewhat like a motion. A *principal* cause, on the other hand, acts in virtue of its own power. Although many finite beings can be used to bring about an effect desired by a principal cause—for example, use of explosives to move earth—nevertheless these beings act by virtue of an *intrinsic principle* of some sort; that is to say, they act by their own power. Hence, they are not mere instruments.

Division of Efficient Causes

We may clarify this problem by distinguishing efficient causes along their most general lines. The most fundamental division is into (1) the *primary* efficient cause, which is the sole cause of be-ing and the primary principle (through secondary causes) even of becoming; (2) the *secondary* efficient causes, the caused causes of *becoming*, which can in no way cause be-ing.

Secondary causes in turn can be (1) *principal* causes acting by their own power; or (2) *instrumental* causes acting by virtue of a power transitorily communicated by the principal cause. With these distinctions, the relation between the various efficient causes should be clear.

SUMMARY

A. Knowledge of Causes through Effects: Proper cause and effect are contemporaneous; the effect here and now depends on an existing cause. From the existence of the effect we know the *existence* of the cause. The effect, however, does not necessarily tell us everything about the *perfection* of the cause, unless the cause is univocal.

B. No Infinite Series of Existentially Subordinated Proper Causes: An *incidentally* subordinated series of causes may possibly extend to infinity (if the universe had no temporal beginning). An infinite series of *existentially* subordinated proper causes is a contradiction; for there would be no primary cause causing, hence no intermediate, nor immediate, cause causing, and hence no effect proceeding (either change or limited beings).

C. Existence of Primary Efficient Cause: (1) Limited beings *change;* they are moved from potency to act. Now, nothing is moved from potency to act except by an extrinsic principle in act. An infinite series of extrinsic principles moved from potency to act is unintelligible. Therefore, there must exist a primary principle of change which is Pure Act. (2) Limited beings *participate* existence; they are not, but *have,* existence. Now, whatever participates (or has) existence exists by derivation (has existence from an extrinsic principle). An infinite series of beings which all derive existence from some extrinsic principle is not intelligible. Hence, there must be a Primary Being which is the Act of Existing itself.

D. Existence of Primary Final Cause: Natural things tend to a distinct end. Now, finality of a limited being to a definite end presupposes an *extrinsic intellect* which knows the end and gives the being its natural inclination to end. An infinite series of limited intellects ordered to a distinct end is not intelligible. Hence, there must exist a primary intellect which is its own end, the subsisting intellect, which orders all other things to end.

E. Existence of Primary Exemplar: The beings of our experience exist according to diverse primary *grades.* But the act of be-ing is more perfect or less perfect insofar as it approaches (imitates) the pure act of be-ing from which the limited beings derive existence. Hence, there must exist the pure act of be-ing, the un-participated exemplar of all beings which participate existence, and their efficient cause.

F. Analogy between Creatures and God: God *is* the Act of Existing; creatures *have* existence; that is to say, they *participate* existence. When we affirm that God *is* (exists), the word "is" sig-nifies an act of existing not limited by a *distinct* essence, or nature. When we affirm that creatures *are,* the verb signifies an act of existing "received in" a limiting essence.

G. Secondary Causes Are True Causes: The Primary Cause is the cause of all other realities, both the limited beings and the changes that occur in them. Nevertheless, finite beings are true causes, contrary to the doctrine of the occasionalists. Causality is either (1) of be-ing or (2) of becoming (change). But finite beings can cause only becoming. Yet, finite beings are true causes (other-wise, we could never know their natures). Hence, finite beings can cause only becoming (change). Finite beings are not limited, how-ever, to being mere instruments.

SUGGESTED READINGS

Anderson, James F.: *Metaphysics of St. Thomas Aquinas,* Henry Regnery Company, Chicago, 1953, pp. 99–117; on metaphysics as "divine science."
———: *The Cause of Being,* B. Herder Book Co., St. Louis, 1952.
Aquinas: *Basic Writings,* edited by A. Pegis, Random House, Inc., New York, 1945, vol. 1, pp. 18–24; on the existence of God.
De Raeymaeker, Louis: *The Philosophy of Being,* translated by E. H. Ziegelmeyer, S. J., B. Herder Book Co., St. Louis, 1954, pp. 282–304; on the absolute basis of being.
Garrigou-LaGrange, Reginald: *The One God,* translated by B. Rose, B. Herder Book Co., St. Louis, 1943.
Gilson, Étienne: *Elements of Christian Philosophy,* Doubleday & Com-pany, Inc., Garden City, N.Y., 1960, pp. 43–87; on the Five Ways of St. Thomas.

————: *God and Philosophy*, Yale University Press, New Haven, Conn., 1941; on what philosophers have thought about God.

Hawkins, D. J. B.: *The Essentials of Theism*, Sheed & Ward, Inc., New York, 1949.

Maritain, Jacques: *Approaches to God*, translated by Peter O'Reilly, Harper & Brothers, New York, 1954; an exposition of the Five Ways of St. Thomas, to which are added other ways.

VII

The Transcendental
Properties

We have studied the intrinsic and extrinsic principles (even the Primary Principle) of participating, changing existents. In this chapter, we shall study the "properties" of existents precisely as existents regardless of their mode of existing. We note that human beings are free, canine beings are barkers, aquatic being freezes at 32 degrees Fahrenheit. Freedom, barking, freezing at 32 degrees are properties of these *modes* of existing. In this context, "property" signifies that which necessarily flows from an essence (from a primary mode of existing) and is inseparably connected with it, although it is not the essence itself.

Are there any properties, or attributes, which are true of *every* being, which, as it were, flow, not from a mode of be-ing, but from being precisely *as being*, regardless of its mode? Are there any attributes which *transcend*, or cut across, the various modes of existing, and are true of anything which exists, regardless of its mode of existing, whether it be angelic, human, canine, aquatic, electronic, or even Divine (which is not a limiting mode)?

Our contention in this chapter will be that every being is one, true, good (and, in a certain sense, beautiful). We shall try to show how unity, truth, goodness are transcendental *properties*.

A. TRANSCENDENTAL PROPERTIES

Transcendental

Unity, truth, and goodness are called *transcendental* properties, because they are true of *every* being *as being*, regardless of its limiting and restricting mode, or manner, of existing; they are properties that cut across generic and specific differences of being. They do not refer to a *special* mode of existing as do the predicaments (e.g., substance, quality, quantity, etc.), which we shall study in the next chapter. Rather, they may be called *general* modes[1] of existing, provided we do not regard them as limiting and restricting modes. They are "modes" coextensive with being; they are "ways" in which every thing which is exercises the act of existing.

Every existent is undivided in itself. Now, to-be-undivided is to be a unit. Every being, precisely as being, is a unit, a "one."

Every being is relatable to (limited) intellect; that is, it is knowable, intelligible. Every being, insofar as it is, can confront a (limited) intellect, by which it can be known. Every being is "true."

Whatever exists is relatable to (limited) will; that is to say, it is lovable. Every being precisely as being can confront a (lim-

---

[1] For the position of St. Thomas on *general* vs. *special* modes of existing (*essendi*), see *De Veritate*, I, lc. Cf. Jacques Maritain, *The Degrees of Knowledge*, translated from the fourth French edition under supervision of Gerald B. Phelan, Charles Scribner's Sons, New York, 1959, p. 211.

ited) will, by which it can be loved, desired, enjoyed. Every being is "good."

Being (ens), then, is one, true, good. Unity, truth, goodness are transcendental "properties"—"attributes" of being as such, regardless of the mode of be-ing.

"Properties"

When we say that unity, truth, goodness are "properties" of being, we are using the term in an extended sense, not in the narrow sense in which logicians understand the term. In logic, we define property as that which is predicated of a subject as flowing necessarily from the essence of the subject, though it is not the essence itself. Thus, "risibility" is said to be a property of human essence, of the human *mode* of existing.

Being (ens), however, is *not an essence,* or mode, though it is true that limited beings always have a limiting essence, or mode, as a constituent principle. We describe being as *that which is.* Does "that which is" express everything that can be said of each and every existent? Or does every being *implicitly* and necessarily contain intelligible aspects which the notion "being" does not *explicitly* express? It is now our task to make such implicit intelligible aspects explicit. These intelligible aspects (unity, truth, goodness), since they are implied in "being" and, as it were, "flow" from being (though not distinct from being), may in an extended sense be called "properties" of being.

Not Mere Synonyms

The one, the true, the good are identical with being. Nevertheless, they are not mere synonyms for "being." [2] Rather, they express the same reality which "being" expresses but in a different

²On the other hand, "thing" and "something" are little more than synonyms for "being" although truly transcendental in that they can be referred to any being. "Thing" (res) stresses the essence of a being but connotes the act of existing (esse) "Being" (ens) stresses the act of existing proportioned to essence. "Something" (aliquid) stresses the division of a being from all other beings. However, "thing" and "something" do not make more *explicit* our understanding of being, and for this reason they are not properties.

way. They make explicit what "being" leaves implicit. They "add" (not from without) to our knowledge of "being" by making explicit its properties, or attributes.

Only Mentally Distinct from "Being"

The distinction, then, between "being" and the transcendental properties, or attributes, is not a real distinction, since the one, the true, the good are identically being. Rather, the distinction is a mental distinction, a distinction of reason,[3] inasmuch as "being" presents *various* intelligible aspects to the intellect confronted by being. The notions which *explicitly* express these aspects are the transcendentals; they are an enrichment of our knowledge of "being."

Not Univocal, but Analogous

Like the notion "being" itself, the transcendentals are predicated analogously. Like "being" they are not restricted to any one species, genus, or mode, as are the predicaments. They are common to all the special modes of being but never in exactly the same way. Such a commonness amid differences is an analogous commonness. Everything *is* in its own way, and is one, true, good in its own way.

B.   EVERY BEING IS A UNIT ("ONE")

Being as Undivided

Every being is a unit of some kind. To-be is to-be-undivided, and to-be-undivided is to be a unit. A divided "house," for example, is not a house. True, it may still be many bricks, rafters, shingles, etc., but it no longer is a housing unit; and not being a *unit*, it (the house) no longer is (exists). A divided being is no

[3] This distinction is a *mental* (logical) distinction. Moreover, it is a *minor* mental distinction, in opposition to the major distinction of reason. In a minor mental distinction, one term implies the other; not so in the major mental distinction; for example, animal does not imply man, although animal potentially contains man.

being; for a thing cannot half be; either a thing is or isn't. Existence, if exercised at all, is exercised in a *unitary* way.

Substantial vs. Accidental Units

Now, unity can be more or less perfect; it can be looser or tighter. For example, both a pile of gravel and a man are units, but in widely different ways. The man is a substantial unit, while the pile of gravel is merely an accidental unit.

A *substantial* unit is an undivided existent;[4] it implies an undivided act of existing proportioned to a limiting essence (in the case of limited beings). Such a unit is a "being" in the proper, or strict, sense of the term. Substantial unity (the abstract term) signifies indivision of the act of existing.

An *accidental* unit, on the other hand, is a composition of many substances (subsistents), of many beings, with some sort of oneness, but this oneness is not based on indivision of one substantial act of existing. Thus, a pile of gravel, a house, a rider and horse, a club, family, nation, United Nations, etc. are accidental units. Such units are truly undivided in some way, but the individual, substantial existents that make up such units remain divided precisely as beings; they retain their undivided substantial act of existing. They do not existentially coincide with the other substantial units which make up the accidental unit.

Various Kinds of Accidental Units

The loosest kind of accidental unity is mere unity in place. A pile of stones, a heap of clothes, a stack of papers is a composite of many beings which are more or less contiguous to each other. When we move elsewhere some of the substantial units that make up the one pile, heap, etc., we no longer have one pile or heap

---

[4] Substantial units are either *perfect* or *imperfect*. Any single substance is a *perfect* unit by reason of indivision of the act of existing. Either such a unit exists and is a perfect unit or it does not exist and is no unit at all. On the other hand, a musician or doctor involves a composition of substance and a quality (musical or medical knowledge), which may be lost. Such a unit of substance and accidents is an *imperfect* unit; the substance can keep on existing without the secondary perfection, or modification, which is an accident of the substance.

but two or more piles, heaps, stacks, etc. Such units based on mere indivision of place are called *aggregates*.[5]

A more perfect type of accidental unit is the *structural* unit, such as a house, an automobile, a typewriter. Such units are composed of many substances occupying more or less one general place. But over and above being in one place, the many substances are parts of one general pattern, or design, for one general end, or purpose. Thus, an automobile is composed of many substances, which together form an accidental structural pattern, or design, for the purpose of transporting human beings.

Another type of accidental unit is the *dynamic* unit, in which one substance directs the activity of another substance or substances. A rider and horse, a chauffeur and his automobile, a pilot and his plane are dynamic units. Here, two or more beings *act* as one; they are undivided in activity but remain divided as beings.

An accidental unit may be composed of many human beings all intending, or willing, one and the same end. Such a unit is a *moral* unit, a society. Examples of moral units are a club, a family, a municipality, a state, a nation, the United Nations, the future interplanetary or intergalactic society. All the individual substances which compose such units remain divided from each other in their very being, but strive together for a common goal, or end. Such units, though real, must never be mistaken for substantial units. The United States, for example, is not one substance.

Simple vs. Composite Units

Another fundamental division of units is into *simple* units (units without parts) as opposed to *composite* units (made up of parts).[6] All the units of our direct experience are composite in

[5] In an atomistic philosophy (not to be confused with scientific atomic theory), certain ultimate particles are regarded as the true substantial units, and everything else is explained as an aggregation of these particles. Such aggregates, whether chemical compounds, cells, plants, animals, men, would be *accidental*, not substantial, units. Obviously, such an explanation fails to account for the unity of organisms.

[6] A *simple* unit is one without parts. It is undivided and cannot be

various ways; they have quantitative parts, essential parts, even existential parts.

Natural vs. Artificial Units

Another division is into *natural* as opposed to *artificial* units. This division depends on whether the unity is brought about by human art or not. Thus, a dog, a fish, a cabbage plant are natural units. A chair, an automobile, a house are artificial units.

Metaphysical vs. Mathematical "One"

We must be careful not to confuse metaphysical (existential) unity and mathematical unity. The "one" of metaphysics and the "one" of mathematics are not the same.

The "one" of mathematics is *univocal;* every "one" in three means exactly the same: one cat plus one more cat plus one more cat is three cats. The "one" of metaphysics, however, is *analogous;* for undivided act of be-ing is never the same. Thus, one dog and one cat and one mouse are neither three dogs nor three cats nor three mice but three *beings* (existents) all of which exercise existence but do not exercise it in the same way. Such a plurality is a *multitude* but not a number in the strict sense. Hence, we cannot strictly enumerate, or count, beings precisely as beings; we can only recognize their existential plurality.

The "one" of mathematics is based on indivision of *quantity.* A mathematical unit is an undivided quantity. The existential "one," on the other hand, is based on indivision of the act of existing. An existential one is undivided being.

Since the "one" of mathematics is based on quantity, which in turn presupposes *matter,* such a "one" can be said only of corporeal being, that is, of beings whose nature is a composition of specifying form and individuating matter. Hence, the mathe-

---

divided. An angel, for example, is essentially simple; its essence is a pure form. But the angel is not existentially simple. God alone is existentially simple, He alone is pure existence

A *composite* unit is one which is made up of parts, which are present actually or virtually. A composite unit may be a substantial unit or an accidental unit.

matical "one" cannot be true of all being; it is not a transcendental "property." On the other hand, indivision of the act of be-ing is true of every existent.

A Transcendental Property

Existential unity is a transcendental property, that is, a property which cuts across all differences of being. Every being precisely as being is undivided in itself. For, if it were not undivided in itself, it would at the same time half be and not-be. Now this is clearly not intelligible. Existence can be exercised only in a unitary way, never in a fractional manner.

Moreover, every being is either simple or composite (composed of parts, principles, etc.). If it is *simple*, it is actually undivided, nor can it be divided. If it is *composite*, the being does not exist unless the parts compose the whole and hence are no longer divided. Every being, then, is a unit.

Opposite of Unity—Distinction

Opposed to being undivided is to-be-divided, or *distinct*. Distinct things are divided from each other in some way; they are not identical; they are not one and the same. Now distinctions are of various kinds, the most significant and important division being that of real and mental distinctions.

Real Distinctions

A real distinction is one which exists between beings independently of the mind. Although it may also be in the mind, the distinction is primarily in the realities outside the mind; the distinction is not *made* by the mind. Thus, gold and lead are really distinct; they were distinct even before any human mind arrived on the earthly scene; their distinction is not owing to the work of the mind.

Between Complete Beings. A real distinction may be one between *complete* beings. Peter and Paul, for example, are really distinct complete beings. A man and his dog are really distinct complete substances. Men simply are not dogs. Real distinctions of this kind are expressed by negative predication.

Between Principles of Being. Real distinctions may also be between *principles* of being, that is, between intrinsic real principles *by which* the unitary existent is, is what it is, is specified, is individuated, is modified. Thus, the act of existing and limiting essence, form and matter, substance and accidents are really distinct, not as complete beings, but as principles (by which) of being. Matter is not form; substance is not the accidental modifications of a being; essence is not the act of existing; they are truly distinct.

Nevertheless, there are no distinct *principles* of being independent of the unitary, total existent which has these component principles. A limited existent *has* an act of existing, *has* a limiting essence. The distinction between the limiting-perfecting, potential-actual components is reflected in the indirect predication of a common subject. A limited essence *has* specifying form, *has* individuating matter. A modified subject *has* modifications, *has* a subject of modifications. Again, the distinction between the intrinsic real components is manifested by the indirect predication of a common subject.

True, principles of being are not separable from another.[7] But separability is not what is meant by real distinction between principles of being. Essence cannot be separated from the act of existing, nor can the act of existing be separated from essence; rather, by these two intrinsic reality factors an existent *is* and is *what* it is, respectively; it exists and exists according to a primary, limiting mode.

Mental Distinctions—Distinctions of Reason[8]

Distinctions can also be made by the mind. One and the same reality, one substantial unit, can be conceived by the mind (according to the essence) through various concepts. Thus, a man's essence, or nature, can be conceived as corporeal, organic, animal, rational. Note that there are several concepts in the mind but only one being (of one essence) outside the mind. Obviously, such

[7] The human soul, however, is an exception. It can be separated from matter without going out of existence. It is a subsisting form. This point will be studied in the philosophy of man.

[8] Sometimes also called "logical" distinction.

a distinction is not a real distinction; it is a distinction produced by the mind itself in forming various concepts of the same essence.

The most important of these distinctions of reason for our purposes is the *virtual* distinction, of which we have given an example in the preceding paragraph. Man, for example, *virtually* is—he has the activities of—animal, plant, chemicals, although actually and existentially he is one being, one substantial unit. The perfection of his nature, which enables him to perform the activities of lower types of being, can be presented in various concepts, which ordinarily would present the *full* essential intelligibility of lower levels of existing—animal, plant, mineral. Such distinctions we shall call major mental distinctions, as opposed to minor mental distinctions.

Major Mental Distinction. The major mental distinction has a *perfect* foundation in reality—the real distinction between matter and form. Matter, which of itself is an indeterminate potential principle, can be informed by various forms of lower or higher perfection. The intellect in its abstract concepts (of the essence) can present to itself the lower forms implicitly, or *virtually,* contained in the higher form. The successive concepts, beginning with corporeal substance, are more and more determinate, thus presenting the essence, or nature, of the existent in a more and more perfect way. The first concept does not actually include the next, but only *indeterminately,* or "potentially." Such is the distinction which exists between the various "metaphysical levels' of existing: rationality, sentiency, organicity, corporeity, substantiality, when applied to the human mode of existing.

Minor Mental Distinction. The distinction between "being" and the transcendental properties is an example of a distinction of reason *without* a perfect foundation in reality. Here, the notions include each other implicitly though not explicitly.[9] "One,"

---

[9] In the major mental (logical) distinction, one concept (the more specific concept) implicitly contains the other (for example, rational implicitly contains animal); but it is not the other way about (animal does not implicitly contain rational).

"true," "good" make explicit what is contained in "being" implicitly. Such a distinction is called a minor mental distinction.

C. EVERY BEING IS TRUE

Being as Object of Intellect

A true Rembrandt was an object of the intellect of the great master who painted it. A faked Rembrandt was not. True gold, we shall see, is an object of intellect even when no human intellects are around to be confronted by the glittering stuff. In this section, we shall discover that every being precisely as being is (or can be) an object of intellect—is intelligible, is *true*.

True Words—Verbal Truth

When we state that someone is speaking the truth (that his words are true), we mean that his words correspond to what he thinks. Verbal truth is the conformity of words (speech) to the mind of the speaker. When a man says what he knows, his words are true; he speaks the truth, at least in the sense that he is not telling a lie. When a man's words are not in conformity with his thoughts (his concepts and judgments) about reality, he is then lying.

True Judgment—Mental Truth[10]

Although a man's words may be in conformity with his judgment about reality, it does not follow that his words are necessarily true, for the simple reason that his judgment may not be true. True judgment, or mental truth, is the conformity of the intellect to reality. Our judgment is true if *what* we think things are is what they actually are, and if we think that they *are*, and they actually are. The opposite of true judgment is error.[11]

True Things—Ontological Truth

Beings themselves are said to be "true." We speak (and think) of true friends and true gold as opposed to false friends and fool's

[10] Sometimes referred to as "formal," or "logical," truth.
[11] The problem of error is studied at length in epistemology.

gold. We speak of real, or true, teeth as opposed to false teeth. We speak of true money and false money (counterfeit). We speak of a true Rembrandt and a false, or forged, Rembrandt. Here there is question of a conformity of being itself to some *intellect*.

In the case of artifacts, it is readily seen that the product is in conformity with the mind of the intellectual efficient cause, or at least *was* under the influence of such an intellect while it was being produced. Thus, the true Rembrandt was under the influence of the great master's intellectual conception as it came into existence; the forged Rembrandt was conformed to the artistic conception of the third-rate artist who perpetrated the fraud. The forged picture is not a true, or real, Rembrandt.

Conformity of Being to Primary Intellectual Cause

Every being is true, or real, even those which we mistake for something else. Fool's gold, for example, is true, or real, iron pyrites. This implies a conformity, or agreement, with intellect. The intellect, however, with which all beings are in conformity cannot be the human intellect, for our intellect does not make things to be *what* they are, nor does our intellect make them *be*; it merely discovers them. The true iron pyrites were true, or real, pyrites long before any limited intellectual beings came upon the scene and were stopped in their tracks by this dazzling mineral.

As we saw in the preceding chapter, all limited beings depend on one Primary Exemplar for their very intelligibility. All limited beings are in conformity with the Divine Intellect, which knows the various ways in which the Divine Essence (the Pure Act of Existing) is imitable outside Itself. Because God knows limited beings, these beings are *what* they are; because He wills them to be, they *are*. Their intelligible structure, or nature, is due to God's knowledge of them. As regards the universe of limited beings, God's knowledge is analogous to that of the artist, whose productions take the form originally in his mind as an artistic conception. Limited beings are in conformity with the Unlimited Intellect.[12]

[12] The Divine Being is in perfect conformity with the Divine Intellect by

Conformability of Being to Limited Intellects

Besides this radical and intrinsic conformity of all being to the Primary Intellectual Cause, beings can be related, or conformed, to limited intellects, by which they can be known. All being is intellectually knowable, or intelligible, insofar as it is being. Insofar as a thing participates *existence* (or is existence itself), it has an intellectual appeal, "glamour," or splendor about it; it can "radiate" into intellect. It is not the quantity of a being, or its matter, or its limitations in general, which are at the root of its ability to wake limited intellects into activity. Thus, a huge elephant has greater quantity than a human being but does not have the appeal for intellect that a human being has, simply because the elephant does not exercise existence on so high a level.

Anything which *is* (exists) can move a limited intellect into act, and the more perfectly it is (exists), the more can it move an intellect, provided it is duly presented to such an intellect.

A Transcendental Property

That is true which is in relation to (or relatable to) intellect. Now, every being is in relation to the intellect of the Primary Exemplary and Efficient Cause.[13] Moreover, every being can be related (is relatable) to limited intellects by which it can be known. Hence, every being is true. The true is transcendental; that is, it cuts across, or transcends, all the different modes of be-ing.

Opposite of Truth—Error

The opposite, or contrary, of verbal truth is falsehood, or a lie. The opposite of mental, or formal, truth is error. There is no strict contrary of metaphysical, or ontological, truth, since only that which is in conformity with the intellect of the Primary Intellectual Cause is "being." "Anything else" simply isn't.

---

identity. God is His own Intellect. All this will be treated at length in the philosophy of God.

[13] Divine Being, of course, is merely *conceived* as so related, since it is really identified with the Divine Intellect.

D. EVERY BEING IS GOOD

Being as Object of Appetite

We call those things *good* which are lovable, desirable, enjoyable. Thus, the good is the object of inclination, of tendency, of appetite. Whatever is loved, desired, or enjoyed has the nature of the good; it either participates in goodness or is goodness itself.

Now, desire for the good is not restricted to beings endowed with knowledge (whether intellectual or sense knowledge as in man and the brutes); rather, beings which have no knowledge also tend toward, or "desire," the good by natural appetite. (This appetite, however, presupposes the knowledge of an extrinsic intellect which moves the being toward its good, or end, by imparting to it a natural appetite.) Hence, inclination to the good— appetite—may be *natural, sense, intellectual.* Here, we shall be concerned largely with the good as object of intellectual appetite, the will.

Just as the true (the intelligible) is the object of the *intellect,* so is the good (the lovable) the object of *will.* In other words, the acts of intellectual appetite—love, desire, joy—are concerned with being insofar as it is good. It is the known *goodness* of beings which moves our appetites into operation, so that they tend to an absent object (by love of desire) and rest in the object when possessed (by love of delight). We love, desire, enjoy things precisely because they are good.

Being as Relatable to Limited Wills

Any being precisely as being need not be related to limited intellectual appetite; a being can exercise the act of existing without being loved, desired, or enjoyed by any limited *will,* just as any being can exist without being known by any limited intellect. However, every being insofar as it exists *can move* limited wills into operation;[14] being can evoke response from will just as it can evoke response from intellect. The reason is that a thing is lovable, or good, insofar as it is perfect; it is perfect insofar as

[14] Provided, of course, that it be intellectually known and judged good.

it is in act; the basic act is the act of be-ing, which everything either participates or is. Hence, every being is good.

Now, our will does not make things good, just as our knowing does not make things true. Beings have metaphysical, or ontological, truth independently of human knowledge; so also beings have metaphysical goodness independently of our willing them. On what is this intrinsic, metaphysical goodness based?

Being as Related to Unlimited Will

Limited beings, whether willed or not by human wills, participate the basic act, or perfection, of existing (*esse*). They are not the act of be-ing; they *have* it. They depend on the Primary Efficient Cause simply to be. This Primary Efficient Cause exercises creative action; it wills to communicate the perfection of existing to limited beings in accordance with the intelligible level of their essence, or nature. The limited beings, existing according to the capacity of their nature, are the object of this Will. Unless they are willed (that is, unless the Cause of be-ing communicates the act of existing), they can in no wise *be*.

Now, "to be" is the most basic act. The higher this act, the higher the perfection of a being. And the higher the perfection, the more a being can be an object of will—a good.

We see, then, that limited beings possess goodness because they are objects of the Divine Will. Because God knows them, they are *what* they are; because God *wills* them, they are (exist). It is not because limited beings are good that God loves (wills) them; rather, it is the other way about: because God loves them (wills them to be), they are good. Limited beings, then, are related to the Divine Will.

A Transcendental Property

If we take the good to signify being as related (or relatable) to will, it should now be obvious that goodness is a transcendental property, for every being is in relation to the will of the Primary Efficient Cause.[15] Moreover, every being can be related to limited

[15] The Divine Being by a "relation of identity," as we conceive it in our nonproper understanding.

wills by which it can be loved, desired, enjoyed. The reason is that every being either is or participates the basic act of existing. Now, insofar as a being is in act, it is perfect. Insofar as a being is perfect, it is appetible, or good.

Every being, then, is good; the good is a transcendental property;[16] it cuts across, or transcends, all the differences of being.

Unqualified Goodness—the Plenitude of Existence

Not every being, however, is unqualifiedly good. Although every limited being has the basic act, or perfection, of substantial existence, not every limited being has all the *accidental* perfection it ought to have in accordance with the capacity, or demand, of its substantial nature. Thus, a sterile fruit tree is said to be bad and is cut down and cast into the fire, although it was still a good shade tree and good insofar as it existed. A fruit tree is unqualifiedly good only if beyond the primary perfection of substantial existence it has all the secondary perfections, or actuations, that a good fruit tree must have: foliage, a certain size, fruit-bearing capacity, etc. If any of the due accidental perfections are lacking, a limited being is unqualifiedly evil, though it remains qualifiedly good, for example, as a shade tree, or insofar as it still exists. That, however, which does not exist is neither good nor evil.

Opposite of Good: Evil—Deficiency of Existence

After discovering that the unqualified good implies the plenitude of existing, we can more readily understand that evil is a deficiency of existence, a *privation* of perfection. The problem of evil and its nature is one of the core problems of philosophy and has evoked a host of proposed solutions in the history of thought.

Two Extreme Positions regarding Evil

An extreme position on the nature of evil is the doctrine that evil is something *positive,* something real. According to this position, blindness, sickness, ignorance would be a positive re-

[16] "Everything which is, regardless of its mode of existing, is good insofar as it is being" (*Summa Contra Gentiles,* III, 7).

ality. In the philosophy of Zoroaster, a Persian philosopher who flourished about 1000 B.C., both good and evil are held to flow from their own first real principle. The primary principle of good (Ormazd) and the primary principle of evil (Ahriman) are locked in a continuous struggle, but in the end, good will prevail over evil. In this view, both the principle of evil and the evils that proceed from it are regarded as positive realities. However, that which is positive is being; and, as we have seen, every being is good. Hence, evil cannot be a positive reality.

Another extreme position is the doctrine that evil is *purely negative*, that evil is a pure negation, or absence, of perfection. Now, we know that not every absence of good is evil. Otherwise, every limited being would be evil simply because it does not possess the perfection of something else. Man, for example, would be evil, since he cannot run as swiftly as a deer and does not have the strength of a rhinoceros. Hence, evil cannot be a pure negation.

Middle Position—Evil, the Privation of Good

As with virtue, philosophical truth is usually found in the middle position between two extremes. The middle position as regards the nature of evil is this: evil is the *privation of good;* that is to say, evil is (1) the *negation* of perfection (2) *due* to (3) a *positive* subject, which has a real capacity, or demand, for that perfection. Thus, absence of sight in a stone is a pure negation and is not an evil. On the other hand, absence of sight in a man is the absence of a perfection for which the nature of the being has a real potency, capacity, or demand. Such a negation of perfection is not a pure negation; it is a *privation,* a deficiency of existence opposed to the plenitude of existence, which the good implies. Evil is, as it were, a "hole in being"; or, more accurately, evil is a "wound" in being.

Although evil is not itself a positive reality, it does imply positive reality. There can be no privation of perfection unless there is an *existing subject* which ought to have the perfection. Thus, there can be no blindness unless a man (or brute) *exists,* who lacks vision. Since every being insofar as it exists is good, evil is said "to be in" the good. If there is no existing subject, there is neither good nor evil.

On the other hand, we must beware of considering an evil—blindness, sickness, ignorance, for example—as a *positive* reality inhering in a subject, although we do ordinarily speak this way. For example, we may say, "Blindness is prevalent throughout the world," "Sickness makes one patient," "His ignorance of the subject is colossal." Evil, we must remember, is a negation; moreover, it is a negation of a *due* perfection—a privation. Now, negations and privations are not "being" in the proper and strict sense of the term. They are "beings of reason" and exist only in the mind; they are conceived as if they were being.[17]

Evil, then, is not a positive reality existing in its own right. Rather, beings exist, which insofar as they exist are good, although they lack some (accidental) good, or perfection, which they should possess; they are deficient; they exist deficiently.

Division of Evil

The principal division of evil is into *physical* evil (evil of nature) and *moral* evil. Physical evil is the privation of a perfection due to a nature, whether the nature be mineral, vegetative, sensitive, or rational. Thus, contaminated water, a sterile plant, a blind dog, an insane man are deficient in perfection and, hence, are in some way physically evil.[18]

Moral evil is the privation of the due order to the ultimate end in a human act.[19] Moral evil, or sin, will be considered in the philosophy of morality (ethical theory).

Cause of Evil

In speaking of the causes of evil, we must keep in mind that evil is not a positive reality. Rather, evil is a "wound in being,"

[17] See Chapter I, section D.

[18] The term "physical" is not synonymous with "corporeal" and "physiological." Even angels are "physical" beings; that is, they have a *nature*. The term is derived from the Greek word, *physis*, meaning "nature."

[19] Moral evil, we shall see in ethics, implies a conversion to a positive false end, besides the privation of due order to the ultimate end.

a lack, a privation, a *deficiency*. The efficient cause which brings about an effect that is deficient (or evil) in some way, cannot intend evil precisely as evil. For only the good, whether true or apparent, can be the object of intention. Hence, there cannot be a direct (*per se*) efficient cause of evil, that is, a producing cause which intends the evil as such. Nor can evil have a final cause. Thus, a sculptor who produces a defective statue does not intend the defect precisely as a defect; he intends a good, but for various reasons, what he produces does not measure up to what he intends. Evil, then, can have only an indirect (*per accidens*) efficient cause, the agent which is good and intends a good.

However, the action of an efficient cause intending a good may be deficient, so that the effect in which the action terminates may be lacking in perfection. This deficiency in the action may be owing to a defect in the *agent* himself. Thus, a sculptor with an injured hand is not able to enshrine the intended artistic conception in the hard marble on which he is working. Moreover, the *instruments* he uses may be defective; dull chisels, worn brushes, poor tools in general will make for deficiency in any production. Lastly, the *material* cause, or subject, may be deficient. As the old adage has it, it is difficult to make a silk purse out of a sow's ear. The material cause must be properly disposed to receive the new form to be imparted by the action of the efficient cause. A lack of such disposition hinders the action of the efficient cause, so that the full perfection of the agent is not realized in the patient.

In brief: evil cannot have a *final* cause, for the final cause, or end, is the good as desired. Evil has no *formal* cause, since it is a privation of a form due to a subject. Evil, however, has an *efficient* cause indirectly, namely, the agent which intends a good and is itself good. In a certain sense, evil has a *material* cause, the being (or beings) which is the subject of the privation.

God and Evil

The problem of God and evil will be treated at length in the philosophy of God, but we shall make some general observations on the subject at this point.

1. God cannot be a direct (*per se*) cause of any evil, whether physical or moral; that is to say, He cannot will evil as evil; only good can be willed.

2. God can be a cause indirectly (*per accidens*) of physical evil; by directly causing the generation of things, He indirectly causes the corruption of others. For example, He causes plants to assimilate the minerals, animals to assimilate the plants, and man to feed upon animals. In causing a higher good, the good of an ordered universe, God directly wills and causes the good to which evil is annexed. Thus, He may be said to cause physical evil indirectly (*per accidens*).

3. God cannot be a cause even *indirectly* (*per accidens*) of moral evil, which is privation of the right order to the Divine Good; otherwise, He would be opposed to His own Goodness. God, however, wills to permit moral evil to be done, and this is a good.[20] For example, He wills to permit the persecution by tyrants because He wills the perfection of martyrs.[21]

E.   EVERY BEING IS BEAUTIFUL

Descriptive Definitions of the Beautiful

We call those things beautiful whose very apprehension gives delight. The beautiful is said to be "that which is a joy to behold," "that which being seen pleases" (*quod visum placet*). These descriptive definitions stress the *effect* which the beautiful object has on the beholder. However, we must not overlook the "that which is beheld," the *being itself* truly beautiful, which being known gives rise to (esthetic) delight. The beautiful is *being* (that which is) insofar as being perceived it gives delight.

[20] *Summa Theologiae*, I, 19, 9, ad 3ᵐ.

[21] This analysis is a metaphysical consideration of "what" evil is. It is not meant to be a "solution" to the *problem* of evil. The problem of evil leads one into the area of revealed truth and is solved only with reference to the Cross. But even with this solution, a certain mystery will always remain concerning evil as long as we sojourn in this life.

Delight in the Beautiful

The beautiful object when known gives delight.[22] Not every delightful object, however, is considered to be beautiful, for example, a delightful steak. The beautiful object gives *disinterested* delight; it gives esthetic pleasure. The beautiful object pleases when *seen;* it need not be possessed. I need not own the sunset to appreciate its beauty; I need not assimilate the painting to appreciate it as a great and wondrous work of art.[23]

The delight in the beautiful flows directly from the *contemplation* of the beautiful object apart from any usefulness the object may have for us and independent of our possession of the object. Thus, a thing of beauty is literally "a joy forever," that is, independent of a passing use for, or possession of, the object.

Moreover, the beautiful gives delight in this special sense, that it causes the knower to "rest" [24] in the thing being known. The beautiful, especially when on a grand scale (mountains, great canyons, the sea, vast plains, an open sky), "arrests" us; it stops us in our tracks; we "rest" and delight in its being known.

Perception of the Beautiful

The beautiful pleases "when known." Although it is ever present to be known, it is not always known. Let us take for an example an autumn sunset confronting (1) a dog, (2) a blind man, (3) a scientist, (4) a poet or artist.

The dog, in our example, knows the sunset but only on the sensory level. He cannot perceive it as beautiful, because he has no intellectual knowledge of it. Certainly, he is not arrested by it; he does not stop to stare at it.

The blind man, on the other hand, has an intellect capable of coming to a knowledge of the object as beautiful, but he lacks

---

[22] Delight can be merely sensible delight (pleasure), intellectual delight (joy), or a combination of the two. Often there is an overflow from the higher appetite to the lower appetite by "redundance."

[23] Intentional possession is sufficient.

[24] This "rest" should not be regarded as cessation of activity; rather, it is the most perfect activity of knowing, an immanent operation.

the important avenue of visual-sense knowledge needed to present the object's sensible beauty to him.

The scientist can give us a precise conceptual definition of the sunset as "a prismatic effect of light filtering through dust particles in the sky," but a definition, no matter how exact and precise, is not a contemplation of the beautiful; at best, it presents only the universal essence, or nature, of the object.

Finally, the poet or artist is confronted by the same sunset. He differs from the others in that he is more or less perfectly "open" to the intelligible splendor of the object confronting him. Not only does he sense it and understand it and judge it to *be;* he also "feels" it; his knowledge is a "loving" knowledge; he delights in the thing known precisely insofar as it is known.

We see, then, that the perception of the beautiful involves the operation of the whole man. Insofar as this operation is cognitive, it is what Maritain has called a sort of "intellectualized sensation," [25] in which the knower comes to grips with the concrete, individual existent in its very singularity. In addition, there is the appetitive response of the knower, a delight or rest (primarily on the intellectual level, but also on the sense level by redundance) in the contemplated object. The perception, or "intuition," of the beautiful is a sort of "loving knowledge" of the real—a knowledge by "connaturality." [26]

Objective Factors

What is there in beings which enables them to evoke such a knowledge? St. Thomas lists three objective factors, which make the beautiful object more readily perceivable as beautiful: (1) integrity, (2) proportion, (3) splendor.[27]

[25] Cf. Jacques Maritain, *Art and Scholasticism,* translated by F. J. Scanlon, Charles Scribner's Sons, New York, 1937, pp. 23–28, 161–173. Cf. also his *Creative Intuition in Art and Poetry,* Pantheon Books, New York, 1953, pp. 163–166.

[26] The term is Maritain's. See *Creative Intuition,* pp 91–145, where he formulates his theory concerning the cognitive process that underlies artistic production.

[27] *Summa Theologiae,* I, 39, 8c.

Integrity is wholeness, or completeness, of perfection. A muti-lated statue, such as the Victory of Samothrace, lacks integrity, and therefore is less beautiful, other things being equal, than if it were whole. It does not have the fullness of being, which is the delight of the intellect.

Proportion, or consonance, signifies order, a unity amid va-riety. Thus, a mere succession of sounds is not music, but a series of sounds unified into a melody, or theme, is the beginning of music. All things being equal, the greater the diversity, provided unity is maintained, the greater the beauty. Thus, a triangle is more beautiful than a line, and a six-pointed star (made out of two triangles) is more beautiful than a triangle; a Gothic cathedral is more beautiful than a simple, shedlike garage.

Splendor designates brightness, clarity, brilliance. The beauty must be able to be perceived. Thus, a fiery sunset is more beauti-ful than a gray dawn, although the latter has its own kind of beauty. The joyous peal of church bells sounds more beautiful than a mournful foghorn. One must be able to see that the ob-ject has integrity and proportion. The splendor, or clarity, of the object intensifies the mental activity of the perceiver and makes for greater delight in the perception of the beautiful. For this reason, beauty (an abstract term) is often called the "splendor of form" (*splendor formae*).

Accidental vs. Substantial Beauty

Often when we refer to things as being beautiful, we have in mind the splendor of *accidental* form.[28] Thus, the figure of a

---

[28] Many things which we perceive to be beautiful are accidental, not sub-stantial, units. Thus, a building, a painting, a musical composition, a statue are accidental units, they have been put together As such, they have an *accidental* beauty, the beauty of structure, pattern, design, or figure.

Moreover, in their own reality, they are *material*. Nevertheless, great art objects can be a striking expression of immaterial qualities, since the artistic productive process enables the artist to isolate a quality from the distracting and irrelevant, concomitant qualities with which it usually appears in the objects of nature.

For an extensive philosophical discussion of art objects, see Étienne Gil-son, *Painting and Reality*, Pantheon Books, New York, 1957.

sleek and graceful race horse may be more beautiful than the figure and face of an aged and decrepit man scarred by the battles of life. The beauty that flows from figure, however, is an accidental beauty. More basic is the beauty that flows from substantial form (*splendor formae substantialis*), which somehow, though often dimly, manifests itself through the sensible qualities. Thus, beneath the withered countenance one can at times discern a beauty that is proper to man. On the other hand, no matter how intently one peers into the countenance of a contented cow, one cannot discern anything beyond a literal bovine bliss. Its level (or form) of (material) existence is such that one should not look for the light of intellect to shine even dimly through its huge bright eyes.

Transcendental Beauty

The ultimate intrinsic source of beauty, however, is neither accidental form nor substantial form, but the act of existing, of which they are the primary and secondary determinants, or modes. The beauty that flows from the act of existing is *transcendental* beauty. By reason of the undivided act of existing, a being is intelligible (true) and desirable (good). Every being precisely as being can confront a knower; every being insofar as it exists can move a knower (who is open to it) to esthetic operation. Its intelligibility, or truth, is like a shining light to the intellect and fulfills its desire to know; and this is a good. Every being, then, is beautiful inasmuch as it participates the act of existing or is the very act of existing itself. Beauty is a transcendental property.[29]

[29] However, transcendental, or metaphysical, beauty, which flows from the substantial act of existing (proportioned to substantial form), is not so readily perceived (in our present mode of knowing) as that which flows from accidental form. Although all beings are beautiful in this profound sense and please "when seen," they are not always *seen*. One may assign reasons for this: (1) on the part of the object; (2) on the part of the perceiving subject.

On the part of the *object*, there may be a lack of the three objective, accidental factors—integrity, proportion, splendor—which are necessary as a condition for our perception of an object's beauty.

On the part of the *subject*, in order to perceive the *accidental*, sensible

It is in accordance with the level, or grade, of the act of existing that a being is beautiful in this most profound sense. Thus, men are ontologically more beautiful than the most perfect animals; animals are more beautiful than the plants; plants are more beautiful than the minerals. God, of course, since He is the unparticipated act of be-ing itself, is Beauty Itself.

Relation to "True" and "Good"

The beautiful agrees with the *true* in that it can be "seen," that is, known; hence, like the true, it implies relation (or relatability) to intellect. It differs from the true, however, in that it adds the element of *delight*, which the true does not necessarily add; in fact, many truths are decidedly unpleasant.

The beautiful agrees with the *good*, since it gives delight by fulfilling the appetite of the intellect. It differs from the good, however, in that it gives delight by being *known;* it need not be possessed. One need nòt eat the sunset to enjoy it; one need not own a painting to admire it.

Thus, the beautiful partakes of the nature of the good and of the true. In a sense, beauty may be called the goodness of the true (*bonitas veri*); that is to say, it is the intelligible radiance and splendor of being inasmuch as this is the good of the knower.

A Transcendental but Not a Distinct Transcendental

It would seem, then, that beauty is not a separate transcendental, distinct from transcendental truth, goodness, and unity, although it is truly a transcendental property. Every being

---

beauty based on accidental form, the perceiver must have good senses, a certain amount of talent and training, and must attentively regard the object. This is certainly within the capacity of many.

The more profound penetration into reality (through the accidents, of course) required for the perception of *transcendental* beauty demands beyond this an ability to discriminate between the superficial and the basic, between the accidental and the substantial, the material and the formal, the essential and existential. Such a knowledge, however, is not the monopoly of metaphysicians; it is possessed in an eminent degree by great poets, great artists, great writers, etc., and is usually the result of a long and often agonizing search after truth.

is one, true, good, beautiful; but, when we say it is "beautiful" (in the transcendental sense), we mean that its *intelligibility* (truth), which flows from the undivided act of be-ing, is the *good* of the intellect and quiets the intellect.

Why Are Not All Beings Perceived as Beautiful?

If we grant that every being precisely as being is beautiful, we must explain why it is that this beauty is not always perceived. The first answer we may give is that ordinarily we refer to *accidental* beauty, when we say that a thing is beautiful, rather than to *substantial* beauty, which admittedly is not readily perceived.[30]

As regards accidental beauty, we may point out that many beings are quite obviously *lacking* in accidental integrity, proportion, and splendor; hence, it is more difficult to perceive them as beautiful. Thus, a broken statue, an off-balance painting, music drowned out by noise are not readily appreciated as beautiful.[31]

Moreover, although these *objective* factors may be present to make the (accidental) beauty more readily discernible, still the beholder may lack the requisite *subjective* qualifications for the perception of the beautiful object. Among these subjective requisites are natural talent (good sense organs, sense memory, ability to concentrate, etc.) and training. Obviously, these conditions are not found in all men.

Often *prejudices* hinder us from seeing the beauty of an object. Snakes, for example, so frighten us that we are unable to appreciate them as beautiful; but a diamondback rattlesnake when viewed safely from the other side of heavy plate glass in a herpetarium can be seen as quite beautiful. Arbitrary presuppositions concerning what is beautiful often hinder us from per-

[30] Even accidental beauty, however, is a manifestation of substantial beauty and does flow from the act of existing, since the total reality of the existent is from this basic perfection.

[31] Every being, however, has existential completeness, or integrity, by being undivided. Every (limited) being has a proportion of act and potency. Every being contains within it the splendor of form or of the act of existing. Hence, these three objective factors are never lacking to make a being substantially beautiful.

ceiving an object's beauty. Thus, a ten-year-old auto or clothes of a quarter century ago are considered out of date and ugly. Unfair comparisons are made between various beings. Thus, apes are sometimes considered ugly when compared to men, whom they resemble somewhat. What one really means, perhaps, is that they are far less beautiful than human beings, that they would make sorry-looking humans. In general, we may say that the ugly is that which insofar as it is *is* beautiful but lacks some beauty it should have or which we expect it to have.[32]

Moreover, beautiful objects that we see frequently lose their original novelty and power to arrest our attention, so that we fail to contemplate them intently and, hence, receive less delight from them. Often, however, when they are taken out of their familiar settings and presented in a new situation, their beauty is again more readily apparent.

Lastly, we are apt to take for granted that all beauty is limited to accidental beauty. Thus, the more profound ontological beauty is not even looked for, much less discovered, even though it is present in every existent.

Objectivity of the Beautiful

Does beauty reside only in the "eye of the observer"? Is beauty only a point of view? Those philosophers who answer these questions in the affirmative hold a subjectivism as regards the beautiful. Perhaps the most influential of the proponents of this position was the German philosopher Immanuel Kant (1724–1804). According to Kant, beauty is fundamentally an experience —the harmonious activity of sense and intellect.

Augustine, on the other hand, in a memorable passage, gives expression to the opposite position, that the beautiful is objective, or real: "And first I shall ask whether things are beautiful because they give delight, or whether they give delight because they are

[33] "To a lady, who, looking at an engraving of a house, called it an ugly thing, he [Constable] said, 'No, madam, there is nothing ugly; I never saw an ugly thing in my life . . .'" (C. R. Leslie, *Memoirs of the Life of John Constable*, Phaidon Press, Ltd., London, 1951, p. 280), quoted by Étienne Gilson, *op. cit.*, pp. 182–183. Cf. Maritain, *Creative Intuition*, pp. 163–165.

beautiful. Thereupon, I will answer without hesitation: they give delight because they are beautiful." [33]

Beauty and Morality

We have seen that all beings are good in themselves and that all beings are beautiful. But not all beautiful and good things are good for me. The latter, of course, is due *to me*. Because of the inordinacy of man's appetites, objects which are good and beautiful in themselves may be morally dangerous. A very artistic novel or play, for example, may not be morally good for an adolescent. One cannot, then, rightly adopt the position: "This is beautiful, and, therefore, my contemplation of it is morally good." Beauty and morality are not one and the same thing.

Nor is the converse true: "This is morally good (produced by a morally good man or depicting a 'moral'), and therefore, it is beautiful." Much bad art is produced by morally impeccable persons. On the other hand, some very good art (objects) has been produced by morally reprehensible artists. The ideal, of course, is that morally good artists produce good art. In any event, let us not confuse morality and beauty.

SUMMARY

A. Transcendental Properties: Unity, truth, goodness are properties of every being regardless of its limiting mode, and hence are *transcendental*. They express explicitly what "being" expresses only implicitly; they "flow," as it were, from "being," and hence are aptly called *properties*. Although only mentally distinct from "being," they are not mere synonyms. Like "being," they are predicated analogously.

B. Every Being Is a Unit ("One"):   To-be is to-be-undivided; existence is always exercised in a unitary way. A substantial unit implies one undivided act of existing. An accidental unit, on the other hand, is a composition of many substances in one place (aggregate), pattern or design (structural unit), acting

[33] *De Vera Religione,* chap. 32.

as one (dynamic unit), intending one end (moral unit). The mathematical "one" is univocal, based on indivision of quantity, and is limited to corporeal being. The metaphysical "one" is analogous, based on indivision of the act of be-ing, and is truly transcendental, since every being is undivided in itself. The opposite of unity is distinction. Distinctions may be real (between complete beings or between principles of being) or mental (major or minor).

C. Every Being Is True: Verbal truth is conformity of words to thought. Mental truth is conformity of thought to reality. Ontological truth is conformity of being to the Primary Intellectual Cause and conformability of limited beings to limited intellects, by which they can be known. The true is being as object of intellect. The opposite of truth is error, or falsity.

D. Every Being Is Good: The good is being as object of will. Every being is related to Unlimited Will, the will of the Primary Efficient Cause. Every being is relatable to limited wills, by which it can be loved, desired, enjoyed. A being is good insofar as it is perfect; it is perfect insofar as it is in act; the fundamental act is "to be"; everything either is or participates the act of be-ing. Hence, every being is good.

Unqualified goodness implies the plenitude of existence. For a being to be unqualifiedly good, it must have, besides the substantial act of existing, all its due accidental perfection. Evil is deficiency of existence. Evil is not positive, nor a pure negation; rather, evil is privation—the negation of perfection in a being which has a positive capacity for a perfection in accordance with its nature. Thus, absence of sight in a man is evil but a mere negation in a stone.

Evil is either physical or moral. Evil cannot have a direct efficient cause nor a direct final cause (end). God cannot be a direct cause of any evil; He can be an indirect cause of physical evil by causing a higher good to which evil is annexed; He cannot be a cause even indirectly of moral evil, but wills to permit moral evil to be done, and this is a good.

E. Every Being Is Beautiful: The beautiful is that which being seen (perceived) pleases (*quod visum placet*). The beautiful when seen gives disinterested, or esthetic, delight; it need not be possessed.

The perception of the beautiful, according to Maritain, is a sort of intellectualized sensation, in which the whole man comes to grips with the concrete, singular existent in its singularity.

Integrity, proportion, splendor are the three objective factors which make a beautiful object more readily perceivable as beautiful. Accidental beauty is the splendor of accidental form; substantial beauty is the splendor of substantial form and the act of existing.

The beautiful partakes of the nature of the true and the good; it is the goodness of the true (*bonitas veri*); it is the intelligible radiance and splendor of being inasmuch as this is the good of the knower. Although beauty is a transcendental property, it is not a distinct transcendental from the one, true, good. Not all beings, however, are perceived as beautiful, either because of a lack of accidental integrity, proportion, splendor on the part of the *object* or because of deficiencies on the part of the knowing *subject*. Things *are* beautiful and hence give us delight when known; beauty is *objective*, not purely subjective. Beauty and morality must not be confused: not all beautiful and good things are good for me; not all art objects produced by morally good persons are good art objects.

SUGGESTED READINGS

Anderson, James F.: *Metaphysics of St. Thomas Aquinas,* Henry Regnery Company, Chicago, 1953, pp. 44–98; on the transcendentals.
Bourke, Vernon J.: *The Pocket Aquinas,* Washington Square Press, Pocket Books, Inc., New York, 1960, pp. 261–282; on beauty and art.
De Raeymaeker, Louis: *The Philosophy of Being,* translated by E. H. Ziegelmeyer, B. Herder Book Co., St. Louis, 1954, pp. 61–69 (on unity and distinction); pp. 76–77, 86–87 (on intelligibility of being); pp. 212–225 (on good and evil).

Gilson, Étienne: *Elements of Christian Philosophy*, Doubleday & Company, Inc., Garden City, N.Y., 1960, pp. 145–163; on God and the transcendentals.

————: *Painting and Reality*, Pantheon Books, New York, 1957; a philosopher's discussion of one type of art object.

Maritain, Jacques: *Art and Scholasticism*, translated by F. J. Scanlon, Charles Scribner's Sons, New York, 1937, pp. 23–28 (on the beautiful); pp. 161–166 (on the perception of the beautiful).

————: *Creative Intuition in Art and Poetry*, Pantheon Books, New York, 1953, pp. 160–167; on the beautiful and the "ugly."

Siwek, Paul: *The Philosophy of Evil*, The Ronald Press Company, New York, 1951.

VIII

Categories of Limited Being

We shall be concerned in this chapter (primarily at least) not with the *fact* of existing—whether or not something is—but with the *modes* of existing, and in particular with the broadest, the supreme, or most generic modes of existing. Our predication reflects these modes of existing, though in an imperfect way. By distinguishing the modes of predicating, we come to a knowledge of the supreme modes of be-ing, of existing, that is, of limited be-ing.

A. CATEGORIES IN GENERAL

Supreme Modes of Predicating and of Existing

The ten categories, or ten predicaments, of limited being[1] are the ten supreme and irreducible modes of predicating, or judging, corresponding to the supreme modes of existing,[2] in which our predication is grounded. To quote the words of St. Thomas on this point:

> . . . there are diverse grades of entity (*entitas*) in accordance with which diverse modes of existing are received, and according to these diverse modes of existing, the diverse genera of things are derived.[3]

The ten highest and broadest genera are the predicaments, or categories.

> . . . being must be limited to diverse genera in accordance with diverse modes of predication, which themselves follow upon diverse modes of existing, because in as many modes as something is predicated, in just so many modes is something signified to be. And for this reason those things into which being is first divided are called predicaments, because they

[1] We should note, at this point, that God cannot be confined within a category, since He does not exist according to a limiting mode. The categories are the most generic modes of limited existence.

We should also note that the categories, or predicaments, can be considered from a *logical* viewpoint or from a *metaphysical* viewpoint. We shall be more interested in the latter point of view.

[2] In the Kantian view, categories are merely a priori forms in the mind superimposed on the empirical data presented by the senses. According to this position, the mind gives the *form* to sensible things. This position, of course, is radically opposed to that of Aristotle and St. Thomas Aquinas, which we are presenting in this chapter. Moreover, there is an important difference in the views of the last two philosophers. It would seem that Aristotle *identified* being and its modes; not so St. Thomas.

[3] *De Veritate*, I, 1c.

are distinguished according to the various modes of predicating.[4]

Being is divided into ten predicaments, not univocally as a genus is divided into species, but according to the diverse modes of existing. Now the modes of existing are proportional to the modes of predicating. For in predicating something of something else, we say that *this* is *that*. For this reason the ten highest genera of being are called the ten predicaments.[5]

Substantial vs. Accidental Modes of Existing

In every (attributive) predication,[6] a mode of existence is affirmed of a subject. Let us consider the following examples: Peter is a *man;* Fido is a *dog;* Felix is a *cat*. In all three instances, the predicate is affirmed of the subject as identified with the subject, as the subject itself. Such a predicate[7] expresses not a secondary mode, or modification, of a subject, but the subject itself. Such a predicate expresses the *substance* of the existent—the fundamental, or primary, mode of existing, not a secondary mode. Men, dogs, cats are substances; human, canine, feline are substantial, not accidental, modes of existing. Predicamental *substance*, then, signifies a primary mode of be-ing (a nature) predicated of real individual existents.

Such a mode of existing is "not to be in another"; that is to say, the total existent (Peter, Fido, Felix) is independent in

[4] *In Met.,* V, 9, 890.

[5] *In III Phys.,* lect. 5.

[6] We are not concerned here with judgments about things *as known* (the science of logic), but with judging about things as they *are* (metaphysics). The predications (or judgments) we are considering here, although put in attributive form (subject, copula, predicate), may be truly existential (for example, Peter is a boy), but we are concerned at this juncture primarily with *modes* of existing, not with the fact of existing. For example, we are concerned that men, dogs, roses are *substances* (the primary mode of existing).

[7] Such a concept is obtained by total abstraction, that is, by a consideration of the whole essence in an indeterminate way by dropping out the individual determinations, e.g., height, weight, size, etc.

being; it exists *in itself* (*per se*), though obviously not *of* itself, since we are concerned here with limited existents. Substance, then, is that mode of existing which does not require "inherence in" something else, but implies existence in itself (*per se*). It is the fundamental mode of existing.

Let us now consider other examples of predication: Peter is *wise;* Fido is *white,* Felix is *fat.* In these cases, the predicate is affirmed of the subject as "inhering in" the subject, that is to say, as modifying the subject (which is already constituted in being according to a substantial, or primary, mode). Such a predication expresses an *accident* of the total existent. Such a mode of be-ing is "to-be-in-another"; that is to say, the accident expresses a modification of the substantial existent. To say this in a different way: an "accident" expresses that the total, unitary, and substantially determined existent exists in a modified way.

Nine Different Kinds of Accidents

Now, accidental modes of existing are of various kinds and the difference between accidental modes is reflected in our predication. That which is predicated *absolutely* (not in relation to something else) as "inhering in," or modifying, the substance may be consequent either upon matter or upon form. That which is predicated as consequent upon matter falls under the predicament of *quantity.* That which is predicated as consequent upon form belongs to the predicament of *quality.*

That which is predicated as modifying, or determining, the substance may be said of the subject not absolutely, but *relatively;* that is to say, it indicates an order to something else, which is the term to which the subject is referred. This predicament is *relation.*

The last six predicaments all involve a relation to something extrinsic which is *as a principle* according to which the substance is modified. That which is predicated of a subject insofar as the subject is the efficient cause of a passage from potency to act in something extrinsic belongs to the predicament *action.* That which is predicated of the subject insofar as the subject is the patient of the action of an extrinsic efficient cause falls under the predicament *passion*.

That which is predicated of the subject as measuring its duration is the predicament *when*. Anything predicated as measuring it in place (the immediate immobile container) is reducible to the category *where*.

Whatever is predicated of the subject according to the relation that the various parts of the subject have among themselves belongs to the predicament *posture*. And lastly, whatever is predicated of the subject according as the subject is related to something merely adjacent to it or joined to it for a human purpose is reducible to the predicament, or category, *habit*.

For a better understanding of the ten predicaments, or categories, let us see examples of them in concrete predications:

John Doe is a man—SUBSTANCE (the fundamental mode of existing)

John Doe is huge, tall, heavy—QUANTITY

John Doe is white, wise, courageous—QUALITY

John Doe is a debtor, owner of an automobile, a father—RELATION

John Doe is striking, pushing, kicking Jones—ACTION (transient)

John Doe is being struck, pushed, kicked by Jones—PASSION

John Doe is a contemporary, twentieth-century—WHEN

John Doe is in room 336, in Omaha, in the U.S.A.—WHERE

John Doe is sitting, standing, reclining—POSTURE

John Doe is clothed, hatted, armed—HABIT (state of apparel)

Accidents Considered as if They Were Complete Beings

We must beware, however, of considering the various kinds of accidents (modifications, or determinations, of substance) as if they were complete, substantial beings themselves. The human intellect is able to divorce them (mentally) from their subject by a formal abstraction and consider them in themselves as if they were beings in their own right. Thus, I may speak of the good qualities that "exist in" a subject; I may speak of the relations that "exist between" beings. For example, I might say, "Smith's virtues are heroic; his knowledge is profound; his height is 6 feet; enmity exists between him and Jones."

It is much easier for us to consider the modifications, or secondary determinations, of a being, as beings in their own right and to speak of them *after the manner of substances* (subsistents) than to use the precise terminology to speak of them and to understand them as they actually are (as principles of being). Thus, the predicamental accidents are a sort of shorthand both for considering and for speaking about the modifications of substances (substantially determined beings).

We must carefully distinguish between the manner in which the predicamental accidents *signify* the modes of being and the modes of being themselves. The predicaments are not mere extrinsic denominations, nor are they mere second intentions (knowledge about an object as known, e.g., genus, difference, species). As first intentions, they are a knowledge of the *kind* of existence of real being, although they present this kind, or *mode,* of existing as if it were an existent.

Ontologically, the Unitary Reality Exists with Modifications

Ontologically, however, it is not the accidents which are the total reality, nor even substance itself. Rather, both substance and the various accidents are *principles* of the unitary, total existent, the subsistent, or supposit, which alone is properly said to be. Substance is the principle by which the being exists in itself. Accidents are the principles by which the total existent is modified in some way, either quantitatively, qualitatively, or relationally. The unitary, total existent exists *in itself* (according to a fundamental, or primary, mode) by reason of substance and exists in a *modified* way by reason of accidents.

Thus, in the example we have given, John Doe is a human substantial unit existing with quantitative extension; is modified qualitatively; is related to various other beings, on some of which he is acting, some of which are acting in turn on him; is related to other moving bodies by which his duration is measured; is contained by some other body; his various parts are variously related among themselves; and, finally, he is related to some things which merely are joined to him for some human purpose.

B. SUBSTANCE

Subject of Determinations

That which the intellect first knows is "being," an existent,[8] a subsistent. That intrinsic principle by which the being exists in itself (*per se*), and not "in" something else, is what we mean by *substance*. Thus, as soon as we know that something is, we implicitly, at least, know substance.

Accidents, on the other hand, are said to "exist in," or to "inhere in," substance; they are the modifications, or determinations, of a subject. Now, our intellect distinguishes in the unitary existent between these *determinations* of a subject and the *subject* of these determinations. The subject of determinations, of modifications, is *substance*.

Substance as Substrate for Accidents

In the period of decadent Scholasticism, substance was conceived for the most part as the substrate, or support, for accidents —as a sort of stabile and permanent principle which remains the same while the accidents "come and go." This conception of substance would reduce accidental change to the mere displacement of unchanging elements, while substance would remain inert and static. This conception of substance was rightly rejected by the English empiricists.

True, limited substance is a substrate for accidents, in the sense that substance is the principle of essential permanence and stability in a being while the being is accidentally modified; and

---

[8] The unitary, total existent with all its modifications and determinations is designated "first substance," or supposit. In this section, however, we shall discuss "second substance," which designates a mode of being

the substance is related to the accidents as potency to act.[9] But to be a support for accidents is not the prime role of substance, although the etymology of the word (from *sub* and *stare*) might lead us to think so.

Substance as Principle of Independence in Existence

A more profound description of substance is "that to which it belongs to exist, not in another subject, but in itself." It belongs to accidents, on the other hand, "to be in" a subject, and this subject is substance, which in turn need not inhere in another. This is to say that substance is a mode of being so perfect that it does not need to depend on another in which to "in-sist"; rather, it belongs to substance to *subsist*.[10] Although a substance if limited must depend on an extrinsic cause to exist, nevertheless, it exists *in its own right*. In other words, the substantial mode of existing implies a certain autonomy, or independence. The same does not hold true for accidents. Thus, man, who is a substance, exists in his own right, but a man's knowledge "exists in" him. The man's knowledge is a modification of the man; unless the man existed, there would be no knowledge "in" the man. Modifications of a subject without a subject which is, and is modified, are naturally impossible.[11]

[9] This, however, is not true of the Divine Substance; there are no accidents "inhering" in God's Substance and modifying that Substance. Besides, this Substance is not potency for accidents. Moreover, Substance in God is not a principle *by* which but is Subsistence itself. Lastly, this Substance is not distinct from the act of existing and, hence, is not the substance of the ten categories of limited being. God is not enclosed in the categories.

[10] "The term substance signifies . . . an essence to which it belongs . . . to be *per se* . . ." (*Summa Theologiae*, I, 3, 5, ad 1ᵐ).

[11] In the Eucharist, however, by God's power, the accidents of what was bread and wine before Transubstantiation exist without inhering in their natural subjects, the substance of bread and wine. The Eucharistic presence, of course, is a mystery. The doctrine of substance and accidents when applied to the Eucharist shows that this presence is not a contradiction. The distinction between accidents and substance, however, does not explain the mystery, although it does throw light on that mystery. See Étienne Gilson, *Elements of Christian Philosophy*, Doubleday & Company, Inc., Garden City, N.Y., 1960, p 328.

Substance a Principle of Being

We must not think that we can directly observe substance and accidents. Rather, what we encounter in our sensory-intellectual experience is "being"—a unitary, though composite, existent.[12] "Substance, as such, is not visible to the bodily eye, nor is it an object of any sense, nor even of the imagination, but solely of the intellect . . . ."[13] The *determinations,* or modifications, of the subject and the *subject* of determinations are grasped by the intellect alone and only after a reflection on the contents of experience.

Since these distinct factors, or elements (substance and accidents), are components of a *single* existent, they are not complete beings, but *principles* of being. Substance, then, as well as accidents, is a principle of being.[14] It is that principle by which a (limited) being exists so perfectly that it need not "inhere in" anything else.

Substance Is Dynamic

Although substance is the principle of essential stability and permanence throughout accidental change, we must not consider substance as a (complete) being which is static and inert. In an accidental change, the limited existent, the subsistent, does truly *change;* for example, when we learn philosophy, we truly change; we become philosophical, which we were not up to now; we become qualitatively different. Moreover, in most accidental changes, the existent changes *intrinsically,* not merely extrinsically (as when an object on my right is moved to the left). Thus, the unitary, total existent does *truly* and *intrinsically* change, while remaining essentially, or substantially, the same. The principle which accounts for the permanence, or "per-sistence," on the same essential level is substance; it is not the total existent itself; rather, it is a *principle* of being. Along with accidents it is a principle of accidental change. It is not correct, therefore, to regard substance as

[12] To express this, logicians use the term "first substance."

[13] *Summa Theologiae,* III, 76, 7c.

[14] We are concerned here with limited beings. In God, of course, substance is His very act of Be-ing, not a principle *by* which He is.

a static, inert substrate, which "remains unchanged, while the accidents come and go." Imagination is a poor substitute for metaphysical reflection.

C. INDIVIDUATION OF CORPOREAL SUBSTANCES

By Matter, Not by Form

In the chapter on participation, multiplicity, and limitation, we saw that matter in some way is the principle of individuation of corporeal substances which are multiplied within the species. Substantial form explains the specific likeness of these individuals; it explains, for example, why Tom, Dick, and Harry are *human*— the same specific type of corporeal being. Matter, on the other hand, is in some way the source, or principle, of individual differences and explains why Tom, for example, is neither Dick nor Harry, though he is essentially the same.

By Matter with Determinate Quantity

Prime matter, however, of itself cannot be the source of individuation, since prime matter is *common* to all corporeal beings whether specifically or only individually distinct.[15] A common factor cannot be the principle of individual differences. Hence, some determination must be introduced into matter so that it may be the source of individuation.

In general, matter does demand that the being to which it belongs be *quantitative,* that it have parts outside of parts, that it have dimensions (length, breadth, thickness). Moreover, matter in conjunction with informing substantial form demands that the

---

[15] "Since matter, considered in itself is indistinct, it is not possible that it should individuate the form received in itself, except insofar as it is divisible. For the form is not individuated for the reason that it is received in matter, except inasmuch as it is received in this matter distinct and determined to the here and now. Matter, however, is not divisible except through quantity. . . . And for this reason, matter is made this and signate insofar as it has dimensions" (*In Boeth. de Trin.,* IV, art. 2).

total corporeal existent (of which it is a principle) have *deter-minate* quantity, determinate dimensions, a determinate place, with the result that the being can be clearly *designated*, or pointed out, as an individual. In this way, matter with its determinate quantity (*materia signata*) is the principle of individuation in corporeal substances of the same species.

By Matter with Determinate but Interminate Quantity

It is not required, however, that the ultimate, or terminate, quantity and dimensions be acquired before a corporeal substance can be individuated. What is required is that the individual substance have *determinate* quantity, or dimension, although the present dimensions may not necessarily be the terminal dimensions. Such determinate quantity is not necessarily the present quantity of the individual being, since some individual beings (organisms) increase in quantity or even fluctuate in quantity. Many of us, for example, gain and lose weight; we increase and decrease in quantity. Our dimensions are always determinate but not always of the same termination.

By *determinate* quantity we mean *this* quantity, these dimensions, as distinct from any other. Thus, the quantity of Tom is not the quantity of Dick, nor that of Harry. By *terminate* quantity we mean the ultimate quantity attained by the individual. Thus, Tom ultimately becomes 6 feet tall and weighs 180 pounds, etc. When we speak of *interminate* quantity, we simply do not consider what the quantity at any one time is, though the individual at every moment of his existence does have determinate quantity. It is matter with determinate but interminate quantity which is the root of individuation.

Abstraction from Matter

In forming the ordinary universal concept of the nature of a corporeal being, the intellect abstracts from (leaves out) individuating matter and presents the essence of the being according to its form, with relation to matter though not with relation to this individuating matter. Since the concept does not present the individuating factor of the essence, the concept can present (cognitively) all the individuals that participate in that essence, but can present them only according to their common nature.

D. SUPPOSIT AND PERSON

First Substance vs. Second Substance

The "substance" of the ten predicaments is a predicate (reflecting a mode of existing), which is said of many and is common to many. For example, substance is predicated of man, dog, rose, etc., in a *univocal* way. In this sense, substance signifies not a unitary, complete existent, but a mode of existing with a certain independence (it need not "inhere" as an accident). In such a predication, substance is a universal and is called *second* substance, in opposition to primary, or *first,* substance, which is the singular substance (the subsistent) which actually exists.

First substance is the singular, individual existent with all its determinations, or modifications. First substance is not predicated of anything else. Rather, it is the subject of predication. At this point, we are concerned not with second substance but with first substance, that is, with the concrete, singular substance which exists (the subsistent).

Supposit

In order to designate such a substance precisely as *individual, complete,* and *subsisting,* scholastic philosophers have coined the term "supposit." Thus, a supposit is of an *individual* nature, not of a universal nature, and hence is not communicable to many. Peter is not communicable to many, but human nature is communicable to billions.

A supposit is *complete,* not merely a part (whether an essential part like matter or form, or integral part like arms and legs, which communicate in the whole supposit).

A supposit is a *substance,* not an accident, which communicates in the substance in which it is said to "inhere"; a supposit exists according to a substantial (as well as accidental) mode.

Finally, a supposit *subsists;* that is, it exercises its proper act of existing, and hence it is absolutely *incommunicable*. For, from two beings in act there can never result one being in act. It is the act of existing which gives the being a certain existential autonomy, that is, makes it a supposit.

A *supposit,* then, is a distinct individual which has its own act of existing; a supposit is an existing, complete individual.

Actions Belong to the Supposit

The supposit is the principle *which acts (principium quod).* The reason is that a being acts because it is (exists) and insofar as it is. Now the supposit, not the nature, is that which *is.* Hence, it is the supposit which acts.

True, nature also is a principle of action, but it is a principle *by which (principium quo)* the supposit acts.

Nor is it the *power* or *part* which acts. It is not the eye that sees—*I* see you—nor the hand that writes; rather, it is the man, who sees with his eyes and writes with his hands.

Actions ultimately belong to, proceed from, and must be attributed to the supposit. The reason is that a being acts insofar as it is in act. Now, the primary act is the act of substantial existence. That which is actuated by this act and rendered substantial, complete, individual, and subsisting is the supposit. The supposit, then, is the total principle which acts. Nature is only part of the supposit, an intrinsic principle by which the supposit acts. And the same must be said of the powers of acting.

Person

A rational supposit is called a *person.* It is a distinct, individual subsistent of a rational nature. Thus, a man is a person; brutes, plants, and minerals are not. Like any supposit, a person in the metaphysical sense is constituted as such by its own act of existing, so that it is incommunicable to anything else.

It is not consciousness which constitutes a *metaphysical* person, for one and the same (metaphysical) person may be conscious at one time and later unconscious. Moreover, one and the same metaphysical person may under abnormal conditions develop distinct *psychological* "persons," or personalities, of which one may not be able to recognize the other or even be conscious of the other. Such personality "splits" are disassociations in the memory system of *one* rational supposit, or *metaphysical* person, which remains substantially the same. Incidentally, the cure usually consists in getting one and the same metaphysical person to integrate the various walled-off memories by recognizing them as his own.

E.   ACCIDENTS IN GENERAL

Modifications of Substance

In our study of the predicaments, we have been primarily concerned up to now with the consideration of substance. In the immediately preceding section (on the supposit and person), we were concerned with *first* substance—the individual, complete subsistent with all its modifications. The other sections of this chapter were a discussion of *second* substance, which signifies a mode of existing with a certain independence, that is, according to a definite substantial mode (it "subsists"). Men, dogs, roses, for example, are substances. Their mode of existing is a substantial, not an accidental, mode (which needs to "inhere in" a subject).

We shall now consider the secondary modes of existing, the modifications of substance; for example, this man is *wise,* that dog is *fat,* this rose is *red.* Whatever is predicated as a modification of a subject (already existing according to a substantial mode) is reducible to one of nine different types[16] of accidents: *quantity, quality, relation, action, passion, when, where, posture, habit.*

We must keep in mind, however, that in the strict and proper sense[17] only the modified being exists (subsists). The modifications

[16] The accidents, however, should not be considered as so many species of a genus "accident." Rather, they are supreme genera which are irreducible.

[17] See Chapter I, section D, for the various meanings of "being." "The accident does not possess existence (*esse*), but by it something is, and for this reason, it is called being (*ens*), just as whiteness is called being, because by it something is white" (*Summa Theologiae,* I, 90, 2c).

In the strict sense, to exist is to subsist, that is, to exist as one complete being. "To be is said properly and truly of the subsistent supposit" (*Quaestio Disputata de Unione Verbi*).

though real do not exist in the primary sense; rather, the modification is a real, intrinsic principle *by which* something exists in a modified way. For example: ". . . whiteness is said to be, not because it itself subsists in itself, but because by it something is white." [18] Thus, in the case of a white man, the human being is the white being, and the white being is the human being. The total existent is (exists) according to a substantial mode (is human) and *is modified* (is white).

Accidents Known by Intellect

In the unitary existent, our intellect is able to distinguish the subject of modifications and the modifications of the subject. The modifications (or secondary determinations) are the accidents. They are the secondary modes of existing. Essence (substance[19]), of course, is the primary mode of existing. Thus, a white man primarily and basically exists according to the human mode (he is a man); he exists according to the secondary mode of whiteness (he is a white man).

Dependence in Be-ing

Substance, we have seen, is a principle by which a being exercises existence with a certain independence. Accidents, on the other hand, are principles to which it belongs to "exist in" another as in a subject. "The subject gives existence to the accident, because the accident does not have existence except through the subject." [20] Accidents cannot even properly be signified unless their subject (substance) is also expressed.[21] For example, we define whiteness as a "sensible quality of a corporeal *substance* (subject)," or we may speak of a white *man*, white *dog*, etc.; that is, we speak of some *substance* having whiteness.[22] We must be careful, how-

---

[18] *Quodlibet* IX, art. 3. Intellect, however, can formally abstract the quality from its subject and consider it after the manner of a subject in its own right. Thus, we say, "Whiteness is a quality."

[19] Substance connotes *independence* in existence according to an essential mode.

[20] *De Principiis Naturae* (*in principio*).

[21] Cf. *De Ente et Essentia*, VI.

[22] Cf. *Summa Theologiae*, I-II, 53, 2, ad 3ᵐ.

ever, not to regard accidents as "being in" a subject as a content is in a container, although such imagery may accompany our philosophical considerations.

Moreover, "in the strict sense, accidents neither become, nor are corrupted; but they are said to become and to be corrupted inasmuch as their subject begins or ceases to be in act according to that accident." [23]

We see, then, that the reality of accidents implies *dependence;* precisely as accidents they have no independent existence; their "existence" is the existence of the subject on which they depend and with which they make composition.[24] For these reasons, ". . . an accident is not called being (*ens*) as if it itself had existence, but because by it something is. Hence, it is better called *of a being (magis dicitur esse entis)."* [25]

Distinct from Substance

As modifications, or determinations, of an already substantially determined subject, accidents are really distinct from the substance of the being which they modify. This distinction, however, like all distinctions between principles of being, must not be exaggerated so that we think of accidents as substances within substance.[26] Rather, accidents combine with substance in a composite unity, in which substance and accidents are related as potency and act. Thus, a doctor is a composite of human substance and medical knowledge (a quality). He is human (substantially); he is medical (accidentally); above all he is *one.*

---

[23] *Ibid*, 110, **2**, ad **3**m.

[24] "The nature of an accident involves imperfection, because the existence of an accident is to be in a subject, to depend on a subject, and to form a composite with a subject" (*In I Sent.,* VIII, 4, 3).

[25] *Summa Theologiae,* I-II, 110, 2, ad **3**m.

[26] "Many have fallen into error with regard to [accidental] forms because of this that they make judgments about them just as they pass judgment about substances. This seems to be due to the fact that forms are designated in the abstract after the fashion of substances, for example, whiteness, virtue, or something of this sort. Therefore, some who follow this way of speaking cast judgment on them as if they were substances" (*De Virtutibus in Communi, quaestio unica,* art. 11).

Proper vs. Common Accidents

Some accidents flow necessarily from a substance and are inseparably connected with the substance. Thus, intellect and will are powers inseparably connected with human substance; a man necessarily and invariably has intellect and will. His essence, or nature, is a quasi-efficient cause of these powers, which "flow" from that essence by a sort of emanation.[27] On the other hand, such powers are not connected with canine or feline essences. Rather, these accidents (these powers) are proper to man and hence are aptly called *proper* accidents.

Other accidents are not proper to man; for example, a man may have sufficient quantity to tip the scales at 200 pounds, but so may a deer or a bear. Such an accident is called a *common* accident; it does not depend on the substance, or essence, as quasi-efficient cause for its production; it does not emanate, or "flow," from the essence as does the proper accident. It can be present or not. It can be present even in other beings which are essentially different.

F.   QUANTITY AND QUALITY

Quantity

Intimately connected with every material substance is the accident of quantity.[28] Every corporeal substance is quantitative; that is to say, it is extended, has parts outside of parts, and occupies a definite place. Our thoughts (judgments, concepts), on the other hand, are not quantitative; they do not "occupy space."

Increase and *decrease* are quantitative changes. Getting bigger, smaller, fatter, thinner, taller, shorter are accidental changes terminating in the genus of quantity. Thus, gaining weight is a quantitative increase; reducing is a quantitative decrease.

Quantity is not matter itself. Quantity presupposes matter. It

[27] The relation of powers to essence, or nature, will be discussed in the philosophy of man.

[28] We are concerned here with continuous quantity. Discrete quantity, number, is properly the study of arithmetical science.

is by reason of matter that a being is quantitative, spread out, extended in three dimensions (or more), has length, height, thickness. The special way in which the being is spread out, so that the parts are organized, for example, into cells, tissues, organs, organism, is due to form.

Whatever, then, is predicated absolutely of a subject as consequent upon *matter* is reducible to the category, or predicament, of *quantity*.

Quality

On the other hand, whatever is predicated absolutely of a subject as consequent upon *form* is reducible to the category of *quality*. Whatever qualities a being has (whether material or immaterial) belong to it by virtue of its form. The four types of quality are: (1) habits and dispositions, (2) operative powers, (3) sense qualities, (4) figure and shape (a quality about quantity).

Qualities are those principles in the being which enable us to answer the question: What sort of a being (already essentially constituted) is it? *Qualis*, the Latin interrogative, means "what sort of." Hence, these principles are aptly called *qualities*.

G.   RELATIONS

Examples

Whatever is predicated absolutely as modifying a subject is reducible either to the category of quantity or to the category of quality. However, we also make predications in which we express an order, reference, or *relation*, of the subject to something else. You are the owner of an automobile; you are really related to it by a relation of ownership; you really own it. I do not. This wall is similar to that wall in color; the two walls are really similar; the relationship between them is one of similarity. An effect is related to the efficient cause from which it proceeds; it really depends on the efficient cause for its becoming or be-ing; it is related to the cause by a relation of dependence. All these are familiar examples of relations.

Elements of Relation

In a relation, a subject is referred, or ordered, to a term on account of a foundation. Thus, one wall is related to another wall on account of the fact that the painter used the same bucket of paint. The *subject* is that which is referred to another; the *term* is that to which the subject is referred; the *foundation* is that on account of which the subject is referred to the term.

Real Relations vs. Relations of Reason

When all three elements of a relation are real, the relation is a *real* relation. Thus, similarity in color, height, weight, etc., paternity, maternity, effect-to-cause relations are real relations.[29]

Sometimes, however, one of the elements of a relation is supplied by the mind. For example, the right side of a round column offers no foundation in reality for a real relation, and so a foundation is supplied by the mind. The same is true for top and bottom, front and rear of a perfectly homogeneous object like a blank sheet of paper. Such relations, in which either subject, term, or foundation is the work of the mind, are called mental relations, or relations *of reason*.

The *predicables* of logic are instances of relations of reason between beings of the mind (second intentions). There are various ways in which a predicate can be related to a subject: as expressing the indeterminate essence (GENUS), the determining "part" of the essence (DIFFERENCE), the determinate essence (SPECIES), something necessarily flowing from the essence (PROPERTY), something contingently connected with the essence (LOGICAL ACCIDENT). We see examples of these relations in the following predications:

Man is animal (genus).
Man is rational (difference).
Man is rational animal (species).
Man is grammatical (property).
(This) man is 6 feet tall (logical accident).

[29] Some relations like similarity and equality are *mutual*. Others like paternity and maternity are nonmutual.

Real Transcendental Co-relations

Besides real predicamental relations, there is another type of real relation, which is in a class by itself—the transcendental relations between the potential-actual, intrinsic principles of being. All the reality of potency is toward act which fulfills the potency; all the reality of (perfecting) act is toward the (limiting) potency which it actuates. Since these relations are mutual to such an extent that the whole reality of the subject consists in its reference to its term, and vice versa, it is better to call this relation the act-potency *co*-relation.

Relation Not a Substance Existing between Beings

Although we often speak of relations "existing between" beings, we must avoid imagining them after the manner of connecting links between subject and term. To speak of relations existing between subject and term (for example, enmity existing between two men) is after all only a manner of speaking. As for the reality, in a real predicamental relation, the subject is real, the foundation is real, the term is real. The subject is *really ordered,* referred, or related, to the term. By relation we mean this order, or reference, *abstracted* from its subject by a formal abstraction and considered as a being "existing between" subject and term. As such, it is a predicate and falls under the ten categories. What is understood, however, by such a predicate is completely real. Intellect understands that one being exists *toward* another being because of a real foundation.[30] This "existence toward" (*esse ad*) is what relation signifies.[31]

H. ACCIDENTS INVOLVING RELATION

The last six predicaments, although not simply relations themselves, all involve a relation. They are action, passion, when, where, posture, habit.

[30] In a relation of reason, however, one (or more) of the elements of the relation is supplied by the mind.

[31] The terms are those used by St. Thomas. Aristotle has an even more cryptic term: *to pros ti* (to another).

Action and Passion

We have seen, in our discussion of efficient causality, that in transient action an agent (in act) acts upon a distinct patient (in potency). The patient passes from potency to act under the influence of the agent in act. Thus, the action of the agent is *in the patient;* for example, when I tear a piece of paper, the tearing is in the paper which is being torn. Strictly speaking, there is only one change in transient action as such,[32] only one passage from potency to act, and this motion is in the patient.[33]

The one motion, however, is the foundation for two relations and together with the relations constitutes two distinct types of predicaments: (1) the motion as proceeding from the agent is called transient *action;* (2) the same motion as in the patient and as modifying the patient is called *passion.*

Action—Motion as from Agent. When we predicate the action of the agent—for example, Smith is striking Jones—we name one being (the agent) from another being, which is distinct from the agent, and upon which the agent is acting, namely, the patient. Thus, the agent is extrinsically denominated (named) from what it does to something else.

Passion—Motion as in the Patient. On the other hand, when we predicate passion of a patient—for example, Smith is being struck by Jones—we name one being (the patient) from another being, which is distinct from the patient, and which is acting upon the patient, namely, the agent. Thus, the patient is extrinsically denominated (named) from what is done to it by something else.

[32] Recall that material action, however, involves an opposed reaction so that the material agent is also patient.

[33] It is well to note at this point that transient action is the perfection of the *patient.* Immanent action, we shall see in the philosophy of man, is the perfection of the *agent.* When we see a landscape, the landscape is not perfected by our action; rather, we ourselves are perfected by viewing it. The immanent operation does not, as it were, pass into the patient. Rather, it remains in, and perfects, the agent, and for this reason the action is called *immanent.*

When (Time)

The predicament "when" denominates the duration of a being from the duration of some other being, which is set up and used as a measure. Thus, many of us have endured (persisted in existence) from, let us say, the five-billionth revolution of the earth around the sun to the five-billion-and-twentieth; others have received many more free rides around the sun while continuing to exist. This predicament, then, clearly involves a relation.

Where (Place)

"Where" is another extrinsic denomination; that is, it names a being through something else. In answer to the question "Where are you?" I might reply, "I am in room 336, in Omaha, in the U.S.A., on earth, in the solar system, in the Milky Way," etc. Thus, in the first example, I am designating myself by stating the immediate, relatively immobile container. "Where" names a being in relation to another being (or beings) which is the container. It is a measure of place, but does not consider the order of parts.

Posture

If the order of parts is considered in the predication, we have the predicament "posture." The order, or arrangement, of the parts of a whole among themselves may vary. A man, for example, may be in various positions in a place: sitting, standing, lying. The order, or relation, of the parts varies; for example, while sitting, one's knees are much closer to the head than while standing.

Habit, or State of Apparel

Lastly, habit extrinsically denominates a being through something else which is merely adjacent to the subject for some human purpose. Thus, a man may be clothed or unclothed, armed or unarmed, hatted or unhatted. The clothes do not make the man; they are merely on the man, cover him, and keep him warm. Is there any real difference in a man when hatted and unhatted? For an answer, ask an unhatted man on a cold, wintry day. He will gladly admit that he wishes he were really related to something merely adjacent to his head.

We see, then, that the last six categories all *involve relation.* Since relation is already posited as a distinct category, this tends to make the division somewhat overlapping. Nevertheless, despite these shortcomings, this classification of the categories, which we owe to Aristotle, has long enjoyed notable success.

SUMMARY

A. Categories in General: The ten categories, or predicaments, are the supreme modes of predicating corresponding to the supreme modes of existing of limited being. The ten predicaments are *substance* and nine different types of accidents: *quantity, quality, relation, action, passion, when, where, posture,* and *habit* (state of apparel). We must beware, however, of considering the accidents as if they were substances themselves; rather, they are modifications of the substance. Ontologically, a substantial, unitary reality exists with modifications.

B. Substance: Substance is the *subject* of determinations, or modifications. Substance may also be called a *substrate* for accidents in the sense that it is the principle of essential permanence in a being undergoing accidental change. In a more profound sense, substance signifies a certain *independence* in existence. It signifies a mode of being so perfect as not to need to depend on another in which to "inhere" (as do accidents), or "insist"; rather, a substance subsists. As such, substance is a *principle by which* a (limited) being exists so perfectly that it need not "inhere" in another. Substance is dynamic, not static.

C. Individuation of Corporeal Substances: Individuation of corporeal substances which are multiplied within the species is (1) by *matter,* not by form; (2) by matter with *determinate quantity;* (3) by matter with determinate but *interminate* quantity. In forming the universal concept of the nature of a corporeal being, the intellect abstracts from individuating matter.

D. Supposit and Person: The substance of the ten predicaments is *second* substance. It is a predicate reflecting a mode of existing, is common to many in a univocal way. Second substance signifies a mode of existing with a certain independence. *First* substance signifies the individual substance (the subsistent) which actually exists and is incommunicable. *Supposit* signifies first substance as individual, complete, subsisting (and for the last reason incommunicable). Actions ultimately proceed from (and must be attributed to) not a part or principle, but the supposit. A rational supposit is called a *person.*

E. Accidents in General: Accidents, in general, are the modifications, or determinations, of a substance. They are *distinct* from substance, to which they are related as act to potency. *Proper* accidents flow necessarily from a substance and are inseparably connected with the substance. *Common* accidents can be present or not and can also be present in other substances.

F. Quantity and Quality: *Quantity* is that which is predicated as modifying the substance consequent upon matter. Every material substance is quantitative. *Quality* is that which is predicated of a subject as modifying the substance but consequent upon form.

G. Relations: In a relation, a subject is ordered to a term on account of a foundation. In a *real* relation, all three elements of the relation are real. If one of the elements of the relation is the work of the mind, the relation is a relation of *reason. Transcendental* co-relations are those which exist between potential-actual, intrinsic principles of being. We must not think of relations as substances existing between beings.

H. Accidents Involving Relation: *Action* is that predicament which extrinsically names (denominates) an agent from what it does to something else. *Passion* names the patient from what is caused in it by an extrinsic agent. *When* names the duration of a being from an extrinsic duration used as a measure. *Where* denominates a being by expressing its measure in place. *Posture* names a thing according to the order of its parts among themselves.

Habit denominates a being according to something which is related to it by being merely adjacent for some human purpose.

SUGGESTED READINGS

Anderson, James F.: *Metaphysics of St. Thomas Aquinas,* Henry Regnery Company, Chicago, 1953, pp. 25–29; on the modes and division of being.

Aquinas: *On Being and Essence,* translated by A. A. Maurer, Pontifical Institute of Mediaeval Studies, Toronto, 1949, pp. 50–54 (on essence as found in substance); pp. 55–59 (on essence as found in accidents).

Aristotle: *Basic Works,* edited by Richard McKeon, Random House, Inc., New York, 1941, pp. 7–37; on the categories.

De Raeymaeker, Louis: *The Philosophy of Being,* translated by E. H. Ziegelmeyer, B. Herder Book Co., St. Louis, 1954, pp. 173–194 (on substance and accidents); pp. 202–205 (on the categories as signifying irreducible modes of being).

Scheu, M.: *The Categories of Being According to Aristotle and St. Thomas,* The Catholic University of America Press, Washington, D.C., 1944.

IX

Analogy of Being
—a Summary

In the first chapter of this book, we gave a brief presentation of the fundamentals of analogy with special attention to the analogy of proportionality between limited beings. It was necessary to introduce this difficult subject early in the course, lest the student get off to a false start by thinking that the principles of metaphysics apply to being in a *univocal* way. In succeeding chapters, we called attention to various other analogies: the analogy of act-potency co-relations within limited beings, the analogy of proportion of principles to the act of be-ing, the analogy of effect and cause, the analogy of participation between creatures and the pri-

234

mary cause, God. In this chapter, we shall give a fuller treatment of the general subject of analogy and discuss each of the principal types of analogy at greater length. The chapter can also serve as a review of many things which have already been presented in preceding chapters.

A. PROBLEM OF ANALOGY OF BEING

Different Beings

Every being (in the proper sense) is an individual. Universals as such do not exist in the world of reality; there is no man-as-such, no universal humanity exercising existence. Each and every existent is an *individual*, and as an individual it is different from every other being. It exercises existence in a manner different from that of every other existent. Some beings are *specifically* different as well as individually different in relation to other beings, for example, men, brutes, plants, minerals; they exercise existence according to essentially distinct modes. Other beings are only *individually* different in relation to some others, for example, Tom, Dick, Harry, or Rover, Fido, Fifi; they exercise existence according to the same specific mode but in an individually different manner. At any rate, all beings differ.

No two beings in the universe of being are absolutely and utterly the same; otherwise, they would be identical. Even so-called "identical" twins are individually different.

Community of Different Beings

Nevertheless, no two beings in the universe of being are utterly and absolutely different; for they both exist. Realities utterly different would have to belong, not to a *uni*verse, but to a *pluri*verse. Such "realities" would be beyond being.[1] The facts are

---

[1] One might add that such "realities" would also be unintelligible, since intellect knows only being. Whatever intellect knows, it knows as participating in being, as related to being, or as the pure act of being itself. The contention of a realistic philosophy is that the intellect's power of knowing is co-extensive with reality, although we admittedly cannot know all being equally well.

that all beings are *similar* in that they exist; there is a true community amid the many different beings. Regardless of their vast differences, they have being "in common." [2]

Problem of Unity of the Many

At first hand, a universe of many (different) beings would seem unintelligible. If all things are similar precisely as beings, how can they differ? Surely, being cannot differentiate being; beings cannot differ by the very factor by which they are alike. Nor can beings differ by something outside being, for beyond being is only nonbeing, and that is not a difference. To say that beings differ in nonbeing is to say they do not differ at all. It would seem, then, that we would be forced to admit intellectually only one being.

But the facts of our sensory-intellectual experience cannot be overlooked; many individually different beings do exist; they all have being "in common"; that is to say, they belong to a universe of "being." And yet they do differ; the one is not the other. How is this to be explained? How can we explain the *plurality* of beings in a *universe* of being?

A universe of many (different) beings, to which experience testifies, confronts us with a startling paradox: only similars (namely, beings) are different from each other; only different beings are similar to each other. Only the things which exist (and for this reason similar) are different from each other; nonbeing is neither similar nor different; it simply is not. On the other hand, no being is similar to itself; it is identical with itself. A being is similar only to something else, from which it differs. If a being did not differ, it would not be similar to another being but identical with it.

---

[2] This phrase must not be misinterpreted. "Being in common" must not be regarded as a "part" by which all things resemble each other while differing according to another "part." Rather, every being according to its whole reality is similar to every other being and by its whole reality is different from every other reality. Our problem is to explain this sameness and difference without falling into the extreme positions found in monism or radical pluralism.

Extreme Position of Monism

In a universe of many (different) beings, a *pluralistic* universe, amid the vast diversity of existents, there is a true unity, a community, and man's intellect (the faculty of "being") is able to recognize this unity. We must be careful, however, not to overstress this unity so as to exclude the differences between beings. Any philosophical interpretation of the universe which attempts to reduce reality to one single principle, or substance, of which the many are mere manifestations, determinations, or participations, is at bottom a *monism,* whether this single principle be identified with "matter" (a materialistic monism) or with the Deity (a pantheistic monism). We must beware of overextending the meaning of such statements as "The universe truly exists" and "The universe has existed a long time." In the strict and proper sense, only individuals, not the complexus of individuals, exist. Moreover, each of them exists in a manner different (at least individually) from every other being. Nevertheless, there is a true similarity, commonness, or community, about them in the fact that they all exist. How can we explain this *unity* and still maintain the obvious diversity of being?

Extreme Position of Exaggerated Pluralism

At a pole opposite from monism, which overemphasizes the unity of being, is the position of *exaggerated pluralism.* According to this position, there is no true unity in being, no true community. Things are absolutely and utterly diverse.[3] Hence, any intellectual endeavor to discover the laws, or principles, which are (analogously) common to all being is a waste of time and effort. In such a view, a science of metaphysics must be regarded as impossible; for there cannot be a unified view of reality if reality offers no ground for such a unification.

A form of exaggerated pluralism is that of *agnosticism* as regards our knowledge of God from His effects. If God and limited beings are absolutely and utterly diverse, so that there is no community whatsoever between creatures and God, it follows that

[3] See William James, *A Pluralistic Universe,* Longmans, Green & Co., Inc., New York, 1943.

limited beings (creatures) can tell us nothing about God; in such a supposition, limited beings could not lead us to a knowledge that God *is*, much less to a knowledge of *what* He is.

Middle Position—Analogy of Being

We see, then, that a universe of many (different) beings presents us with a thorny problem: How can we explain the diversity of beings and still maintain unity? If we overemphasize the unity, community, or similarity, of beings, we are apt to fall into a monism of some sort. If, on the other hand, we lay too much stress on the differences between beings, we logically are driven to an extreme pluralism. The middle position respects both the obvious plurality of beings and the community of beings. The universe is pluralistic. It is not, however, a "pluriverse." It is a *pluralistic universe* of *being*. To explain just how being is common to everything in such a universe is the principal problem of this chapter. In general, our answer will be that being is *analogous*.

B. ANALOGOUS PREDICATION OF "BEING"

Predication of "Being" as Attributive Noun

In the strict sense, only individuals exist (subsist), each of them different from every other individual existent. Nevertheless, there is a similarity, a commonness, or community among them in that they all exist. To express this similarity, or this community amid differences, we may use the noun "being" as a predicate and affirm it of various beings. We may say, for example: God is a *being*, I am a *being*, Fido is a *being*, and so on down the various levels of existing. Such a predication is not univocal, nor equivocal, but analogous.

The notion expressed in such a predication unifies our knowledge of being. This notion, obviously, is not the direct knowledge we have of an existent in a sensory-intellectual experience of the material beings that surround us.[4] Rather, it is a complex

---

[4] Such knowledge delivers only material-sensible being. It is not the metaphysical knowledge of being. See Chapter I, section B.

knowledge derived by reflection on our conceptual-judgmental knowledge of existents; it is a knowledge which has been "separated" from the limiting conditions that do not apply to being as such.[5] Hence, it can be predicated of any thing which is, but its predication will be *analogous*. This term must be carefully explained.

Univocal Predication

When a term is predicated of various subjects, it is predicated either univocally, equivocally, or analogously. A term is predicated *univocally* when it is said of various subjects according to exactly the same meaning, for example, "man" when predicated of Tom, Dick, Harry, and the other billions of human beings on the face of the earth. The meaning, or intelligibility, of "man" is exactly the same in each of these predications—rational animal— regardless of the considerable differences between individual men. The individual differences (height, weight, color, size, etc.) have been "dropped out" by *abstraction* in forming the common, or universal, concept. Hence, this "meaning," or intelligibility, can be predicated of all the individuals that participate, or share, in that nature. The knowledge expressed by a univocal term is a *common* knowledge, a knowledge common to all the individuals of which the term is predicated.

We must carefully note, at this point, that the notion of "being," or the "real," is not formed by an *abstraction* from individual differences. We cannot "drop out," or abstract from, any differences in the real because the differences themselves are real; they pertain to "being." For example, men are really different from brutes because they are *really* rational; their rationality pertains to being. We see, then, that the notion, or concept, of

[5] Such a concept will be quite meaningful in connection with our knowledge of God's essence through analogous predication, where it is the first of all predicates. Such a notion can also be highly significant when used in a critique of positions such as those of Plato and Plotinus regarding the "One," the source of all other reality. (For Plato and Plotinus, the "One" is beyond being and yet is "real.") It is meaningful to say in criticism, "God is a *being*." See George P. Klubertanz, S.J., *Introduction to the Philosophy of Being*, Appleton-Century-Crofts, Inc., New York, 1955, p. 286.

"being" cannot be arrived at by the ordinary process of abstraction terminating in a universal concept (which is a species or a genus in relation to the individuals, or inferiors, of which the concept is predicated univocally).

Moreover, we must keep in mind that such abstract terms (and knowledges which they signify) express a *mode* of existing, not the act of existing, nor the common knowledge of the "existent," or "being." An existent, or being, is not purely and simply a mode of be-ing (although it does not exclude a limiting mode). Hence, such abstract terms cannot express the common knowledge of "being."

Equivocal Predication

A term is predicated *equivocally* when it is said of various subjects[6] according to a meaning which is entirely different in every predication. For example, "bank" may be predicated of the place where one's money is kept; it may also be said of the confines of a river. In such a predication, two (or more) concepts, meanings, or intelligibilities are expressed by one and the same spoken or written term.

Only terms can be equivocal; concepts cannot be equivocal. The reason is that the same word (an oral or written sign) may be used to express different concepts, that is, more than one concept. Concepts, however, express only one nature, one mode of existing, and hence cannot be equivocal.

One may wonder how equivocal terms can have meanings "entirely different," since no two beings (as beings) are entirely different. The reason is that such predications (attributive judgments) are concerned with differences in *modes* of be-ing (existing), not with the difference between being and nonbeing. Thus, two things can be of entirely different modes, while still being alike in that they both exercise existence in accordance with a mode. Since one and the same word may be used to express two different concepts (which present the mode of existing, not the act of existing), we can readily see that the meaning of the term may be entirely different as far as modes of be-ing are concerned.

[6] Or of the same subject, for example: "John Smith is a criminal lawyer"

Analogous Predication

A term is predicated *analogously* of various subjects when it is said of these subjects according to a meaning, or intelligibility, which is simply different but somewhat the same. For example, this is my head; Jones is the head (of the class); Smith is the head (of the corporation); that is the head (of the bed). In all these predications, the term "head" signifies the upper part, either of the body, or in rank, or in authority, or the place where the upper part rests. Hence, the meaning is somewhat the same; there is a common meaning. And yet the meaning is simply different in every predication. Such predications are analogous.

An analogous predication expresses the similarity between (different) things, whether this similarity be real or only imagined. Moreover—and this is the fundamental meaning of analogous predication—this type of predication is at bottom a recognition and expression of a relation, reference, or order of one thing to another, or of many things to one, or of many to many.

That subject to which the perfection expressed by the predicate belongs primarily (*per prius*) is called the *primary analogate*. The other subjects, to which the perfection belongs because of a relation to the primary analogate (whether this relation is made explicit or remains implicit in the predication) are called *secondary analogates*. Thus, in the example we have given, the head of the body is the primary analogate; the other subjects are secondary analogates.

"Being" Is Not Predicated Univocally

Surely, when "being" as an attributive noun is predicated of various subjects, it is not predicated *univocally;* that is to say, it is not predicated according to exactly the same meaning as an abstract universal. The reason is that no two beings exist in absolutely the same way, manner, or mode. Our predication must reflect these differences in the real.

The logical outcome of univocal predication of "being" is a monism. The meaning of "being" can be absolutely the same only if all reality *is* absolutely the same. Such a philosophical position would hold that all reality is one, or at least, reducible to one principle. In a pantheistic monism, this principle is identified with the Deity, of which the "many" are manifestations, determinations, or participations. In a materialistic monism, this primary principle, or substance, is matter, which receives various configurations. Needless to say, both positions go counter to the overwhelming evidence of our direct experience that there are many beings and that they are distinct from one another.

Some Christian philosophers (e.g., Duns Scotus, 1266–1308), who certainly did not consider themselves monists, have held a univocal predication of being, owing to a faulty explanation of the derivation of the notion of "being." In their view, "being" is the most abstract of concepts formed by dropping out, or abstracting from, the different modes of being. What is left is a sort of supreme genus, a concept with perfect unity of meaning, which when predicated of its inferiors requires the addition of a mode of being. For example: God is being (of Himself); creatures are being (from another); substance is being (in itself); accidents are being (in another).

The difficulty encountered in this position is that the differences, which have been dropped out (abstracted from), pertain to being. They are real differences and may not be left out of consideration; otherwise, being would differ in nothing. It follows that the notion "being" cannot be an abstract genus, or species, with perfect unity of meaning. For this reason, it cannot be predicated according to exactly one and the same meaning. In other words, "being" cannot be predicated univocally.

"Being" Is Not Predicated Equivocally

Nor is "being" predicated *equivocally,* that is, according to entirely different meanings, since entirely and absolutely different from "being" is only nonbeing, which can properly be predicated of nothing. No matter how different two beings may be, their difference is not that of "being" and "nonbeing." No beings are that different—not even God and electrons—since they both exist.

An equivocal predication of "being" would imply that there is no true unity in being nor in our knowledge of being. Metaphysical knowledge, the supreme effort of the mind to unify its knowledge, would be impossible. In such an exaggerated pluralism, there would be no unity even in our knowledge of limited beings.

Rarely, however, in the history of philosophical thought has an extreme pluralism regarding limited beings been held explicitly and consciously. We must not forget, however, that *agnosticism* as regards the existence and nature of God is one form of extreme pluralism. A philosopher who overemphasizes the transcendence of God's reality—and he may do this with the most profound intellectual reverence—cuts from under his feet the very ground on which his knowledge of God must rest. To deny that there is a community between God and limited beings (for example, between God and electrons) is to deny that we can rise from a knowledge of limited beings (God's effects) to a knowledge that God *is* and to some knowledge of *what* He is.

"Being" Is Predicated Analogously

We have seen that predication is either univocal, equivocal, or analogous, since the meaning of a predicate must be either entirely the same, entirely different, or somewhat the same though different; there are no other alternatives. Now, as we have shown, "being" is predicated neither univocally nor equivocally. Consequently, "being" must be predicated *analogously*, that is, according to a meaning, or intelligibility, simply different in every instance though somewhat the same. For, as we have shown, all beings are simply different though somewhat the same, and our predication to be true must reflect this difference amid similarity.

The analogously common knowledge expressed in such a predication is not arrived at by an *abstraction* from the differences between beings. If that were the case, the predication would need to be univocal. Rather, this knowledge is achieved by judgments of "separation," in which the existence of a being is known as distinct from the essential factors of the being without at the same time excluding those essential factors. In such a mental operation, nothing is dropped out. This operation is not an abstraction and does not terminate in an abstract concept. Rather, it terminates in a meaning, or intelligibility, all its own, since this meaning has an indeterminate *diversity* despite its true (analogical) *unity*.

Our position avoids the two extremes of (1) monism (univocal predication of "being"), which would logically reduce reality to one principle, and (2) an extreme pluralism (equivocal predication of "being"), which would logically need to admit reality "beyond being" and would implicitly deny the principle of intelligibility —that the intellect can know all reality, since it knows being as being.

C. NOT BY ANALOGY OF EXTRINSIC ATTRIBUTION

Extrinsic Analogy

It now remains to determine by what type of analogy "being" is predicated. Analogy is fundamentally a *proportion,* that is, a relation, reference, or order, of one thing (or principle) to another, or of any things to one (or one principle), or of many to many. Such relations are either extrinsic or intrinsic.

Let us consider the traditional example of "healthy" as predicated of John Doe, food, climate, complexion. In these predications, the perfection predicated is found properly and intrinsically only in the primary analogate, John Doe. He alone is healthy (in the proper sense of the term); the food is healthy (as cause of health); the climate is healthy (as a condition of health); the complexion is healthy (as an effect, or manifestation, of health). The perfection is predicated primarily of one subject, John Doe (the primary analogate), and is predicated of the secondary analogates only because of a *relation,* reference, or order, which they have to the primary analogate.

This is to say that the perfection is not predicated as being intrinsic and proper to the secondary analogates. It is predicated of the secondary analogates only by way of *extrinsic denomination,* because the secondary analogates have some relation, reference, or proportion, to the primary analogate. This relation is often one of cause or effect; for example, the good food causes health in John Doe, the good complexion is an effect of health in John Doe. Such an analogy is an *extrinsic* analogy of attribution (or proportion).

Intrinsic Analogy

An *intrinsic* analogy, on the other hand, is one in which the analogous perfection, the perfection predicated, is intrinsic to *all* analogates (to all the subjects of predication) and is present in the *proper* sense of the term in each of the analogates.

"Being" Is Intrinsic to All Analogates

Is the analogy of "being" an intrinsic or an extrinsic analogy? Having proved the existence of God as the Pure Act of Existing and the Cause of all other beings, we can readily see that He is the Primary Analogate, the subject of which "being" must be predicated first and foremost (*per prius*); He is the Being par excellence. Other beings (limited beings, which have, or participate, existence) are effects and hence have a relation of dependence to this Primary Being simply to exist. They, then, are the secondary analogates, of which "being" is predicated secondarily (*per posterius*).

Do we predicate "being" of the secondary analogates solely because of their relation to the primary analogate, their Cause? True, the secondary analogates, the limited beings, *exist* solely in virtue of their relation (of dependence) to the primary analogate, the Pure Act of Be-ing. This relation of dependence, to an extrinsic cause, however, is not what we mean when we call things "being." Rather, we call them "beings" because the perfection of being is found *intrinsically* and in the *proper* sense in each of the secondary analogates. They exist in their own right (though with a relation of dependence on the primary analogate).

From this it should be clear that "being" is not analogous by analogy of *extrinsic* attribution (or proportion), in which the perfection is found properly and intrinsically only in the primary analogate. Rather, the perfection of being is found properly and intrinsically in all the analogates of which it is predicated. Being is common to all things in a proper and intrinsic way. The analogy of being is an *intrinsic* analogy.

D. NOT BY ANALOGY OF METAPHORICAL PROPORTIONALITY

Metaphor

A metaphor is a figure of speech in which one thing is said to be like another different thing by being spoken of as if it were that thing. Consider, for example: "foot" when predicated of the bottom part of a table, mountain, or class; "king" as predicated of the lion and the leader of the promenaders; "night owl" when predicated of a man.

Metaphorical Proportionality

.   In a metaphor, a term ordinarily and primarily predicated of one thing is predicated of another because of some imagined similarity between two (or more) different sets of relations (proportions). Thus, one thing is imagined to be related to another (or others) as one thing is really and properly related to another.

Consider this example: Baudouin is *king* (of the Belgians); the lion is *king* (of the animals); John Doe is *king* (of the promenaders). In every case, there is a relation of ruler (or "ruler") to ruled: Baudouin, the lion, John Doe all rule their subjects (or "subjects"). Thus, there is a similarity of relation (proportion) of ruler to ruled.[7] The comparison implicit in such metaphors involves a similarity of relations, or proportions—a *proportionality,* which we may indicate in this way:

Baudouin : Belgians *as* the lion : brutes *as* John Doe : promenaders

Although there is a similarity of relation, or proportion, nevertheless there is an important difference: Baudouin alone (the primary analogate) rules by political power; the lion rules by physical power; while John Doe rules merely for one night by

[7] And, we may add, there is also a similarity of relation of ruled to ruler.

make-believe power. Thus, there is a relational, or proportional similarity, which is truly different in every case.[8]

"Being" Is Proper to All Analogates

We must carefully note that in analogies of this type, the analogy of metaphorical (nonproper) proportionality, the term predicated (e.g., king) applies properly only to the primary analogate (e.g., Baudouin) and does not properly apply to the other subjects, the secondary analogates; that is to say, it applies to the secondary analogates in a transferred sense. The term "being," however, is predicated in the proper sense of all things, of all the analogates (both God and creatures). Hence, the analogy of "being" cannot be of this type.

E. ANALOGY OF PROPER PROPORTIONALITY (Between Limited Beings)

Analogous Predication of Noun "Being"

When "being" is predicated as an attributive noun of various subjects, it expresses the similarity between beings, which nevertheless are simply different; that is to say, it expresses the analogy of being. This similarity, we have seen, is not a univocal similarity, or commonness. And yet it is a true similarity, commonness, or community. In what does this community consist?

Since our first knowledge of being is restricted to limited beings, this first analogous predication of "being" must reflect how being is common to all *limited* things. How is being common to them?

Act of Existing Proportioned to Essence. In every instance of limited being, an act of existing is proportioned, or related, to some individual limiting essence; the exercise of existence is "on a level with" the capacity of the essence, which is the potency for this act and determines the act, thus limiting it to a specific grade

---

[8] There is truly a relation in every instance, but not a relation of real kingship except in the case of the primary analogate.

of existing. In each and every limited existent, we discover an "is" factor and a "what" fáctor, a principle of existence and a principle of limitation of existence, proportioned to each other as correlative principles of the unitary existent. These factors are never twice the same, but they are always present as basic, metaphysical, "structural" principles in every limited existent. Without the "is" principle, nothing *is;* without the "what" principle (essence), no*thing* is, no *kind* of existent results. The mutual correlation of these intrinsic principles constitutes the limited existent.

Proportional Similarity between Limited Beings. In the analogous predication of the noun "being," we recognize and express the proportional likeness of limited beings to each other, a likeness between beings which truly differ but have a similar relation of intrinsic components proportioned to each other.[9] True, the knowledge of each individual limited existent cannot be expressed in any one notion, but the knowledge of proportional similarity between beings can be expressed in one notion. And that is precisely what we do when we analogously predicate the attributive noun "being" of limited existents by the analogy of proper proportionality.

Relation to Mathematical Proportion and Metaphorical Proportionality. For the purpose of clarifying the analogy of proportionality between limited beings, it may help to consider other proportions, or relations, of paired terms. Let us consider, for example, the case of doubling: "These windows are *double;* those doors are *double;* those beds are *double.*" Now, windows, doors, and beds are simply different. And yet, in our example, since there is a doubling of them, these simply different things are similar; there is a commonness, or community, among them owing to a *proportion,* and this commonness amid differences is expressed in the "analogous" predication. (A more careful consideration,

---

[9] The analogy between limited beings is *based* on the transcendental corelation of the potential-actual, intrinsic principles But formally this analogy is between the *complete* beings composed of similarly proportioned principles.

however, will make it clear that "doubling" is a univocal term and that our example is not a true case of analogy of proportionality.)

Another example may be borrowed from *mathematical proportions:* for example, 1 : 2 as 3 : 6 as 7 : 14. Here again there are two elements involved, of which one is related to the other. The two elements are always different numbers. Nevertheless, there is a common proportion of one to the other: the first number is a half of the second and the second is double the first. Thus, there appears to be some sort of proportional similarity. (But again on closer examination the commonness turns out to be univocal; there is an identity, not similarity, of proportions.)

The *metaphorical proportionality,* often called nonproper proportionality, is perhaps the most helpful in throwing light upon the analogy of proportionality between limited beings. But since in such an analogy the term predicated is found properly only in the primary analogate, this analogy cannot be the analogy of being. Although the various examples of proportion of paired terms, whether mathematical or metaphorical, may help us to come to an understanding of the analogy of being, we must keep in mind that the proportional similarity between beings differs from that in any examples we may propose. It cannot, and must not, be reduced to any "type" of analogy.

Analogous Affirmation of Existence

More fundamental, however, than the analogous predication of the attributive noun "being," and underlying this predication, is the analogous *affirmation* of the act of existing. The existential act (to be) affirmed in the existential judgment is never twice the same. Although we affirm that men *exist,* dogs *exist,* roses *exist,* we never affirm the act of existing in exactly the same way, since act of existing is always proportioned to the capacity of the essence of the existent. A man, for example, could not exist with the existence of a dog. And yet in all these affirmations there is a commonness amid difference: we do affirm something to exist, to *be;* we do affirm an act of existing proportioned to an essence. In brief: we affirm existence analogously.

The word "yes" in reply to questions concerned with the existence of something never has exactly the same meaning. For example: "Are there whooping cranes?" "Yes." "Does God exist?" "Yes." "Is there a snake in the tent?" "Yes." In all these affirmations, there is a unity of meaning, and for this reason we can use the same word to convey this meaning. Nevertheless, the meaning is never univocally the same. In other words, we affirm existence analogously.

Analogy of Existents

Ultimately, the analogous predication of the attributive noun "being" and the analogous affirmation of existence is grounded in the *existents* themselves. Our analogous predication and affirmation reflect an analogy of beings themselves: every existent differs from every other existent; that is to say, it exercises the act of existing in an essentially (specifically or at least individually) different way; the mode of existing, the manner of be-ing, of any two "be-ers" [10] is never absolutely identical. Nevertheless, every (limited) existent is similar to every other existent by a similarity of proportions. In every limited existent, no matter how diverse, whether a human existent or an electronic existent, we discover a proportion between the act of existing and essence. Every existent *is,* and is according to its own unique, individual mode.

Analogous Application of Metaphysical Principles

The perennial temptation of the student of metaphysics is to regard metaphysical principles as univocal, much like the principles and laws of the other sciences, which are acquired by some kind of abstraction and are concerned with modes (not the act) of be-ing. It should be clear to the student at this point that the

[10] As we noted in the first chapter, an existential metaphysics is badly in need of terms which the English language does not provide. Several attempts have been made by writers of textbooks to remedy this deficiency, but these attempts have met not a little opposition from our colleagues in the English departments. Hence, it is with a certain hesitancy that we venture another coinage—"be-er." A "be-er" is one who exercises the act of be-ing (existing), as a runner is one who exercises the act of running.

principles which the science of metaphysics formulates regarding being *as being* must be understood in an analogous way and applied analogously, since no two beings are exactly the same.

F. ANALOGY OF PROPORTIONALITY WITHIN LIMITED BEING

Analogy within Being

In the preceding section, we considered the analogy *between* limited beings. There is also an analogy *within* each limited being, an analogy not between beings (in the proper sense) but between correlative, intrinsic, constitutive principles of the limited being.

Composition in Three Orders

In Chapter III, we examined the evidence which led us to admit participation, multiplicity, and limitation in the order of existence, the order of substance, and the order of accidents. We saw that this participation, multiplicity, and limitation require a *composition* of intrinsic, constitutive principles in the subsistent, individual reality: (1) of the act of existing and limiting essence; (2) of accidents and substance (a composition within the individual essence); (3) of substantial form and primary matter (a composition within substance).

Similarity amid Differences in Composition

None of these compositions is exactly the same. Nevertheless, there is a common feature in all of them. In each of these compositions, there is a *perfecting* principle, that is, a principle which confers perfection: "to be," accidents, substantial form. Correlative to the perfecting principle there is also a *limiting* principle, which, as it were, "receives" the perfection and restricts the perfecting principle: essence, substance, matter.

The composite is neither of its component principles. Thus, the limited existent (the subsistent) is neither essence nor existence. Individual nature (essence) is neither accidents nor substance. And substance is neither matter nor form. Ultimately, the reality is the unitary (albeit composite), total existent, in which by philosophical analysis we have discovered a multiple composition of intrinsic principles.

Act-Potency Co-relation

Of these intrinsic, constitutive principles within the total existent, "to be," accidents, substantial form are perfecting principles—*acts*. Essence, substance, and primary matter are their correlative limiting principles—*potencies*. Thus, there is a *similarity* between these various sets of potency-act principles, whose mutual relation constitutes the limited existent.

At the same time, there is a *difference* between these various sets of potential-actual principles. Existence, accidents, substantial form are all *acts,* but they are not act in the same manner. Existence is the actualizing principle of the total, unitary existent making it be. Substantial form determines it to be what it is primarily. Accidents determine it to be what it is secondarily. On the other hand, essence, primary matter, and substance are all *potencies,* but they are not potency in the same way. Prime matter is pure potency, an indeterminate potency for substantial form. Substance is a determinate primary mode of existing in potency to accidental modification. Essence, the composite of substance and accidents, is directly potency for the act of existing.

Analogy of Proportionality within Limited Being

The similarity between these sets of potential-actual constitutive principles despite their differences constitutes an analogy *within* being. And since it is a similarity of relations, or proportions (of act to potency and of potency to act), this analogy is an analogy of *proportionality* within being. The pairs of intrinsic, constitutive principles are proportionally similar to each other though simply different. Thus, "to be" is related to essence *as* accidents are related to substance, and *as* substantial form is related to prime matter. The following mathematicized formulation may make these relations more apparent:

"To be" : essence *as* accidents : substance *as* form : matter

(*act*) (*potency*)   (*act*)   (*potency*)   (*act*) (*potency*)

G. ANALOGY OF PROPORTION OF INTRINSIC PRINCIPLES TO "TO BE"

No Reality apart from Subsistent

The intrinsic, constitutive principles of a being do not exist in themselves; they have no reality apart from the unitary, total existent of which they are the principles; they are not separate existents (subsistents). Rather, they are intrinsic, constitutive principles by which the unitary existent *is*, and is *what* it is (primarily and secondarily). Thus, by reason of substantial form, the total existent is of a definite species; by reason of matter (with its due quantity), the "entire" being is individuated; by reason of accidents, the existent is modified; and by reason of the act of existing, it *is*. Apart from "that-which-is" (the whole existent), these principles have no reality.

Principles of Being Are Correlative

All the reality of a limiting principle, or potency, is an order, or relation, to the act which it limits. The reality of a limited act, in turn, is a relation to the potency which limits it.[11] In this way, potential-actual principles are mutually related (co-related); that is to say, they are correlative principles within being.

Unless one keeps in mind the *correlative* character of potential-actual principles, one is apt to consider them as little substances within another substance, as beings within being, a position which does violence to the obvious unity of beings.

Beings by Analogy of Proportion

Existence, "to be" (*esse*), is the act of acts, the basic, intrinsic, actualizing principle. In any limited existent, the potential-actual, constitutive principles (with the exception of existence itself) are related, or proportioned, to the act of existing, which they determine in some way. By reason of this relation, or proportion, all these principles pertain to being, and in this sense, may be called

[11] Not every act, however, is ordered to potency. If a being's essence is pure form (an angelic nature), such a form, which is essential act, is not ordered to potency Nor is the Pure Act of Existing (God) ordered to potency.

"being" by an analogy of *proportion* to the act of be-ing. We must not forget, however, that "being" in the proper sense signifies the unitary, total existent—the supposit. It is only within a subsistent, as its intrinsic, "structural" principles, that the potency-act correlations have any reality.

Moreover, this proportion, or relation, to existence *differs* in the various potency-act correlations. Essence, as existential potency, is directly related to existence, its act. Within essence, substance (potency) is related to accidents (act) and through the composite essence both principles are related to existence. Within (material) substance, matter as pure potency is related to substantial form (its act), thus composing the substance, which together with its accidents constitutes the essence, which is directly related to existence.

Existence, however, is the basic act and is not proportioned, or related, to a higher act. It is the act to which all other acts (and potencies) are ultimately related within the existent; it is the act to which they pertain. In virtue of this pertinence, relation, or proportion, the other acts (and their potencies) are being and are called such by an *analogy of proportion*. They are acts and potencies only by reason of their proportion to the act of existing, "to be," the supreme act. These proportions are suggested in the following diagram:

H. ANALOGY BETWEEN EFFECTS AND (SOME) CAUSES

Agent Acts in a Manner Similar to Itself

We saw in the chapter on efficient causality that every agent acts insofar as it is in act. In every transient action, the agent is in act; the patient is in potency; the agent communicates the perfection (to which it is in act) to the patient, causing the patient to pass from potency to act as regards the perfection to which the agent is in act. The actuation in the patient, then, must be similar to the agent's perfection.

Univocal Efficient Causes

In some causations, this similarity is a *univocal* similarity; that is to say, the effect and cause are of the same nature. Thus, a heating agent, for example, a hot radiator, will heat the surrounding cold air. Also, in animal generation, the parents, who are of a definite species, or form, will produce offspring of the same species, or form (unless other lines of causation intervene); like generates like.

Moreover, by knowing the actions caused by such agents (and the result in which the action terminates), we can rise to a knowledge of the nature of the agent. For example, from the nature of offspring, we can know the nature of the animal parents. Since in such causations the effect and the cause are of one and the same nature, the agent is aptly called a *univocal* efficient cause.

Analogous Efficient Causes

Not all causes, however, are of the same nature as the effects they cause. When an effect proceeds from an *intellectual* efficient cause (or from a sentient efficient cause, for example, a beaver), the effects may be of various kinds. Human causality is not limited to the univocal causality of reproduction. Besides generating offspring, which are of the same nature, human beings can produce many kinds of effects: buildings, vehicles, paintings, statues, novels, etc. In such causations, the cause is not of the same nature as the effect; a man is not of the same nature as the house he builds, nor is the beaver the same in nature as the dam he so skillfully "engineers."

Nevertheless these effects, so different from their cause, do resemble their cause; the effects are similar to the thought (or at least sense knowledge) of them existing in the mind of their producer. Thus, the assembled steel, glass, and fabric of an automobile have the stamp of man's intellect upon them. The auto, however, does not resemble the man who designed and built it in the same way as his human offspring resemble him. Although all children resemble their parents, there is a great difference in the way in which "brain children" and natural children resemble their progenitors.

Since the cause in such cases, although somewhat similar to the effect, is strictly speaking different from the effect, we may aptly call causes of this kind *analogous.*

Perfection of Effect in Cause Virtually

Nevertheless, the cause must be somewhat similar to the effect, since the perfection of the effect must be precontained in the cause somehow. Although not present formally (according to the same nature), the perfection of the effect is present *virtually;* that is to say, the power to produce that perfection is present in the cause. A silver dollar, for example, is virtually a dime, a quarter, a half dollar, but actually and formally is none of these. Yet it has the same buying power across the counter; it is virtually a dime, quarter, etc. The silver dollar though strictly different is like the smaller coins in that it has their perfection, their buying power; thus, it is "analogous" to them. The smaller coins in turn, though strictly different are similar to the silver dollar; they have some of the buying power of the silver dollar though not all its buying power; they are "analogous" to the silver dollar.

Analogy of Effects and Some Causes

In somewhat similar fashion, there is an analogy between some effects and their causes, and for this reason, the effects manifest somehow the perfection of their analogous cause. For example, the Sistine Chapel murals tell us what a genius Michelangelo was, but no doubt he had even greater artistic conceptions that were never executed. Also, a carefully fabricated beaver dam manifests what a smart little "engineer" a beaver is but tells us nothing about his other abilities. Thus, these effects have the perfection of their cause in some way and for this reason are *similar* to the cause on which they depend. But since the perfection of the effect is not formally of the same nature as the cause, the effects are simply *different*. The relation of such an effect to the nonunivocal cause in which the perfection of the effect is found virtually is an analogy of proportion.

I. ANALOGY BETWEEN CREATURES AND GOD

The Basic Analogy

None of the analogies which we have considered so far, however, is the fundamental analogy. The basic analogy is that between limited beings (which are effects) and their Primary Efficient and Exemplary Cause. It is the analogy between creatures and their Creative Cause, the analogy between participants in be-ing and the Pure Unparticipated Act of Be-ing, the analogy between relative beings and the Absolute Being. This analogy is more fundamental than the analogy within individual beings (of principles to their act of be-ing, of proportionality of potency-act correlations); it is more fundamental than the analogy of proper proportionality between limited beings (creatures). This is an analogy within the *universe of being;* it is a proportion, or relation, of all limited existents, of relative beings, to their ground in being, namely the Absolute Being.

All other analogies presuppose this fundamental analogy.[12] There can be no analogy within limited beings, nor an analogy (of proportionality) between limited beings, etc., unless limited beings *exist*. And, for them, to exist implies that their whole reality is related (proportioned) by a relation of dependence to the Primary Being, Which is the cause of limited beings.

A Relation of Many to One

Analogy, let us recall, is a relation, proportion, or order, of one thing to another, of many to many, or of many things to one.[13]

---

[12] However, we rise to a knowledge of this most profound analogy only after proving that God is the Pure Act of Be-ing (since He is the Primary Efficient and Exemplary Cause of the beings which participate existence).

[13] See section C of this chapter.

The analogy we are considering now is the relation of the *many* to the *one* in the most fundamental order, the order of existence. In an order of many beings (and beyond there is only nonbeing), there must be a relation, or proportion, of the many to a unique One, Who as principle of unity (and be-ing) of the many is not related to a higher "one."

An Intrinsic Analogy

Moreover, this most radical of analogies must be an *intrinsic,* not an extrinsic, analogy. Being belongs intrinsically to all the analogates, both the primary analogate and the secondary analogates. Creatures are truly beings. Each of them exercises its own existence (though always with a relation of dependence); their existence is "innermost" to them; it is their core reality principle. The existence they exercise is not the existence of the Primary Cause; the existence they participate is not the existence of God; existence is *proper* to them. Every limited being, every creature, exercises existence in its own unique way, even though its whole ·reality implies a relation of dependence to the Creative Cause.

Relation of Creatures to God

". . . whatever is said of God and creatures is said according as there is some relation (*ordo*) of the creature to God, as to its principle and cause, in which all the perfections of things pre-exist most excellently." [14] The perfection of all perfections, of course, is the act of be-ing. Hence, this perfection preexists most excellently in God. And when we predicate "being" of God, we signify not only that God is the *cause* of limited beings, but that the perfection of being *preexists* in Him most eminently,[15] as the Primary Efficient and Exemplary Cause of the many, limited beings.

Proportion of Many to One

This analogy, then, is a proportion of many to one. The entire reality of limited beings, although distinct from each other and distinct from God, implies a relation, or proportion, to one

[14] *Summa Theologiae,* I, 13, 5c.
[15] *Ibid.,* 6c.

unique Primary Principle, on which they depend for their very reality, and whose perfection they manifest imperfectly by existing according to the diverse capacities of their various essences. The many, relative beings are proportioned to the one Absolute Being.

A Universe of Being

The universe of being has a true unity. It is a community of being. ". . . the things which are from God are assimilated to Him insofar as they are beings, as to the primary and universal principle of their entire reality." [16] As beings which *participate* existence, they depend upon, and manifest, Him Who is the *Unparticipated* Pure Act of Existing.

SUMMARY

A. Problem of Analogy of Being: Beings are individually different. Nevertheless, they are similar. How can different things be similar? If we overstress the similarity between beings, we fall into a monism of some sort. If we overstress the differences, we are driven to an extreme pluralism. Our explanation of commonness amid differences, of unity amid diversity, is a recognition of the analogy of being.

B. Analogous Predication of "Being": Predication may be univocal, equivocal, or analogous. The predication of "being" is neither univocal (monism) nor equivocal (extreme pluralism). Therefore, it must be analogous.

C. Not by Analogy of Extrinsic Attribution: In such an analogy, the perfection is found only in the primary analogate and is predicated of the secondary analogates only because of a relation to the primary analogate. Obviously, this cannot be the analogy of being, since the perfection is intrinsic to all the analogates. The analogy of being, then, must be an intrinsic analogy.

[16] *Ibid.,* 4, 3c.

D. Not by Analogy of Metaphorical Proportionality: In such an analogy, the perfection predicated belongs properly only to the primary analogate. It is predicated of the secondary analogates only because of an imagined resemblance between two or more different pairs of relations. Nevertheless, this analogy helps us to understand the analogy of proportionality.

E. Analogy of Proper Proportionality (between Limited Beings):   The relation of the act of existing to limiting essence is never quite the same, but such a relation is discovered in every limited being. Thus, limited beings are proportionally similar to each other; they have a similar relation of constitutive principles in the existential order. This analogy is expressed by using the attributive noun "being" as a predicate. Moreover, the act of existing affirmed in existential judgments is never twice the same; it is always proportioned to the capacity of the essence of the existent. Ultimately, the analogous predication and affirmation are grounded in an analogy between the limited beings themselves.

F. Analogy of Proportionality within Limited Being: The various potency-act correlations within a limited being are proportionally similar to each other. "To be" is related to essence as accidents are related to substance as substantial form is related to matter.

G. Analogy of Proportion of Intrinsic Principles to "to Be":   The intrinsic, constitutive principles (with the exception of "to be") can be called "being" (and are such) insofar as they are related, or proportioned, to the act of existing, which is the primary, or fundamental, act.

H. Analogy between Effects and (Some) Causes: In univocal causation, the effect and cause are of the same nature. This is not the case in analogous causation. The analogous cause is similar to the effect but simply different. In like manner, the effect is similar to its analogous cause but simply different. The perfection of the effect is found not formally, but virtually, in the analogous cause.

I. **Analogy between Creatures and God:** This is the basic analogy. All other analogies presuppose it. In a universe of being, creatures participate act of be-ing; their entire reality implies a relation to the Unparticipated Act of Being, on which they depend and which they imperfectly manifest.

SUGGESTED READINGS

Anderson, James F.: *Metaphysics of St. Thomas Aquinas,* Henry Regnery Company, Chicago, 1953, pp. 36–43; on the analogicity of being.

——: *The Bond of Being,* B. Herder Book Co., St. Louis, 1949; a book-length discussion of the analogy of being.

Bourke, Vernon J.: *The Pocket Aquinas,* Washington Square Press, Pocket Books, Inc., New York, 1960, pp. 163–168; on analogy in predication and in being, proportion and analogy, analogy between God and finite beings.

Cajetan: *Analogy of Names,* translated by E. Bushinski and H. Koren, Duquesne University Press, Pittsburgh, 1953; sixteenth-century commentary and exegesis of the doctrine of Aquinas on analogy.

Foote, Edward: "Anatomy of Analogy," *The Modern Schoolman,* vol. 18, pp. 12–16, November, 1940; a short article on the fundamentals of analogy.

Klubertanz, George P.: *St. Thomas Aquinas on Analogy,* Loyola University Press, Chicago, 1960; a recent textual analysis and systematic synthesis.

Lyttkens, H.: *The Analogy between God and the World,* Almquist and Wiksells, Uppsala, 1952.

Phelan, Gerald B.: *St. Thomas and Analogy,* Marquette University Press, Milwaukee, 1941.

INDEX

263

Metaphor, 246
Metaphorical proportionality, 246–247, 249
Metaphysics, formal object of, 27
material object of, 26
point of departure, 22
primary object of, 22
primary principles, 28–32
of accountability, 31–32
of intelligibility, 30
of noncontradiction, 29
Modes of existing, 16, 28, 78, 209–211, 240
conceivable by intellect, 30
expressed by predicate, 76n., 210–211
general vs. special, 179
manifestation of, 125
and modes of activity, 127
primary, 68–69, 80–81
secondary, 69–70, 83–84
substantial vs. accidental, 211–212
Monism, 237, 241–242
Moral cause, 129
Morality and beauty, 205
Motion (see Change)
Multiplicity, in accidental order, 69–70
of being, 236
in essential order, 69
in existential order, 68
(See also Participation)

Natural finality, 142–144
presupposes intellect, 143
presupposes intentional order, 143
Nature, and natural appetite, 141–142
necessity of, 143–144
(See also Essence)
Necessity, of nature, 143–144
of principle, of efficient causality, 117

Necessity, of principle, of final causality, 137–138
Negation, pure vs. privation, 194
Noncontradiction, principle of, 29
Notion of being, 248

Object, formal, 27
material, 26
Objectivity of the beautiful, 204
Occasion, 108
Occasionalism, 172
One, 181–185
metaphysical vs. mathematical, 184
transcendental character of, 185
(See also Units)
Order, of discovery, 126
intentional, 138–139, 143
metaphysical, 126
of universe, 145–146

Parmenides, 46
Participant, limitation of, 70–71
Participation, 67–104
of accidents, 69–70
analogy of, 169–171
of essence, 69, 80–83
of existence, 68, 78–80
problem of, 113–115
fact of, 168
Neoplatonic theories of, 73
Plato's theory of, 72
(See also Limitation)
Passion, 119–120, 229–230
Patient in transient action, 119
Perception of the beautiful, 198–199
Perfection, accidental, 193
of effect, in cause virtually, 256
and limitation, 73–86
in accidental order, 83–87
in essential order, 80–83
in existential order, 74–80
limited or unlimited, 103